THE LOGIC
OF THE ABSURD

THE LOGIC
OF THE ABSURD

On film and television comedy

Jerry Palmer

BFI Publishing

First published in 1987
by the British Film Institute
21 Stephen Street
London W1P 1PL

Copyright © Jerry Palmer 1987

Design Ray Carpenter

Typeset by K.C. Graphics Ltd., Shrewsbury

Printed and bound in Great Britain by
St Edmundsbury Press
Bury St Edmunds, Suffolk

British Library Cataloguing in Publication Data

Palmer, Jerry
    The logic of the absurd: on film and
    television comedy.
    1. Wit and humour — History and criticism
    I. Title   II. British Film Institute
    808.7   PN6147

    ISBN 0-85170-204-X
    ISBN 0-85170-205-8 Pbk

CONTENTS

ACKNOWLEDGMENTS

Various parts of this book have been given or published as papers, and I would like to thank the relevant editors and audiences for their attentiveness and comments:

British Sociological Assn., Sociology of Literature and Sociology of Humour Working Groups; Bjørn Ekmann and the *Jahrbuch für Internationaler Germanistik*, 1984; English Department, University of Copenhagen; Communications Department, University of Aalborg; English Department, University of Aarhus; Faculty of Foreign Languages, University of Dijon; English Department, University College, Cardiff, Critical Theory Seminar; Professor Avner Ziv and the Fourth International Symposium on Humor, Tel Aviv; *National Styles in Humor*, edited by A. Ziv; *Esprit*, March 1985.

DEDICATION

To who else could I possibly dedicate this book except those people who have made me laugh more than any others over the years; in alphabetical order, then:

Woody Allen, John Cleese, The Communist Party of the Soviet Union, Bob Edelman, Bernard Esmein, Oliver Hardy, Stanley Laurel, Stephanie and Christy Palmer and all the performers who between them are called Alternative Cabaret, and who collectively made me realise there was a connection between politics and humour.

Introduction

▬

A personal story, by way of introduction.

Among my friends is a professional saxophone player. One evening he was playing with a rock'n'roll band in a South London working men's club, playing to an all-white audience with a singer who turned out to be something of a racist. Towards the end of the evening the singer announced, to everyone's amazement, that they were going to play some reggae. The song turned out to be a pastiche, a deliberate satire, very anti-black. My saxophonist friend could not stomach this and walked off in the middle of the number – a dramatic breach of musical ethics. At the end of the evening the singer demanded to know why he had walked off in the middle of a song, and was told; his response was: 'What's wrong with you? That song's just a joke, that's all – can't you take a joke?'

Regardless of the actual answer, what are the possible answers to such a question? One can say: 'No it isn't – it's racist propaganda.' Mrs Whitehouse once accused *Till Death Us Do Part* of being political propaganda masquerading as humour (*"Who Does She Think She Is"*, p.74). But clearly the song *was* a joke – the audience was laughing. One can say: 'Well, I don't think it's very funny,' which attracts the withering 'You've got no sense of humour, that's your trouble.' Or one can say: 'Yes, it's a joke, yes, it is funny – and that's why it's racist propaganda, and evil'; but that involves shifting from the realm of the humorous to the non-humorous, which is apt to arouse resentment if not derision. In the 1960s the American cartoonist Al Capp created a caricatural folk singer called Joanie Phoanie, and was duly threatened with a lawsuit by Joan Baez, who felt that the character was a libellous

9

reference to herself. The cartoonist said he was surprised and sorry if she saw her reflection there, for 'Joanie Phoanie is a repulsive, egomaniacal, un-American, non-taxpaying horror' (quoted C.P. Wilson, p.191).

These stories raise, in exemplary form, fundamental questions about humour and comedy. Firstly, and most obviously, the question of the limits of humour: At what point does a joke become, or cease to be, funny? But more profoundly, lurking behind this question, is a second and ultimately more significant one: What is the nature of humour? It is more significant because it implicitly includes the first: it is so built into humour that it can easily fail, or offend (or both), and therefore any account of the nature of humour must include, as an integral part of itself, an account of what the limits of humour are. Thirdly, it raises the question of the effectivity of humour: what types of effect is humour capable of having? In each of the cases quoted above humour appears to have the effect of neutralising opposition, of bypassing the possibility of criticism. A few years ago I was confronted by a group of football fans, rather aggressive. One of them yelled at me 'You look a right prat!' (the term he actually used was even less flattering). I replied, cheerfully, 'That's because I am one': laughter all round, incident closed. A more elegant example is to be found in an anecdote told by C.E. Schutz (p.250) about the nineteenth century American politician and wit, John Randolph of Roanoke, who was reputed to be impotent. He was assailed in Congress by Tristram Burges, member for Rhode Island:

BURGES Sir, Divine Providence takes care of his own universe. Moral monsters cannot propagate. Impotent of everything except malevolence of purpose, they cannot otherwise multiply miseries than by blaspheming all that is pure and prosperous and happy. Could demon propagate demon, the universe might become pandemonium; but I rejoice that the Father of Lies can never become the Father of Liars. One adversary of God and man is enough for one universe.

RANDOLPH You pride yourself on an animal faculty, in respect to which the slave is your equal and the jackass infinitely your superior.

Burges' attack is witty, and had Randolph attempted a rational, critical, serious reply he would have got nowhere. Instead he replied in kind, out-ridiculing his opponent. His reply, in turn, bypassed the possibility of a serious response. The implication is that any model of humour must also be able to account for this particular effectivity, if this indeed turns out, on closer inspection, to be its effectivity.

These points indicate the place that *The Logic of the Absurd* aims to occupy. On the one hand, it offers a descriptive theory of how humour works, a task undertaken many times before – whether the attempt has anything more to offer will no doubt be decided on the basis of the traditional pudding test. On the other hand, the form that humour takes, the way in which it works, makes it suitable for some purposes and not for others, and therefore its use in everyday life creates a series of dilemmas, indicated above by examples – dilemmas which are moral, political and rhetorical. The nature of these dilemmas, as we shall see, derives from the nature of humour, and therefore any discussion of the sorts of situation found in our examples must eventually refer to a theory or theories of humour.

In 'The Art of Donald McGill' George Orwell considers the impact of a very traditional form of British humour, the mildly bawdy seaside postcard, featuring small hen-pecked husbands, caricaturally voluptuous young ladies, loud, fat, aggressive wives, etc. Orwell's argument is essentially that these postcards, although sufficiently close to obscenity to risk occasional prosecution (his essay dates from 1942), only make sense 'in relation to a fairly strict moral code' (p.172): their repetitive jokes about nakedness, chamber pots, mothers-in-law and illegitimacy, testify to the framework of a social order in which marriage and family solidarity are taken absolutely for granted. Yet at the same time, asserts Orwell, they are deeply subversive:

Whatever is funny is subversive, every joke is ultimately a custard pie, and the reason why so large a proportion of jokes centre around obscenity is simply that all societies, as the price of survival, have to insist on a fairly high standard of sexual morality. A dirty joke is not of course a serious attack upon morality, but it is a sort of mental rebellion, a momentary wish that things were otherwise (p.176).

11

Orwell's thesis, shorn of his eye for telling detail, is traditional and commonsensical. But it contains an unresolved dilemma: how can it be that something is simultaneously conservative and subversive, simultaneously supportive and destructive of the status quo? Orwell's answer is that everyone has two sides to their nature, the Quixote side and the Sancho Panza side, the noble and the ignoble, and that such jokes give temporary pride of place to Sancho; on the way they reaffirm his indissoluble relation to Quixote, acting as a kind of safety valve for the only quasi-avowable appetites that all our Sancho sides have, thus reaffirming the ultimate dominance of the Don. The jokes are so to speak a holiday from the pressures of nobility. Of course, this scarcely resolves the dilemma, it merely displaces it to the psychological plane: to assert that bawdy reinforces morality by subverting it is no less paradoxical in its psychological formulation than in its political one. Now it is not that this paradox is incorrect: it is just that it is a paradox, and therefore in need of exploration; we shall see that it is indeed capable of elucidation, and that without reducing it to homogeneity.

Orwell's article brings us to the heart of one of the most contentious aspects of humour: the relationship between comedy/humour and non-comic values – which was of course already implied by the theme of 'Can't you take a joke?' in the opening story.

Take the case of feminism and dirty jokes. Many feminists find the bulk of sexual humour unacceptable – to the extent that one feminist of my acquaintance has started a collection of acceptably feminist dirty jokes. The unacceptability is based on the analysis that sexual humour implicitly asserts that woman = vagina, and is therefore demeaning. Now the appeal of dirty jokes to those who like them is probably that they speak the unspeakable – that is why (all other things being equal) a sexual pun is usually considered funnier than a non-sexual one – and it is fairly unlikely that anyone enjoying a dirty joke would be aware that (if the feminist analysis is correct) they were implicitly demeaning women by enjoying it. Where the appreciative audience sees nothing but humour, others see a serious implication. The question thus arises: how is it possible for two different groups of people to see two entirely different things in the same artefact?

One answer is of course to say that when you are on the receiving end of ridicule it is difficult to appreciate the joke. Some comedians deliberately use comedy as a weapon. Ulster playwright Bill Morrisson, for instance, explicitly uses comedy to ridicule those who use violence in Ulster; his way of writing about 'the troubles' is to create 'black farce', 'appalling farce', for he thinks that those who use violence want to be taken very seriously indeed, and he refuses:

> If you are a person who tries to pursue a civilised value and if you forswear the use of force, what have you got? What can you put against the weapons of force? . . . the only weapon I possess is the weapon of scurrilous humour, and I believe that comedy is a final resort of civilisation . . . ('Conversation Piece').

And he creates a form of comedy where he 'rolls in the jokes like hand-grenades'. No doubt his victims find it difficult to appreciate his humour. But this is not quite a parallel instance to dirty jokes and feminism, for no matter how demeaning feminists may find them, they are unlikely to feel that they are intentionally insulting.

If we stick with comedy that is intended to ridicule, or that has given offence, we can draw some limited conclusions. If feminists are angered and insulted by dirty jokes, it is because they feel that such humour, by demeaning women, helps to perpetuate the status quo, the status quo of patriarchy; dirty jokes, to them, are an act of aggression whose purpose is to continue male dominance, like pornography. To them, therefore, sexual humour is intensely conservative. For appreciative males (and perhaps females), the pleasure of sexual humour derives from making comedy out of something which is the source of constant emotional tension, that derives in fact from subverting inhibitions (in simplified form, this is Freud's theory, as we shall see); to them, therefore, sexual humour is experienced as something subversive and liberating. Obviously similar considerations apply to explicit satire. What happens in cases like this, it would seem, is that in order to attack something by ridicule, or to give offence, a joke must by contrast validate something else. If McGill's postcards make nakedness and chamber pots seem funny, it is because modesty is implicitly normal, and therefore to find nakedness and chamber pots funny is to accept the normality of modesty. Indeed, such implicit presuppositions may well reinforce the attitudes in question – if we find dirty jokes funny it is because we accept the normality of sexual reticence, and all the other implications that are commonly present, such as the centrality of genitalia to male/female relations. If John Randolph of Roanoke can ridicule his opponent by comparing him unfavourably to a slave and a jackass, it is because we implicitly accept that he (and we) are or ought to be superior to both; that is why the slave reference in his reply is likely to be offensive in the twentieth century if not at the time it was made. Or to use a current joke: 'How do you become a millionaire?' – 'Invest £900,000 for a year'; implication: you can't. Do such implications in fact reinforce attitudes? We shall see that there is a major snag with such an equation.

If we were to restrict ourselves to such examples, perhaps on the grounds that they are the most interesting and important type of humour, we would conclude something along these lines: that humour can be used to attack some things and defend others, and we might then investigate, à propos any individual or group of individuals, what the tendency of their humour was: what did they mock and what implicit values did their humour promote. This method has recently been applied to television sitcom in the BFI Sitcom Dossier. We might perhaps even find out that there were some universal topics of humour (sexuality would obviously be a prime candidate – though we shall see that even this is dubious). We might also find that certain groups found some topics absolutely unsuitable for humour.

Interesting though such material might be, especially for the social scientist perhaps, it would have a clear disadvantage: failure to take account of the form of humour or comedy in itself; for by reducing comedy to the play of serious values (attacking A, promoting B) the nature of the process, the pleasure which is specific to comedy and humour, is lost. (Conventionally, this question is referred to psychology or philosophy, though we shall see that there are good reasons for preferring another approach.) This involves an impasse, and it is the impasse evoked in the story that opened these pages: 'Can't you take a joke?' To evoke values in the mode of humour is to evoke them in a special, unique way, a way which cannot ultimately be reduced to the serious presentation of the 'same' material; hence, perhaps, the special effectivity of humour – this will be the subject of Chapter 9. Therefore the final element which any theory of humour and comedy has to include is the capacity to explain how humour mobilises the materials it uses – such as serious values – how it transforms them into humour, and how by so doing it gives them an impact which is unique to it. A theory of humour must, in short, be able to account for the special effectivity, the special pleasure itself independent of 'what' the joke is about.

These matters are addressed, in fictional form, in Trevor Griffiths' play *Comedians*. A group of would-be professional stand-up comics are being taught their craft in an evening class by an old professional, and the play is set in the evening when they get their first try-out in a local working men's club, with a talent scout in the audience. The focus of the play is a series of conflicts about what comedy ought to be: should it be nothing but the creation of laughter, as the talent scout holds? Or should it be a means of getting at the truth, of confronting fears and insecurities, as the teacher maintains? Or should it be the expression of hatred of the oppressors of the working class, as one of the hopefuls insists? The play clearly rejects the first opinion – commercialism – on the grounds that it involves pandering to all the worst prejudices that the audience holds: racism, sexism, etc. But it comes to no conclusion with regard to the other two possibilities: they are simply stated as two alternatives, and the audience is left to make its mind up. Griffiths has made it clear in interviews that the situation shown in the play, the conflicts to which it gives voice, is to be seen as a condensation of different aspects of the working class, or different positions which those on the left may adopt: the kindly rational humanism of the teacher and the explosive anger of the pupil (Poole and Wyver, Chapter 5). However, what is central for our purposes is the means Griffiths uses to dramatise these conflicts.

In the first act of the play, the teacher asks the student comics to do an exercise, which consists of responding to a cough in the audience. Gethin Price, the pupil who subsequently voices the thesis that comedy is essentially about class hatred, responds with an obscene limerick, which the teacher criticises on the grounds that it 'hated women' (*Comedians*, p.22); in his opinion, comedy should not pander to vicious stereotypes. In the second act, the would-be professionals try out their acts, but since they have been warned that what the talent scout is looking for is rather different from what their teacher values, some of them change their acts in order to accommodate his commercialism; the changes involve a series of racist and sexist one-liners. Since the comics address the theatre/TV audience as well as the fictitious audience of the working men's club, the real audience is directly implicated, by its own response to the comics' jokes, in the conflict between different comic styles, and the wider political implications of this conflict. If we, the real audience, laugh at the racist and sexist one-liners the comics improvise to accommodate the talent scout, then – Griffiths implies – we are making ourselves accomplices of the processes of racism and sexism. This is a technique which David Edgar has used too:

> I think, there is a moment in . . . *Destiny* which is very funny, for example, when a chap says, about the factory he's working in, there are so many turbans in the canteen it looks like a field of bloody lilies, whereupon the audience has tended to laugh. He then says, 'and smells like the Black Hole of Calcutta', and you can see people throughout the theatre pretending they didn't laugh the first time (p.12).

This scene in *Destiny* is clearly intended to confront the audience with their own collusion in racism, just as is the contrast between the different acts in *Comedians*.

The core of Griffiths' drama is thus the clash between different comic styles and the consequent political positions that derive from them. In this process the decisive moment is Gethin Price's act, which is the last of the would-be comics' presentations at the club and the point at which the divergence between comic styles becomes most heavily underlined. Price appears dressed as a skinhead Manchester United supporter but made up as a clown, with a thick white mask of make-up. He starts his act with a gag about a violin bow with a loose string, which he burns; then he stomps on the violin, and launches into a short soliloquy about smashing up trains accompanied by Kung Fu exercises. At this point the spotlights show up a pair of tailors' dummies, in evening dress; Price alternatively attempts to befriend them, berates them and insults them, cracks jokes, and finally pins a flower on the girl's immaculate white gown, which draws blood. His act finishes with the alternation of football chants and comments about not needing the upper classes, finishing with a horrendously out of tune rendering of the *Red Flag* on another violin.

The reaction of the onstage audience in the TV version is stunned silence, and in the following act the other comedians respond negatively as well: the talent scout describes it as repulsive, the teacher as brilliant but terrifying, one of his fellows calls it putrid; in a final conversation with his teacher, Price defends it in terms of his vision of the truth. So unfunny is his act that even the two jokes he tells in its course – both of which could be funny in a different context – are killed stone dead by the pervasive aura of hatred that emanates from the performance as a whole. The outrageousness of what he has done underlines as heavily as possible the link between comic styles and political commitment that is the core of the play, and at the same time introduces a new dimension: the possibility that the opposition between commercialism and decency (the talent scout and the teacher) may have been bypassed and rendered obsolete by the anger and hatred that Price's act expresses.

The act which precedes Gethin Price's is a catalogue of insults against women, most of which women find difficult to laugh at (the televised version is somewhat cleaned up); but it contains one joke which many women do find funny:

I took my wife to the zoo. Belle Vue, to see the orang-utan. Enormous, great painted whatsits, like rump steak. . . . She falls right over the wire, as sure as I'm standing here, she trips clean over and lands on her back with her legs parted, her skirt up and her drawers flapping in the wind. I couldn't look, it was horrible. I can remember when I'd a given a week's wages for half what was on show. The big feller kinda sniffs and ambles towards her, and there was this music from his rear end, a slow tolling, dong, dong, dong. . . . he ends up poised above her, like that, and the wife whispers: (Breathless terror) 'George, what shall I do? What shall I do?' And I said: (Whisper) 'Tell *him* you've got a headache . . .' (pp.47-8).

Is this a joke that 'hates women', like Price's obscene limerick in the previous act? If so, why do women find it funny? For Griffiths, laughing at this joke implicates the audience in sexism, but there is another possibility: that laughter at this joke is dissociated from hatred of women, or from sexism, by the absurdity of the situation evoked in the punch line. That is to say, if the situation evoked was plausible, or realistic, then the audience's response to it would necessarily involve hatred of women, or sexism; but because it is impossible to believe in the situation – no husband would in fact behave like this – the laughter which it evokes may perhaps be innocent of hatred, precisely in so far as no one can *take the situation seriously*. Clearly, for a member of the audience who does hate women such a joke would have a reverberation that would feed, and feed off, this hatred; but for anyone else – and especially a woman, perhaps – laughter would not necessarily imply anything other than the perception of the absurdity of the situation. In any event, the overall thesis of this book is that such ambiguities are built into the reception of comedy and humour, and this for reasons that are fundamental to their nature.

The subject matter of this book is film and television comedy, and it has been chosen for several reasons. The first is that it is probably the most pervasive form of comedy in our society, despite the common-place activity of joke telling, for there is a clear connection between the forms of TV comedy and the form of the joke as it is told in everyday life: both lay primary stress upon a form that delivers a laugh at a controlled moment – the punch line – and both involve the narrator as a focus of attention (contrast mutual enjoyment of a humorous situation, or a dialogue with no audience, where each amuse the other). The second reason is that in these forms the relationship between individual joke and the larger-scale narrative in which it is placed is extremely visible precisely because of their reliance upon the form of the joke; the obvious contrast here would be a writer like Dickens, whose comic effects depend upon far more diffuse processes. The third reason for this choice of subject matter is that it enables us to focus upon the relationship between verbal and visual humour, for in film and TV comedy (with the obvious exception of the silent screen) both are omnipresent. To anticipate somewhat, we shall see that the fundamental mode of operation of both is the same, and that in order to demonstrate this, we shall need to refer to certain recent theories of how signifying systems function.

1
Taking Humour Seriously

A review of current theories of humour and comedy would be a book in itself, and a large one: most major thinkers have included a theory of humour in their systems, and there is a mass of psychological and sociological theorising on the subject, as well as commentaries on comic texts and aesthetic theories based on them. Fortunately, major thinkers' theories of comedy cannot readily be disintricated from the overall systems of which they form part, and brief summaries rarely make much sense. For Henri Bergson, for example, laughter is a feature of man's inherently social nature; life in society demands adherence to rules, but in order to function properly across historical change society must be flexible, akin to a living organism that develops as circumstances change. Laughter derives from man's natural spitefulness, but it has a beneficial social function: it is to shame those people who are unwilling or unable to fit in with the demands of a flexible social order. The common feature of all butts of humour is that they have ossified, their behaviour has become mechanical and inflexible and thus a threat to the capacity of the social fabric to develop: so it is that the nature of laughter is such as to promote social ends.[1] Clearly such a theory makes little sense outside the context of Bergson's theory of society – what, for example, does 'social flexibility' mean? Should we take his theory to imply that all laughter has the function of promoting socio-political change? Such a brief account is necessarily a travesty, and this would be true of any similar account of other major thinkers.

The alternative to a survey of current and classic theories of humour and comedy is the analysis of themes which dominate such writing. Recent theorising on the subject is dominated by two themes, each of

19

which is in fact an area of unresolved debate; these themes are:

1) the question of whether the comic – regardless of the medium of its transmission – is an immanent property of a given event, utterance or text, or whether these latters' comic quality is something which is established in a process of negotiation with the audience;

2) in the case of the analysis of what are formally designated as comic texts – a film, a TV show, a book, a play, as opposed to a remark in a conversation that arouses laughter – is the analysis to be based upon the minimum unit of comedy, the individual joke or gag and its structure, or upon larger scale units, comic narrative or comic character, for example?

This matrix of themes could be represented diagrammatically, thus:

Unit of analysis

		Maximum	Minimum
Status of the comic	Immanent	A	B
	Negotiated	C	D

In this diagram any given analysis would fit into one or other of the boxes A,B,C or D: Freud's theory, for example, would be in box B, as it is based upon the supposition that the unit of analysis is the individual joke, and that the comic is immanent rather than negotiated. Most literary or film criticism would fit in box A, since it is based on the large scale units of narrative and character, and assumes that the comic is immanent; interactionist sociology and social psychology is in box D, as it argues for the inherently negotiable nature of comedy, and is usually based upon minimum units of analysis, although in principle there is no reason why it should not be based on the analysis of units such as character.

The rest of this chapter is devoted to a fuller exploration of these themes and to arguing for an option within them.

Humour: Immanent or Negotiated?

In 'The Social Control of Cognition' Mary Douglas argues that a joke must be both perceived as a joke and permitted as a joke, in other words that two processes must occur. A given utterance or event must be seen as having something funny about it (intentional or otherwise), and this something funny must be allowed to be funny; thus a joke told in a pub might be permitted to be funny, while the self-same words uttered during a funeral might be refused this status by the listeners and regarded as offensive instead, because under these circumstances any joke would be offensive. Similarly, we may recognise humorous intention, but simply not be amused – the intended humour may strike us as banal, for instance. Arguably, however, failure through banality is not really a question of permission for humour: failing to laugh at a bad pun is a very different reaction to being offended at a sick joke during a funeral. In the case of a bad pun, we might prefer to say, humour has been permitted but has simply failed. In any event, within this framework it is clear that humour is something negotiated rather than an immanent property of utterances, and that this negotiation has two fundamental axes: in the first place, whether such-and-such a topic and/or occasion is appropriate for humour ('Do you mind! There are ladies present', etc.); in the second, whether such-and-such an utterance, intended as humorous, succeeds in creating mirth: the bad pun or banal joke greeted with stony silence, the elaborate, recondite witticism that meets blank incomprehension – both are examples of something permitted as humour but failing.

Analyses of literary and cinematic comedy tend to ignore these considerations. Certainly criticism is concerned with aesthetic success or failure, but success or failure at mirth creation is usually passed over rapidly in favour of analysis of plot and character. In any event, it is rare for professional comedians to fail to make somebody laugh, and criticism is usually directed towards analysing other features of comic performance. In general, criticism is premissed upon a concern with the properties of texts rather than the properties of audiences. Furthermore, the objects of such criticism (comic texts) are entities which are formally designated as sources of entertainment and made available in institutionally appropriate forms (clubs, books, theatres, broadcasts, etc.): it is difficult to be exposed to formal comedy under inappropriate circumstances – short of listening to tapes on a personal stereo during a funeral! As a result, such texts are unlikely to be refused the status of comedy-in-intention; the exceptions derive from real mismatch between audience and comedian – telling Nazi jokes at a bar-mitzvah, for example – or those moments when there is a sudden shift in comic styles, and what one audience thinks is hilarious is seen as offensive by others. The reception of Lenny Bruce is an example of this, as is the fate of the 1960s British TV satire show *That Was The Week That Was* – despite its remarkable success, increasing its audience from around two million to around twelve and a half million in three months, it was never repeated, presumably because it was too controversial in its satire. Similar examples are to be found in the fate of comedians and comic institutions in more repressive régimes: the fate of the Weimar cabaretiers after the Nazi takeover is well-known.[2] However, if the status of comedy-in-intention is rarely refused, the status of comedy-as-success may certainly be refused by a particular audience on the grounds of banality, poor performance, etc.: an audience which appreciates alternative cabaret is unlikely to appreciate a 'Carry On' film, for instance.

These considerations may explain why the question of the negotiation of humour is likely to be relatively insignificant in the analysis of comic texts, therefore in film and literary criticism. The place where it may be expected to be crucial is in the analysis of humour in everyday life, for here the institutional designation of utterances as sources of entertainment has a low profile, restricted virtually to introductory sentences such as 'Have you heard the one about . . . ?' Under circumstances where the audience may have very restricted indications of whether a given utterance is to be considered funny or not, we may expect that disagreement over whether to permit it the status of comedy/humour would be more likely than under the sort of institutionally clear circumstances outlined above. Unsurprisingly, therefore, it is in social scientific literature that such considerations are to be found.

Handelman and Kapferer's study of joking activity, for example, discusses an episode in which an insult is deflected by joking: X says, audibly and maliciously, in a small group, 'Y is fat', to which Y – an elderly male – replies 'No I'm not, I'm pregnant', and the group respond by laughing. Under these circumstances another response would have been equally plausible, and Handelman and Kapferer are able to give an explanation of the emergence of this response rather than any other in terms of the dynamics of the group in question: in oversimplified form, this consists of interpreting X's use of the insult as an attempt to establish his status in the group, and the group's unwillingness to grant it him, expressed in accepting the joking response as such, which effectively undermined the first speaker's interpretation of the circumstances which gave rise to his insult. In this analysis, Y's reply is not to be considered inherently funny: the absurdity of his comment could be interpreted in several ways (as childish, for instance), and it is only as the result of a process of negotiation of its meaning that it is declared funny. We shall see later whether this interpretation is necessarily correct: for the moment, what is significant for our purposes is to recognise that this interpretation is indeed plausible, and that it points very clearly in the direction of a theory of the negotiation of comic meaning, as opposed to a theory of its immanency.

Similar conclusions can be derived from Gail Jefferson's study of how participants in a conversation indicate that a given utterance is to be considered humorous. Jefferson observes that it is a frequent feature of everyday conversations that a speaker should indicate that a remark was intended humorously by inserting a laugh in the flow of speech at the end of the remark in question; the listener can then either accept the implied invitation to laugh or reject it; if acceptance occurs the conversation can then start up again, if rejection occurs then the speaker may repeat the laughter invitation and logically this could be an interminable process. Jefferson observes that the potential relevance of laughter as a response has to be positively denied, in the form of pursuing the topic of conversation in a non-humorous vein, that is taking up the serious cues that are contained in the previous utterance and basing the development of the conversation upon them, bypassing the possibilities offered by the invitation to consider the preceding remark as humorous. The implications of such a study are clear; remarks are not intrinsically humorous, their intention as humour has to be indicated by a para-linguistic marker and their status is then available for negotiation between interested parties; the outcome of such negotiation may be recognition as humour or the reverse.

23

Not all those who are concerned with humour in everyday life consider it to be subject to a process of negotiation. No doubt the most eminent of such immanentist theories is Freud's *Jokes and their Relation to the Unconscious*, to which we shall return at a later stage of the argument. A more recent example is to be found in the application of the theory of psychological reversals to humour.[3]

Psychological theories of humour have tended to assume a homeostatic model of the mind, a model in which the normal state of the mind is psychic equilibrium rather than its opposite; in this context humour is seen as a process of paradox creation and resolution, where the paradox creates disequilibrium and its resolution restores equilibrium. The theory of reversals is based on the general hypothesis that there are certain mental states in which disequilibrium is the norm rather than its opposite; these states are non-goal-oriented (para-telic) rather than telic – states of mind such as playfulness and humour. Under these circumstances forms of disequilibrium which would be experienced as unpleasant in a telic state are experienced as pleasant instead. The form of disequilibrium which is specific to humour consists in attributing to any one thing or person two conflicting identities or attributes. Thus, in the old slapstick standard of slipping on a banana skin the two attributes would be normality and abnormality, comfort and discomfort, dignity and indignity, for example. Such conflicting identities are not exclusive to humour and are equally to be found in other forms, such as metaphor or sport. In metaphor things which are dissimilar are joined together – 'The slings and arrows of outrageous fortune', for example – and the pleasure of metaphor derives from this junction of the dissimilar; in sport the context in which it takes place assures the spectator that the excitement (s)he feels is not accompanied by danger.

Clearly any theory which cannot distinguish between humour and limitrophic phenomena is defective, and we shall have occasion to return to this question later. Reversal theorists distinguish the identity conflicts of humour on two grounds. Firstly, humour always involves the conflict between the real and the apparent; secondly, the replacement of the apparent by the real always implies denigration of whatever is the subject of these conflicting identities; for example:

CUSTOMER: I've been waiting here for ten minutes!

WAITER: That's all right, sir. I've been waiting here twenty-five years.

Here the apparent meaning of 'waiting', the customer's meaning, is replaced by a second 'real' meaning which undermines the value of the customer's complaint. Another example involves an attack with a dagger that turns out to be a toy with a retractable blade: again the replacement of the apparenty identity with a real identity involves belittling the original.

This theory is subtle, and an assessment of its validity lies outside the scope of an essay on film and television comedy. In the meantime, we should note that it clearly implies that humour is an immanent feature of utterances, and not something that is subject to a process of negotiation.

Maximum or Minimum Unit Analysis of Comic Narrative?

Pre-twentieth century studies of comedy tended to concentrate on the didactic function of laughter: laughter was considered a pleasant way of discouraging misbehaviour through its mockery. In this respect the publication in 1914 of F.M. Cornford's *Origins of Attic Comedy* marks a watershed, for Cornford considers literary comedy no longer prescriptively, in terms of a moral function, but descriptively, in terms of the vision of the world that it encapsulates. Tracing its origins to religious ritual, he considers its essential content to be a celebration of the renewal of life, the expulsion of the forces associated with old age and death and the assertion of youth and vigour, whence its 'erotic tone' and its 'canonical ending in marriage'.[4] This shift in perspective not only changed the dominant approach to comedy from prescriptive to descriptive, but also set the agenda for much future commentary, for the theme of life-enhancement has become a commonplace since.

One of the most influential versions of this theme has been the chapter devoted to comedy in Suzanne Langer's *Feeling and Form.* Her account is marked by two fundamental drives: firstly, by the desire to provide a descriptive basis for a theory of comedy; secondly, by the attempt rigorously to separate comedy as an art form (one of the 'great dramatic forms') from mere everyday humour. The descriptive base consists of an account of the urge to self-preservation which she takes to be the basis of our species, indeed of all organic life, and which takes the form of the 'sense of life' or 'enjoyment' (pp.327ff); thus the morality of comedy, central to earlier theories, is no more than an excuse – one among many possible – for the creation of fictional form (p.326), a form which is no more than the surge of vitality. Anticipatably, Langer is led to repudiate any identity between comedy and 'funniness': the essence of comedy is the conflict between the forces of destiny and the sense of vitality, where the protagonist is irreducibly vital and the forces of destiny are entirely external to him/her; whereas in tragedy, destiny is interior and the protagonist is forced into an *agon*, the fundamental total reappraisal of self and the world that is the basis of the tragic vision. The comic confrontation does not even have to end happily, since Fate hands out definitive misfortune even to the irreducibly vital; it is the externality of the relationship between protagonist and fate that is central to comedy, and thus Langer can include the whole of classical French tragedy in the category of comedy (p.336).

Nevertheless, laughter and the funny, the 'comical' as she calls it, is readily associated with comedy. But it is important, she claims, both to see that all forms of humour are versions of the same drive to the expression of felt vitality, and that there is a clear distinction between everyday humour and humour in art, that is, comedy. Discussing Marcel Pagnol's theory that humour consists of the sense of superiority, she produces anomalies to demonstrate its insufficiency: gallows humour and the baby laughing at the repetition of simple actions; in both cases the explanation is the surge of the feeling of vitality, through wish gratification (baby) and self-assertion (gallows humour), which they have in common with Pagnol's sense of superiority. Here, therefore, is a theory of everyday comedy, not dependent upon artistic form. Everyday comedy is the product of 'stimuli' that only work if we are in the mood for them (p.347), whereas humour in comedy is carefully articulated on to the structure of the narrative, and therefore little things that would not make us laugh in everyday life do make us laugh in fiction (pp.344ff); for example, 'political and topical allusions in a play amuse us because they are *used,* not because they refer to something very funny' (p.347). This distinction is paralleled by the distinction between farce and comedy. In farce, comedian TV shows and the like, 'the laughs are likely to be of a peculiar sameness, almost perfunctory, the formal recognition of a timely "gag" . . .' (p.345), and the 'flood of shows' based on topical allusions do not outlive their topicality (p.348).

At this point it is clear that Langer has edged over the awkward dividing line between prescription and description: farce is not comedy for the same reason that everyday humour is not comedy, that neither of them have any artistic shape, any 'organic form' (p.326). Does this surreptitious transition contaminate her descriptive base, the 'sense of life'? Laughter and humour are only one of the forms that comedy (in her sense) may take, as we have seen; and therefore humour is subordinate to comedy, logically: what are we to make, in this case, of humour which is not part of comedy? For humour is apparently given its meaning by its subordinate participation in the order of comedy – is non-comedy humour still part of the surge of vitality, but not taking an artistic form? Or is it some other awkward entity? And are there other forms of surges of vitality, which escape comic artistic form – sexual passion, for instance (p.332)? How are we to place these various phenomena in relation to one another? Clearly the fundamental principle which animates these distinctions, their taxonomic base therefore, is artistic creativity manifest in organic form; but this in itself can tell us nothing about humour, funniness, or about contiguous, limitrophic phenomena.

It is no exaggeration to say that this approach has dominated commentary on literary comedy; for example, a recent essay on the comic hero suggests that he is 'comic . . . primarily by virtue of the festive values that he celebrates and embodies: values of biological life and imaginative freedom, of dogged humanity and belligerent self-hood'.[5]

Two themes in Langer's argument are of particular relevance for our purposes. The first is her assertion that the essential meaning of comedy is created by the 'comic rhythm', that is to say by the form of the comic narrative as a whole, whose basis is the externality of the relationship between fate and the protagonist. The second is that Langer explicitly distinguishes between comedy and 'mere funniness', and that she is necessarily obliged to by the structure of her argument: it would be difficult to assert that a whole story was in itself funny just because of its overall narrative shape; nor are the festive values, the sense of vitality, in themselves funny even if they are the basis of comedy.

In this tradition the units of analysis are the narrative pattern and the nature of the hero – what I have called the maximum units of analysis. Such an approach is not without its difficulties, as can be seen from Gerald Mast's attempt to classify the plots of film comedies into groups. He distinguishes eight varieties:

1) young lovers succeed in marrying despite various obstacles;
2) the parody of other genres;
3) the *reductio ad absurdum* in which a single mistake produces utter chaos;
4) 'an investigation of the workings of a particular society, comparing the responses of one social group or class with those of another';
5) the picaresque, where the picaro's 'bouncing off' people and events reveals his superiority to his surroundings;
6) a sequence of gags;
7) the heroic endeavour, notably Buster Keaton;
8) the discovery of a life-long error or foible.

Quite apart from the fact that several of these categories are far from specific to comedy, two things are striking: firstly, that most of the plot categories are based upon narrative shape (1,3,4,7,8) or the nature of the hero (5,7); secondly, that the two exceptions (2 and 6) demand a theory which is based upon the minimum unit of comic narrative, the individual joke or gag – for the distinguishing feature of a sequence of gags is precisely that it is nothing but a sequence of gags, that it has no other narrative structure, and a parody must consist of a series of episodes, each of which is a distorted version of some other text. In other words, the weak point in Mast's theory is that the plot structures *either* are not specifically funny, not specific to comedy in any sense of the word, *or* they are not in fact plot structures, but refer to the minimum unit of comic plot, the individual joke or gag. The reason for this aporia is clear: even if we accept Langer's distinction between comedy and everyday humour, we would nonetheless be obliged to refer to 'funniness' in texts as one way in which certain comic texts, although certainly not all those Langer classfies as comic, in fact embody festive values and incarnate the sense of vitality which Langer sees as central. In other words, there must be some relationship between funniness and the overall shape of the comic narrative and the nature of the comic hero. At this point, two things occur: firstly, the distinction between comedy and humour starts to break down; secondly, an obvious question poses itself – what is it about humour that casts it in this role? Why is it appropriate? Both of these considerations point in the direction of an analysis of the minimum unit of comedy, the individual joke or gag, since it is here that 'funniness' is located.

At this point, our survey of the two main debates in theorising about comedy and humour is complete, and we can turn to the third element in this argument: an option within these debates.

We have just seen that the theory of comic narrative demands a theory of the joke or the gag as its necessary counterpart. Similarly, it can be demonstrated that theories of humour that regard it as inherently a matter for negotiation also demand a theory of the joke as their counterpart, and this for a reason that is as easy to show logically as it is difficult to prove empirically: either the negotiation about humour takes place at completely random points in discourse, or it takes place at points which have some feature that marks them as humorous or potentially humorous. This is easiest to demonstrate using Gail Jefferson's study of laughter invitation. For Jefferson, the point at which negotiation occurs is the point at which a para-linguistic marker is inserted in the discourse (a laugh), and therefore, to this extent, the process of negotiation does not occur at a random point. However, what determines the decision to insert a marker at this point rather than at some other? Again, either it is random, or there is some reason for it, and that reason can only be the perception that the remark in question is (potentially) humorous; in its turn, this ascription of potential humour is either random or it has a reason, and commonsense suggests that the latter is more likely.

Empirically, it may be intensely difficult to see what it is about a particular remark that strikes the speaker as humorous and this for a good reason: the laughable features of the remark may be buried deep in the network of perceptions that the individual has of his world – perhaps that is why so many invitations to laugh are declined – or equally deep in the structure of the group among whom the remarks are made: one of the strengths of Handelman and Kapferer's study is that they are able to trace such threads. In parenthesis, it is worth commenting that taking a laugh as necessarily indicating the perception of humour is problematic: it may equally well indicate nervousness or embarrassment.

Thus there are clear and pressing reasons for opting for an approach to the study of comedy and humour which is based upon the analysis of the minimum units of narrative and of those features of them which are intrinsically funny. Not that this approach will be any less fraught with difficulties than the others, as we shall see. However, on the grounds with which we are now familiar, here seems a more fruitful starting place than the alternatives. Freud's *Jokes and their Relation to the Unconscious* is a convenient point of departure.

At the core of Freud's theory is a single, simple assertion: jokes give a form of pleasure that is specific to them, and this form of pleasure, because of its specific nature, is capable of subserving the interests, so to speak, of the 'major purposes and instincts of mental life' (p.183); Freud calls this the 'principle of assistance or intensification' (p.185). Seen in this context, the long section on joke techniques which opens the book has a clear purpose: it is to establish a definition of the form of the joke, and to analyse what Freud calls 'joke-work', a process whose nature is thought out on the basis of an analogy with 'dream-work', that is, with the manner in which dreaming brings disparate elements of everday experience into relation with each other and with the fundamental drives of the unconscious. 'Joke-work' takes words and their associations and brings them into relationship with each other and with the major drives in a way which is specific to them just as dreaming is an activity which is distinct and specific.

Freud divides jokes up into groups on the basis of their techniques. These groups are then arranged in a hierarchy, in which the most important distinction is between verbal and conceptual jokes. The distinctive feature of a verbal joke is that if the words are changed, the joke disappears: when asked about the professions of his four sons,

Professor Rokitansky replied 'Two heal and two howl' (two doctors and two singers); the same information is contained in the words in brackets, but the joke has disappeared, for it is the assonance of 'heal' and 'howl' that provides the joke (p.179). In a joke based on conceptual play, much of the wording can be changed without losing the joke:

> A horse-dealer was recommending a horse to a client. 'If you take this horse and get on it at four in the morning you'll be at Pressburg by half-past six' – 'What should I be doing at Pressburg at half-past six in the morning?' (p.91).

Here much of the wording and the details could be changed without losing the joke provided the basic equivocation was maintained: it could be said à propos any form of transport, anywhere, and even the exact nature of the final reply is not essentially invariable – it could equally well be something like 'What's so great about Pressburg in the morning?'

This major distinction is then broken down into a series of sub-categories, whose complete scheme is diagrammatically represented overleaf.[6]

However, Freud does not appear very interested in a taxonomy of joke techniques for its own sake; indeed, as soon as he comes to discuss the purposes of jokes he abandons the question of technique and its sub-divisions, and approaches the question instead from the point of view of the relation of jokes to the unconscious. Here, he distinguishes between 'innocent' and 'tendentious' jokes: jokes whose pleasure derives entirely from their technique, and jokes which act as a mask for one of the drives of the unconscious, notably aggression and desire. It is at this point that the distinction between verbal and conceptual jokes takes on its real importance, for – despite some terminological confusions – this distinction is essentially isomorphic with that between innocent and tendentious jokes. We shall see shortly the importance of this relationship.

Freud's thoughts on the subject of joke technique have one final significant characteristic: the techniques of jokes are explicitly not specific to them, they are equally characteristic of other forms of statement. Unification, for instance, is equally a characteristic of

```
                                          ┌─ with composite words
                        condensation      └─ with modifications

                                          ┌─ whole words and
                                          │     their components
                                          │  inversion
                        use of the same   │  slight modification
                        same material     │  same words,
                                          │     in their full or
                                          └─     watered-down sense

          verbal                          ┌─ proper name and
          jokes                           │     name of object
                                          │  metaphorical and
                                          │     literal sense
                        double meaning    │  word play
                                          │  equivocation
                                          │  double meaning
                                          └─    and allusion

jokes
                        puns

                                          ┌─ displacement
                        faults of         │  contraction
                        reasoning         └─ other faults

          conceptual    unification
          jokes

                                          ┌─ by the opposite
                        indirect          │  by something similar
                        representation    └─ comparisons
```

riddles (p.105n), and the principal techniques of jokes are also typical of dream-work: faults of reasoning, condensation and displacement; representation by the contrary is also the basis of irony, which is – as we shall see in Chapter 4 – far from universally comic. It is tempting to assert that these remarks miss the point, that it is central to Freud's method to underline a parallel between dream-work and joke-work, for instance. However, the core of Freud's theory of jokes is that jokes give a form of pleasure specific to them, and that it is this pleasure which is responsible for the contribution they make to the processes of the unconscious; but by conflating joke and non-joke techniques Freud denies himself this possibility. This is controversial, no doubt, and needs to be demonstrated.

Freud insistently repeated that the essential characteristics of jokes are to be found in tendentious jokes. The specificity of the joke is that it overcomes repression and inhibitions; the demonstration of the mechanism whereby this is achieved is based on the example of tendentious jokes, which are defined in the process: at the moment at which the joke overcomes repression there are present in the mind three tendencies:

  a) to do something that is the object of social disapprobation – for
     example, insult someone;
  b) the repression of that tendency;
  c) the pleasure specific to the joke.

In the absence of (c), (b) will usually succeed in repressing (a); but if a joke is introduced into the overall situation – that is, if (c) is introduced – then the combined pleasure of (a) and (c) will be sufficient to overcome (b). Under these circumstances, Freud argues, a thought which would be an insult if it was not expressed in joke form will be expressed (in the form of a joke) and tendency (a) will find expression. Clearly the pleasure which is specific to the joke is central to this schema; it consists, Freud explains, of the capacity to subvert the norms of adult rational thought – which he also often calls 'rational criticism' – for it is in these norms that repression occurs. Through this subversion the adult manages to recreate the sense of pleasure in play that the child loses in the process of maturation. Jests and jokes prolong 'the yield of pleasure from play' by silencing 'the objections raised by criticism which would not allow the pleasurable feeling to emerge' (pp.178-9); this is achieved by combining the yield of pleasure with the demands of criticism: 'the meaningless combination of words or the absurd putting together of thoughts must nevertheless have a meaning' (p.179).

Thus, as Freud insists in the following pages, it is not the techniques of jokes that define them, but the capacity to subvert criticism and give pleasure through the prolongation of the childlike sense of play. This pleasure that is brought about by the subversion of rational adult criticism derives from the pleasure created in general by the subversion of inhibition, for rational criticism is in itself an inhibition; its subversion corresponds therefore to an economy of psychic expenditure.

We are now in a position to understand the logic of Freud's paradoxical argument that jokes could not be separated from other linguistic forms on the basis of their techniques:

> The technique which is characteristic of jokes and peculiar to them, however, consists in their procedure for safeguarding the use of these methods of providing pleasure against the objections raised by criticism which would put an end to the pleasure (p.180).

This procedure, which protects the sources of pleasure, is precisely psychic economy, for a procedure which does not consist of the techniques of jokes must be based on the relationship between the joke and the mind of the listener. That is to say, the technique of jokes is to be found equally in things that are not jokes, and the distinction between jokes and non-jokes is displaced to the manner in which the mind appreciates the technique.

Now it is true that certain other affirmations made by Freud somewhat undermine his insistence that joke techniques do not have a central place in the schema, notably the way in which he returns to the question of the mixture of sense and nonsense in jokes ('the meaningless combination . . . must have a meaning'); for if this combination was specific to jokes it could be considered a way of distinguishing the joke from other linguistic forms on purely technical grounds. Freud's statements are inconsistent on this point: on the one hand he says ' . . . there is no necessity for us to derive the pleasurable effect of jokes from the conflict between the feelings which arise . . . from the simultaneous sense and nonsense of jokes' (p.181), and nowhere does he indicate that in his opinion the combination of sense and nonsense is a technical matter.

These assertions and lack of assertions are consistent with the position that there is no technical distinction between jokes and nonjokes. On the other hand, he says (also p.181), 'the pleasure in a joke is derived from a play with words or from the liberation of nonsense, and the meaning of the joke is merely intended to protect that pleasure from being done away with by criticism'. Two pressures are at play in this sentence: on the one hand, Freud appears to feel obliged to admit that the mixture of sense and nonsense is central to the joke process, for it – more specifically, the presence of sense – protects pleasure from criticism; on the other hand, it 'merely' does this, and the presence of 'merely' indicates very forcefully the drift of Freud's thought.

Freud is therefore in a position characterised here by two contradictory pulls: either jokes are technically distinct, because of the mixture of sense and nonsense; or they are not. If one opts for the first possibility (which is arguably faithful to the letter of Freud's text, but not to its spirit) then two further problems arise. Firstly, is it true that the mixture of sense and nonsense is specific to jokes? (We shall see in Chapter 3 that it is not.) Secondly, it would no longer be true that the essence of jokes was to allow free rein to the drives of the unconscious, for what was true of tendentious jokes would also be true of innocent jokes – we shall see that this problem is in fact capable of resolution. If we opt for the second possibility, then a further problem arises: what mechanism is responsible for the psychic economy which protects the technique of the joke from rational criticism? If Freud wishes to maintain the affirmation that joke techniques are not distinct from other linguistic forms, then it is clear that the source of psychic economy cannot be in the techniques: but at the same time there can be no other possible source. The pleasure of play cannot be the source because the joke produces the pleasure of play precisely by subverting criticism – that is to say, it is thanks to jokes' subversive capacities that psychic economy is created. *But it is psychic economy that protects jokes and play from rational criticism.* The argument is thus strangely circular, precisely in so far as Freud has refused to distinguish between jokes and other linguistic forms.

In Freud's theory humour is an immanent feature of the signifying system – with the proviso, noted above, that there is a point of incoherence in the letter of Freud's text, and that that incoherence indicates the site of this immanence. Clearly the feature of the signifying system that is responsible for its efficacity in this respect is the mixture of sense and nonsense to which Freud refers somewhat equivocally. Now this notion of sense and nonsense mixed is something of a commonplace in writing about humour in the twentieth century. To take an example: in the opening chapter of *The Art of Laughter,* N. Schaeffer refers the source of humour to the notion of incongruity, which he defines in these terms:

> With incongruity we see two things which do not belong together, yet which we accept at least in this case as going together in some way. That is, when we notice something as incongruous, we also simultaneously understand it to be in some minor way congruous. Our mental task is to find this slender element of congruity amid the predominating elements of incongruity (p.9).

This definition is subtle, in various ways: in the first place, because it insists upon the relationship between congruity and incongruity – or sense and nonsense, to use Freud's terms; in the second place, because it insists on a disequilibrium between the two, with incongruity predominating, which we shall see in the following chapter to be crucial. The problem which it raises is one which we found also in Freud: how to distinguish between humour and other phenomena which fit the same description? In Freud these were riddles and dreams, in Schaeffer it is primarily poetic metaphor; we may consider all these under the same heading since all involve incongruity, in one way or another. Freud, as we have seen, makes no attempt to distinguish between them as elements of signifying systems, since he refers their operations to the workings of the subconscious. Schaeffer distinguishes between joke and metaphor on two grounds: firstly, the ground of context – the poetic context predisposes us to look for serious connections rather than hilarious ones; secondly, in terms of the distinction between a search for truth and a search for pleasure – metaphor points us in the direction of truth, which takes effort, while humour points us in the direction of pleasure, which involves no effort. None of these grounds seems entirely satisfactory.

As Todorov has pointed out *à propos* Freud's theory, one cannot summarise signifying systems in such a binary way: between truth and its opposite – and by implication between effort and pleasure – lies the realm of the symbolic, which is characterised neither by truth in the empirical sense, nor by nonsense, and which while it may give pleasure certainly demands effort too. In any event, it seems a strange theory of the mind which opposes effort and pleasure, especially in the context of the pleasure of poetry. Secondly, the question of contextual cues. Certainly common sense tells us that we know in advance the difference between a poem and a farce – there are ample institutional and experiential cues available – and that such awareness will prepare us for different types of pleasure. But what do these cues consist of? Gerald Mast suggests that film comedies use things such as the title, the presence of actors who are well known as comedians, anti-illusionistic devices such as talking to camera and 'funny dialogue'; the latter is of course a tautology, and the former present us with the problem of infinite regression: how do we know that such things indicate comedy? Because we have previously seen them introduce comedy: but at what point, and how, did we learn that what they introduced was comedy?

There is no possible end-point to this experiential series, unless we posit one of a different order: it is only when we have experienced something as funny that we are able to know what comedy is, and thus we are back at square one: what signifying element is it that produces the experience of comedy, in other words provokes mirth? In any event, even if cues predispose us to laugh, we still in practice laugh at particular points, not at random points, and we shall see that these points have clearly defined features.

The argument pursued here has now reached a stage at which a change of direction is necessary. What we have learnt so far is that existing theories all raise problems which they are unable to solve within their chosen frameworks, and that all these problems will revolve around a single point: what is it that produces humour? For it is only when that question is answered that we can show how the other processes referred to in the debates summarised above can occur: how comic narrative incarnates the festive values that literary criticism associates it with, why negotiation about what is allowed to be funny should take place at one point in time rather than another, and how jokes are able to release us from certain inhibitions.

Notes

1. Summarised in M. Gurewitch, *Comedy – The Irrational Vision*, 1975, pp.30-4.
2. See L. Appignanesi, *Cabaret*, 1984, especially Chapters 7-8.
3. The theory of psychological reversals is a general theory of motivation, which has been applied to humour among other things. See M. J. Apter, *The Experience of Motivation*, 1982, and M. J. Apter and K. C. P. Smith, 'Humour and the theory of psychological reversals' in Chapman and Foot (eds), *It's a Funny Thing, Humour*, 1977.
4. Summarised in Gurewitch, *Comedy – The Irrational Vision*, pp.34ff.
5. R. Torrance, *The Comic Hero*, 1978, p.viii.
6. Schema translated from T. Todorov, 'La rhétorique de Freud', in *Théories du symbole*, 1976, p.288.

2

The Semiotics of Humour

The Logic of the Absurd

In the second reel of *Liberty* (1929), escaped convicts Laurel and Hardy try to swap trousers on the scaffolding of a half-completed skyscraper, a process that is rendered somewhat more complicated by the fact that one of the pairs also contains a large live and aggressive crab. During these cavortings in the ionosphere they have periodically and unintentionally bombarded the cop at the foot of the half completed structure with a variety of near-lethal objects: a bag of cement, a ladder, . . . Successfully negotiating their way back to the builder's lift on the side of the skyscraper, they descend at exactly the moment that the cop decides to take shelter from the hail of descending objects – in the lift shaft. Laurel and Hardy land squarely on top of him, apparently reducing him to pulp as the lift settles on the ground; they exit rapidly. The lift goes up again to reveal a midget in policeman's uniform.

This is one of Laurel and Hardy's more audacious, surrealistic gags, and one that is entirely successful. It is also an excellent – though in no way privileged, or exceptional – starting point for a theory of gags.

The gag is analysable into two moments, for which the terms 'syllogism' and 'peripeteia' are appropriate.

1. *Peripeteia*

In classical aesthetics the peripeteia is the moment when the fortunes of the principal character are reversed. The example which Aristotle gives is that of Oedipus in Sophocles' eponymous tragedy: Oedipus is eventually forced to recognise that Tiresias has seen the situation correctly, and that he himself has in fact murdered his father and married his mother in exactly the way that the prophecy foretold. In the film of *Tom Jones*, to take a modern example, the peripeteia occurs when Squire Weston cuts Tom down from the gallows at just the moment he is supposedly launched into eternity, and bears him off to marry Sophia. The peripeteias of comedy are of lesser stature, but their essence resembles that of textbook examples such as these two: it is the construction of a shock or surprise in the story the film is telling.

In the example of the lift/cop gag from *Liberty*, the surprise that the narrative constructs for us is the survival of the policeman, albeit in a changed form, when common sense tells us that the result of a squashing in a lift shaft is not reduction in size, but death. But although this surprise results from common sense (this problematic term will be discussed below), it is nonetheless constructed in the narrative of the film: in order for the surprise to occur we must know that the policeman is a normally constituted human being, not Superman or the Incredible Hulk, that the lift is a lift containing two human beings, descending at such and such a speed, etc. In other words, we have to see the immediately preceding segments of the film, in relationship to which the revelation of the cop's new status functions as does the punch line in a verbal joke. That is to say: all jokes, verbal or visual, have two stages, the preparation stage and the culmination stage; and this is true even of the most minimal gags, such as the traditional custard pie in the face, for the custard pie in the face is the culmination of a brief sequence in which the preparation consists, minimally, of the face without custard pie all over it.

Thus the first moment of the gag consists in a form of surprise, for which I have reserved the word peripeteia on the grounds that this form of surprise is constructed in the film narrative and is thus a specifically aesthetic form of surprise. However, it is clear that not all surprise, not even all aesthetic surprise, is funny: to take Aristotle's example again, the moment when Oedipus reappears on stage, his face running with blood after he has gouged out his own eyes, is certainly surprising, in some sense of the word; but it is not funny. What specific feature of comic surprise is responsible for the fact that it is funny? Or: what specific feature of comic surprise turns it into *comic* surprise?

The narrative of a gag:

*Laurel and Hardy decide
to return to safety*

*Their bombardment of the cop
(notice the burst bag, frame
lower left) leads to the same
decision*

*The result of their conference
is disaster . . .*

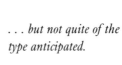

*. . . but not quite of the
type anticipated.*

41

2. *Syllogism*

For the second moment of the gag I have reserved the term syllogism, in order to underline its intensely logical nature.[1] In traditional logic, the syllogism is a system of reasoning in which one moves from a well-known state of affairs (called the major premiss) through an empirical observation (the minor premiss) to a conclusion which is as a result of the nature of the reasoning inevitably correct. A favourite textbook example was:

a) all men are mortal – major premiss, a well-known state of affairs;
b) Socrates is a man – an empirical observation, the minor premiss;
c) therefore – conclusion – Socrates is mortal: an inevitably correct deduction given the nature of the form of reasoning.

However, the syllogistic forms of comedy are more complex, for each gag is constructed out of two, contradictory syllogisms. In the lift/cop gag one line of reasoning tells us that what we see on the screen is intensely implausible:

a) the result of squashing in a lift shaft is death – a well-known state of affairs, the major premiss;
b) i) the cop is squashed – empirical observation, the minor premiss;
     ii) second minor premiss: he survives;
c) conclusion: the event is implausible.

But a second, contradictory, line of reasoning tells us that the event does in fact have a measure of plausibility:

a) the result of squashing is a reduction in size;
b) the cop comes out smaller;
c) therefore the event has a measure of plausibility.

However, we should not imagine that these two syllogisms are of equal weight. The first of the two (implausibility) is clearly a much stronger line of argument than the second, as it has the not inconsiderable merit of being true to the world as we know it on the basis of everyday life; whereas the second is clearly only tenable on the basis of a piece of false reasoning which serves as its basis: the assumption that what is true of inorganic or non-animate forms of being can be unproblematically transposed to the realm of the animate. This manner of reasoning on the basis of a false and unstated premiss was known to traditional logic as the *syllogismus in modo barocco*, the baroque syllogism; a favourite textbook example was: the grass is green, the sea is green, therefore the sea is grass.

The falsity of the second syllogism, and the fact that it is therefore of less weight than the first should not lead us to suppose that it is any the less essential, or that it is any less important in the composition, or structure, of the gag, than the first. The essence of the second moment of the gag is that it is characterised by the simultaneous presence of both modes of reasoning, which are maintained in tension, or balance with each other – provided we do not interpret balance to mean that they are of equal weight; for the tension which characterises their relationship is based precisely on the fact that the second is a false, inferior, type of reasoning.

In summary therefore: the gag can be analysed into two moments, thus:

1) a peripeteia, a shock or surprise that the narrative constructs for us;
2) a pair of syllogisms, leading to contradictory conclusions:
   a) that the process is implausible
   b) that the process nonetheless has a certain measure of plausi-bility, but that this is less than the implausibility.

The peripeteia is prepared and then sprung at a specific moment in the narrative, and this moment also unleashes the process of reflection analysed in the two syllogisms. (It hardly needs underlining that this process is not a conscious, verbalised one on the part of the spectator: it is a spontaneous, intuitive reaction of which the two syllogisms are an elaborated, analytic form.) Finally it should be stressed that the two moments of the gag are in practice absolutely inseparable: without the moment of surprise, there is no estimation of the gag as simultaneously plausible and implausible, and without the preparation for the gag, we would have no means of knowing that the action in question is both plausible and implausible: it is only because we see the lift squash the cop that the emergence of the dwarf is to be characterised in this way. On the other hand, as we have already seen, it is the balance between plausibility and implausibility that makes the peripeteia into comic surprise, and not some other form of surprise, horrific surprise, for instance. For the totality of these processes it seems appropriate to reserve the title: the logic of the absurd.

Thus the gag, considered as an aesthetic form, has a clearly delineated structure, which is in fact responsible for its nature and for the type of pleasure that it gives: humour, or laughter. To this extent, therefore, this analysis has already dealt with an objection raised earlier to other analyses of humour, in which the specific difference of comedy was seen to be lacking: this difference, which enables comedy to perform the various functions ascribed to it, consists precisely of the structure which is outlined here, for – it is my assertion here – this structure is nowhere to be found except in the fundamental forms of comedy. Not that this should lead us to suppose that the topic of the structure of comedy is exhausted by these remarks, for the implications of the structure delineated here are extremely wide.

The first of these implications concerns the nature of the surprise that we have seen to be one of the two moments of comic structure: where do these surprises derive from?

It is possible to distinguish, analytically, between two distinct sources of comic surprise, or peripeteia. The first is the contradiction of knowledge, or values, or expectations about the outside world that the audience may be assumed to derive from their ordinary everyday experience of the outside world – this may be summarised under the heading of the discourses of the social formation. The second is a series of expectations concerning the future course of events on screen that are the product of the narrative up to that point. It should be stressed that this distinction is analytic, and that in most gags both elements are to be found simultaneously, and this for reasons that will turn out to be fundamental.

1. *Peripeteia and the discourses of the social formation*
Perhaps the commonest of all the peripeteias of traditional farce is the infliction of pain and/or indignity on the human body; its most basic form is the custard pie in the face and the banana-skin pratfall. Such comic forms J-P. Coursodon calls 'effects of nature': walking under a ladder and getting a pot of paint on the head is such an effect which produces laughter as a 'purely mechanical reflex', in which there is no

intellectual involvement. A gag, on the other hand, is the intellectual organisation of such effects of nature, such as carefully walking round the ladder and still getting the paint pot on the head (Coursodon, pp.30ff). The exclusive reliance on 'effects of nature' Coursodon calls the pre-history of the gag; the gag starts, he says, where such effects finish.[2]

This distinction does not seem satisfactory, for several reasons. Firstly, it is far from clear that seeing suffering and indignity always produces laughter, whether as a mechanical reflex or in some other way – we have already referred to the example of Oedipus. Minimally, we need some form of reassurance that the suffering is not real, or not serious, a mechanism which could be called 'comic insulation' and which will be discussed shortly. Secondly, the idea that laughter is a mechanical reflex is hard to reconcile with the fact that the production of such laughter occurs in an aesthetic form which is historically specific: if all cultures had art forms in which indignity produced laughter, it might be plausible, but it seems unlikely that this is so; if that is true, then laughter at indignity can hardly be a mechanical reflex, but must be thought of as a product of culturation. Thirdly, to take the example he uses, it is clear that he is describing two stages of a gag: in stage one the actor walks under the ladder and suffers for it, in stage two he tries to avoid a repetition of the situation and still comes to grief. Coursodon's distinction would thus involve us in thinking of a non-gag followed by a gag, of something involving no intellectual involvement followed by something characterised by the opposite.

It seems more sensible to think of the basic indignities of farce as contradicting some commonplace expectation held by the society for which farce is produced; in our culture such an expectation would be closely related to the traditional belief that the human body is the locus of dignity, the dignity which is immanent to the human species, and that it ought to be treated in a way that is consistent with that sense of dignity. Pratfalls, custard pies in the face, etc., all contradict such a belief.

On many occasions in silent screen comedy the individuals who suffer such indignities are figures of authority (the upper classes, the police, etc.) and it is likely that the fact of subverting established authority may magnify the extent to which indignities are felt to contravene basic cultural expectations. One might also account for the frequent role of women, especially well-dressed and beautiful women, as the victims of these indignities: a male audience at least may well think of the status of women as analogous to that of authority, and thus see an assault upon her dignity as an additional element of subversion of a cultural commonplace. If the infliction of the indignity is deliberate, this may also contradict the further cultural commonplace to the effect that one should refrain from giving way to the desire to inflict pain upon others, that one should control one's aggressive impulses unless there is some sort of authorisation for indulging them, such as previous aggression on the part of the victim.

It has often been pointed out how frequently predictability and unpredictability play a central role in the impact of gags. Thus the outcome of the lift/cop gag is utterly unpredictable, and there can be little doubt that this is in some measure responsible for its comic impact. On the other hand there are many moments where the production of laughter is based upon an absolutely inevitable outcome. Thus in Laurel and Hardy's *From Soup to Nuts* (1928), where our heroes are waiters, there is a gag in which Oliver Hardy slips on a banana skin and falls face first into the monstrous cream gateau he is carrying; in a fit of pique he hurls the banana skin away, across the room, and goes back to the kitchen to get another monstrous cream gateau. While he is out a small dog that is playing under the dining table gets the banana skin and deposits it in the kitchen doorway; just in case anybody misses the point there is a cutaway shot to Stan who sees what is happening and covers his eyes in horror, and then an iris-in shot focusing on the banana skin. The results are an absolutely predictable re-run of the previous disaster; in fact, 'predictable' is something of an understatement here, for it is totally impossible not to know what is coming next.

Thus gags can be either totally unpredictable or totally predictable, but never neither: the universe of the gag is always one or the other. This contradicts our common sense everyday knowledge of chains of events in the ordinary outside world, for common sense tells us that causality is such that events are neither totally predictable nor totally unpredictable. Totally predictable events, moreover, commonly contradict such commonsense items as 'nobody's that stupid', or 'once bitten, twice shy'. Totally unpredictable events are likely to be so because the natural laws of the known universe have been apparently dislocated, as they were in the lift/cop gag.

In *The Finishing Touch* (1928) Ollie closes a sequence involving a footful of nails and a disappearing bucket by hurling the bucket out of the nearest window in a fit of pique. With the inevitability that characterises so much of the silent comedy of the 1920s, the bucket heads straight for a passing policeman and knocks him sideways into a large pile of wood, which his impact demolishes. While it is certainly true that this gag works in part by contradicting our respect for the human body and (perhaps) for authority, this is not the source of the main impact of this gag, which rather derives from the contradiction of a common sense knowledge of stochastic processes: Hardy's ejection of the bucket is done at random, and common sense tells us that random processes have random results, whereas here the process has resulted in something which defies the laws of chance; indeed, it is commonly the case in farce that objects travelling randomly in fact have the determination of a homing pigeon – the aleatory becomes the fateful.

The purpose of these examples of extra-textual expectations has been twofold. In the first place it was simply a question of giving some examples of what the term meant and how it applied to the structure under analysis. But in the second place, and more profoundly, it is also a question of demonstrating the sociological nature of this concept. This can be most easily demonstrated using the final example, the example of random processes. Apparently the knowledge which is contradicted by gags of this type is of a universal nature, since it refers to statistical processes which are by definition universal. However, in practice this is not so, as a simple anthropological comparison shows. The Azande of central Africa regard what we would call coincidence as the result of witchcraft. If a man contracts meningitis, if someone is gored by a buffalo, or if a roof whose beams have been eaten away by termites falls on someone's head, then this is an instance of witchcraft. Witchcraft it not felt to be responsible for the existence of the germs, the buffalo or the rotten beams: but what, they ask, can be responsible for the fact that such and such an individual and not another is infected, or gored, or that the roof should happen to fall at just the moment that someone was passing underneath? The answer that the common sense of our civilisation would probably give is coincidence (this is not to deny the possibility of alternatives: epidemiological, stochastic . . .), but the Azande prefer witchraft, for that answer allows them to ascribe a cause to an event that otherwise would not have a cause, and thus to prescribe a corrective: get rid of the witch and the affliction will not recur.[3] This is not of course to suggest that the Azande answer is in any sense superior or preferable, it is simply to demonstrate that the common sense of one culture is not necessarily the same as the common sense of another. Indeed, it seems likely that the aleatory processes described above would not seem at all funny to the Azande, but would rather seem threatening since they would give the appearance of witchcraft.

The same is to be said of the two syllogisms. Although it may appear that the process of reasoning that brings us to the conclusion that the midget policeman is implausible is universal, in fact this is clearly not so: it is only implausible to a culture that has at its disposal a certain – admittedly rudimentary – physical knowledge, and which does not believe in magic, or has an insufficiently deep belief in it to overcome its knowledge of the physical laws of the universe.

2. Narrative expectations

We have already seen that expectations deriving from the discourses of the social formation are articulated in the narrative, and indeed have to be in order to put in an appearance in the text. To repeat, it is because we see the policeman squashed that the peripeteia of the midget occurs, and is evaluated in the two contradictory ways that it is. To this extent therefore, *all* expectations in the text are narrative ones despite their links to the social formation, the culture of the society, at large.

To take an example: in *The Finishing Touch* there is a running gag involving a ramp up to the porch of a half-finished house that Laurel and Hardy are building.[4] Finding a portion of the ramp in his way, Stan Laurel removes it just as Ollie is going up carrying a door, with predictable results: Ollie falls into the gap, putting his head straight through the door. Stanley quickly replaces the plank and Ollie bangs his head on it as he gets up. Mystified, Ollie leans on the plank to consider the situation; the plank promptly breaks in half and Ollie goes flying. Stanley then 'repairs' the plank by fitting the two broken halves together on top of a very thin, visibly weak little board. Ollie checks that the 'repaired' plank is in place, balances another door on his head, walks across and promptly falls through. Many minutes and gags later the plank is replaced by a good solid beam and Ollie nips across unscathed; the entire porch collapses in a heap of rubble.

The early stages of this running gag – each of which is a gag in its own right as well as being the preparation for the culmination, the collapse of the porch – depend largely on the discourses of the social formation: we do not expect workmen to be so stupid and cavalier about safety at work as Stan and Ollie visibly are. Such stupidity is rather implausible, as indeed is anything that contradicts the discourses of the social formation; the modicum of plausibility that is required to make the actions comprehensible and funny derives from the individual circumstances of each: Stanley does not notice, the first time, that Ollie is about to walk up the ramp; Ollie does not see Stanley's 'repair' of the plank and it looks, superficially, solid; etc. But the instance of the collapse of the porch, towards which all the earlier, somewhat conventional, gags are tending, does not depend for its main impact upon the contradiction of the discourses of the social formation. Clearly it is in part dependent upon them: we need to know what a porch is, etc., in order for the gag to be understandable, in just the same way as the understanding of a novel depends upon competence in the language in which it is written. Furthermore, the collapse of the porch is funny in part because it contradicts our expectation of the solidity of houses. But the main impact of the gag does not derive from these considerations, but from a complex dislocation of our narrative expectations, which have been carefully constructed during the earlier, preparatory stages of this gag.

In the preparatory stages our attention has been focused on the plank, and the porch, which supports one end of it, has been external to the structure of the gag(s). In the second place, once Ollie has crossed the plank we regard the incident as closed, and its re-opening in the collapse of the porch is an integral part of the comic effect, the contradiction of a narrative expectation. In the third place, the sturdiness of the porch is not only a matter of commonplace knowledge external to the film text, but it is also built into the structure of the narrative: up until the moment of its collapse the porch has been supporting the ramp, and this in itself lends credibility to its sturdiness.

James Agee discusses a gag with a similar structure in 'Comedy's Greatest Era': a very large man gets out of a very small car, followed by a large number of similarly large men, as many as the joke will stand; pause, then out climbs a midget; pause, then the car collapses. This gag depends upon the discourses of the social formation to the extent that it needs knowledge of smallness and largeness, cars, etc., but the main source of humour derives from the way that events are ordered in the flow of the text. The contrast between the small car and the large man is a starting point only, though the small implausibility implied in the contrast may in fact get a laugh as well. The sequence of large men gets increasingly implausible, but, after all, they might have been packed in like sardines; we deduce, inter alia, that the car is sturdy. The emergence of the midget is highly implausible for there is no reason why a figure who makes such a neat contrast should have been there at all, let alone be the last one to emerge, but is made plausible by the calculation that there cannot have been room for any more large men. Lastly, the collapse of the car is highly implausible in that it was far more likely to collapse while full than empty, and very surprising because the emergence of the midget has focused our attention completely away from the question of the sturdiness of the car; plausibility is given by the size of the load. All of these jokes depend in part upon commonsense knowledge, clearly, but the main impact derives from the sequential ordering of the incidents.

Again in *The Finishing Touch*, we see a policeman standing in the middle of the frame and out of our right hand side of the frame there emerges the end of a plank, at shoulder height, obviously being carried by someone who is as yet hidden by the edge of the frame. The end of the plank crosses the entire frame and continues out of the left hand side, still moving; at this point we realise that it is a very long plank indeed, and the policeman starts scratching his head in bewilderment. Finally, Stanley appears, carrying the far end of the plank. We may deduce at this point that far from the plank being balanced about its midpoint, as we had assumed (albeit that it was implausibly long) one end was in fact entirely unsupported. As Stanley reaches the policeman he stops, turns round, and walks back out of the right hand side of the frame, still carrying the end of the plank which continues to move across the frame after his exit. The policeman continues to watch

Stanley's departing back as if trying to make sense of the situation. Finally, the first end of the plank comes back into frame – carried by Stanley!

Of course, this excellent surrealistic gag works in part by referring to commonsense knowledge about balancing long heavy objects, in other words by reference to the extra-textual. But it is primarily a question of references to the cinematic apparatus and to the narrative of the gag itself, short and self-contained though it is. As the plank travels across the frame we expect that it is balanced about its mid-point, and we assume that eventually its bearer will appear out of the side of the frame; we expect this because we assume that the space surrounding the frame will be unproblematically continuous with the space within the frame: if the camera follows John Wayne across a tract of the Arizona desert, we do not expect it to reveal the Taj Mahal with a giant crab singing on one of its minarets. This expectation is of course controverted in much surrealist and avant garde film – Godard's *Weekend* (1967), for instance – but it is the normal commonplace expectation of anyone brought up on Hollywood, and is a fundamental tenet of realistic film narrative.[5] It is utterly implausible that a plank could be carried in this manner, but because of our assumptions about the nature of film grammar, we assume that the plank is balanced until the last moment. This assumption leads us to give the image a measure of plausibility, and when Stanley and the far end appear this implausible moment gains a further paradoxical plausibility, for by that time we are beginning to think that the plank is so long that it can't possibly be balanced at its mid-point: and lo and behold, it isn't. The second half is based upon the absurd development of the premiss established in the first half of the gag: it is Stanley alone who is carrying the plank. Once this premiss is granted then the conclusion of the gag makes sense to the extent that it is now granted a measure of plausibility: if no one other than Stanley is carrying the plank, and it is not balanced at its mid-point, then clearly it is logically essential for Stanley to be carrying both ends!

A final example. In Buster Keaton's *The General* (1926), Buster, accidentally involved in the American Civil War, uses a railway engine towing an enormous mortar mounted on a flat-bed truck to chase an enemy train. He loads the mortar and tries unsuccessfully to fire it as

51

they both rush down an interminable length of straight track. He reloads it and lights the fuse on the mortar bomb; at this moment the mortar gradually lowers its muzzle until it is pointing directly at Buster's engine, about six feet away. Since they are on a straight track and the mortar is pointing down the centre-line of the track . . . Panic and agony, protracted, on Buster's part, as he tries to uncouple the truck carrying the mortar, at which point the audience, armed with an elementary knowledge of ballistics, swiftly calculates that the different speeds of railway engines and mortar shells make his efforts entirely nugatory. The mortar fires, at the exact moment that the train enters a curve that was hidden by the frame of the previous shots. The shell whistles past Buster and scores a direct hit on the enemy train. It is true that extra-textual knowledge is the foundation of this gag: what a mortar is, what explosives do, what a trajectory is. But the essential is the train and the track: Buster is towing his own destruction, and the straight track ensures that it will indeed be such; it is the narrative expectation created by the continuing progress of the train that is responsible for the force of this gag.

Thus far all the examples of humour have been taken from silent comedy. It is time now to apply the model derived originally from the realm of the purely visual to the case of verbal humour as well. The examples chosen are graffiti and one-liner jokes, whose compact form makes them especially amenable to this type of analysis.

JESUS
SAVES!

is written on a wall; underneath, in different handwriting:

and Keegan scores on the rebound!

Of course, this joke depends absolutely on certain visual features: the spatial distribution of its segments, and the difference in the handwriting of the retort, for it is essential to realise that the second section is in fact a reply to the first by someone else.[6] Nevertheless, the core of the comic impact derives from the play on two of the senses of the word 'saves'. The context given by the grammatical subject 'Jesus' clearly imposes a particular meaning on 'saves', which is then subverted by its subsequent association with a grammatical subject ('Keegan') who imposes a very different meaning. This subversion of the earlier sense of 'saves' is also iconoclastic. These dislocations are absurd (in the sense defined above by the model of the gag): they are also implausible because the discourses of our social formation tell us that the concepts 'Christ' and 'goalkeeper' are incompatible with each other, and yet they have a measure of plausibility because (give or take a little anachronism) there is no reason why Jesus Christ, like any other fit member of the human race, should not keep goal.

But there is a further level of both dislocation and reintegration of meaning in this joke: part of our surprise derives simply from the fact that a word is revealed, against our expectations, to have more than one sense. This is against our expectations because it is basic to our culture that words do not have more than one meaning in the same context. At the same time, the fact that the word does objectively have both the meanings that are successively attached to it here serves to justify (to give a degree of plausibility to) the juxtaposition of the two. Herein lies the secret of the pun ('Jesus Saves', etc., is in fact a complex example of a pun): in this form of humour a word is given a specified meaning by its context, and then the fact that it can have another meaning becomes in itself – without the motivation of a set of fictitious circumstances, here supplied by Keegan – the source of humour; all the components of the logic of the absurd are supplied by the normal resources of the lexicon.

The second example is a line from Groucho Marx: 'I'd horsewhip you if I had a horse!' The structure of this line is essentially no different from that of the previous example: the dislocation of narrative expectations is obviously created by the substitution in the final word. Yet the line is also plausible, in a twofold way: firstly, the syntagmatic and semantic association of 'horse' and 'whip' in the term 'horsewhip', which in some measure 'justifies' Groucho's choice of word; secondly, the line is syntactically correct, in the sense that the word 'horse' is a noun and is in the correct place in the sentence for a noun object of the verb 'had'. The sentence is thus correct in the sense that Chomsky allows a measure of correctness to the sentence 'Colourless green ideas sleep furiously'. Syntactic correctness and syntagmatic association are also responsible for the plausibility of these lines from Laurel and Hardy's *Way Out West*: on finding they have been betrayed, Ollie denounces the traitor in his most dignified manner: 'You snake in the grass!'; unwilling to be left out, Stanley follows up: 'You toad in the hole!'. We have already seen the role of syntactical correctness in visual humour, *à propos* Stan Laurel and the endless plank.

A further example, also a graffito:

Bureaucracy rules OK
OK
OK

Once again the joke depends upon the spatial distribution, therefore upon visual impact as much as upon verbal play. This spatial distribution has two aspects, both intertextual: in the first place the reference to the bureaucratic preference for triplication, in the second place to the reference to football supporters' slogans and the conventional form that they take (in Southern England at least). But clearly the core of the humour is again verbal: in the first place the intertextuality of the reference to football slogans is as much verbal as visual, as much contained in the shape 'X rules OK', as in the choice of a wall as a space to write; in the second place, the moment of the peripeteia lies in the link established between 'OK' and whatever precedes 'rules': there have been many variations on this theme, and all of them obey this fundamental rule – for example 'Dyslexia rules KO', 'Sycophancy rules – if it's all right with you', 'Apathy rul'. In all of these cases, the nature of this link both dislocates a specific intertextual expectation (team X rules OK), thus creating a peripeteia; and is simultaneously plausible and implausible – implausible because it disrupts a specific intertextual expectation, and always substitutes for the aggressiveness of the original something which is signally unaggressive, plausible because of the nature of the link which is established in each instance: the apathetic disinclination to even complete its own slogan, bureaucratic triplication, etc.

A final example, a line from Bob Hope (quoted by Wilson, p.189): 'I knew Doris Day *before* she was a virgin'. This line is somewhat more complex because of the cultural knowledge it presupposes. On the one hand its disrupts our expectations because of the obvious impossibility of the circumstances – and is therefore implausible; on the other, the kind of roles Doris Day played during the period when she was type-cast by the Hollywood star system, the roles that created her public persona, were certainly characterised by a certain 'virginal purity', and a cynic might well be led to speculate on the divergence between this persona and the practices necessary – according to the worldly wisdom current then and now – for a woman to achieve star status in Holly-wood, practices usually summarised under the heading of 'the casting couch'; all of this could be said to give this literally impossible state of affairs the degree of plausibility necessary to turn it from impossible to absurd.

In the pages devoted to sight gags, to purely visual humour, some stress was laid on the manner in which even the briefest gag is com-posed of two stages, preparatory and culmination, and an analogy was drawn with the punch line of a verbal joke. The examples of verbal humour quoted here demonstrate the same structure: the double meaning of 'saves' is only possible because of the linear structure of the graffiti; Groucho's choice of 'horse' is only funny because of the previous mention of 'horsewhip'; the triple 'OK' only makes sense be-cause of the previous 'bureaucracy'; and Bob Hope's crack at Doris Day's expense depends upon the word 'before' implying a state which can be preceded by another. In each of these cases, therefore, the first stage of the joke sets up an expectation which the second stage contra-dicts, thus creating a peripeteia; and as we have seen, in each case the peripeteia is simultaneously plausible and implausible. Thus it can be seen that the structure of verbal humour is identical to the structure of visual humour.

We are now in a position to start to apply this model of humour on a slightly wider scale.

In the first place, we can now make sense of the notion of 'comic in-sulation'. When we see – for instance – Tom receiving yet another dynamite blast from Jerry the mouse, it is often argued that the pre-condition of finding this funny is that we know perfectly well that it isn't serious, that the character will in fact be restored to normal in a very short time, none the worse for very rough wear. This seems per-fectly correct, but says nothing about *how* we know that Tom will be none the worse for his explosive experience; the model of comedy proposed here, however, has the capacity to generate an explanation of the source of our emotional certainty. We know that what we see on the screen is funny in so far as it is simultaneously plausible and implausible, but more implausible than it is plausible, absurd, in short; it is precisely because it is absurd, more implausible than plausible, that we 'don't take it seriously', that we have the emotional certainty that all will be well immediately after. In other words, it is not a question of us feeling free to laugh at something that might otherwise be nasty because we are 'emotionally insulated' from it by some mechanism that is separate from what we laugh at: it is the very mechanism of humour itself that insulates us.

Ray Durgnat discusses this in *The Crazy Mirror*, under the heading 'the emotional anatomy of the gag'. The controlling quality of a gag is its capacity to deflate tensions, he argues:

> The phrase 'a general in long underpants' is a little joke ... [it] is funny because the prepared tensions (respect, authority, etc.) are subverted by the association of the underpants (vulnerability, unpreparedness, fear of the cold, near-nudity). A mere contradiction of the general's authority ('a general in confusion') would not in itself be funny, for such a contradiction could sustain and increase rather than deflate the overall tension (p.33).

Allowances made for discussing these images out of context, the contrast Durgnat intends is clearly correct: 'a general in confusion' clearly does not have the same type of impact as 'a general in long underpants'. In terms of the logic of the absurd, the general in confusion is not funny because it is all too plausible: why should generals not be confused? But the general in long underpants is implausible to the extent that the two components of the phrase derive from such dramatically different conceptual vocabularies: if all men are equally likely (or unlikely) to be seen in long underwear, it is still the case that the association of generals with smart uniforms as well as with authority makes this sight more implausible than plausible. Thus the different emotional impacts which Durgnat postulates can be explained in terms of the logic of the absurd.

This explanation has been couched in terms that restress the importance of a point made earlier, that it is the balance between the two syllogisms that constitute the second moment of the absurd that is crucial, not just their simultaneous presence. This balance can also be alleged as the explanation of comic failure.

Many contemporary audiences find the humour of the silent screen simply silly, and therefore fail to find these comedians funny. Contemporaries, on the other hand, sometimes found them excessively 'black', too abrasive to be funny.[7] Those who find these films merely silly are only seeing the implausible side of the actions portrayed, and are failing to give sufficient weight to the plausible aspects; alternatively, they may see in these actions nothing but a series of cinematic conventions, and thus find them merely boring, because they are conventional. Those who find them excessively abrasive are no doubt over-emphasising the plausibility syllogism. If it is unlikely that many of our contemporaries would find Laurel and Hardy and the other silent clowns excessively abrasive, it is certainly the case that some contemporary humour is greeted with that reaction, as we shall see when we discuss *Fawlty Towers*. In any event, the comments made here have established the most important principle: that the logic of the absurd is capable of offering not only a model of gags and verbal jokes, but also a model of comic failure too. We shall have occasion to return to this question on several occasions.

Notes

1. The logical nature of gags was observed by French critics of the silent cinema. See J-P. Coursodon, *Keaton et Cie*, 1964, and F. Mars, *Le Gag*, 1964.
2. The question of the 'pre-history' of the gag will be dealt with in Chapter 5.
3. See E.E. Evans-Pritchard, 'Witchcraft', 1955.
4. Running gag: a gag based on repetition of the same or very similar incidents. The commonest form is triadic: A does X, with disastrous results; he repeats the action, perhaps with a variation intended to avoid repetition of the disaster, which in fact occurs in the same way; on the third occasion he takes considerable precautions, but the same or a similar disaster occurs, in a new and unforeseen way. On comedians' terminology in general, see James Agee, 'Comedy's Greatest Era', in *Agee on Film*, Vol. 1, 1963.
5. See N. Burch, *Theory of Film Practice*, 1973, pp.10,19.

6. The presence of distinct social roles within the joke will be discussed again under the heading of Freudian theory.

7. See contemporary reviews of Laurel and Hardy's *Block-Heads*, in the opening sequence of which Ollie thinks Stan has lost a leg; quoted in W.K. Everson, *The Films of Laurel and Hardy*, 1967, p.187.

3

The Semiotics of Humour

The Comic and the Metaphoric

The model of humour proposed here, under the heading of the 'logic of the absurd', has so far been presented in a highly informal manner, in so far as many of the concepts which have been used have been presented as if they were entirely unproblematic, which is in fact far from the case. Thus, for example, one of the terms in which analysis of jokes and gags has constantly been couched, is 'expectation': the peripeteia 'contradicts expectations', for instance.

The concept 'expectation' apparently derives from psychology, in the sense that an expectation is conventionally conceived as something located in the mind of the individual; thus if it were to be formalised, one would expect it to be done in terms deriving from psychological models. But we have seen that the expectations discussed here (and the same would be true of any others) are derived from the forms of knowledge which are clearly also part of the social structure, as in the earlier example of the Azande tribe and their conception of causality. Thus clearly there is already a problem here, one which is usually posed in the social sciences in terms of the opposition phylogenesis/ ontogenesis. Is the origin of any mental phenomenon to be explained in terms of attributes of the individual psyche, or in terms of the social structure? Furthermore, we have also seen that the distinction between 'preparation' and 'culmination', or punch line, in joke and gag structure shows that any expectation that the audience may have is necessarily produced in the text as well as deriving from the 'discourses of the social structure'.[1] This raises a further problematic relation: that between the narrative flow of the text, which is a form of production following its own logic, and the discourses of the social structure which clearly have an existence which is in some measure at least independent of comic texts. (We shall see that resolution of this problem has implications for the phylogenesis/ontogenesis opposition.)

This relationship (narrative/social structure) can also be considered from another point of view, which is equally problematic. If the words and images that compose jokes derive their meaning from discourses that are in some sense external to them, then from where do such discourses in turn derive their meaning, since such discourses are nothing more than a very large (but finite) collection of texts, statements, etc? In other words, if each text derives its meaning from an entity that is external to it, where can the source of meaning lie, since once all the finite set of statements composing a discourse have been enumerated, there is nothing left which is external to them. On this hypothesis, there would apparently be no source of meaning.

All of these problematic concepts are in fact capable of being reformulated in a satisfactory manner, and it is all the more important to do so because it is in the process of clarification that it will be possible to resolve another major problem, raised in the introduction: what is the relationship between laughter and the object of mockery?

That all these problematic relationships can be clarified within the framework of a single reformulation is due to the nature of this framework: the semiotic tradition and the developments of it known generically as 'post-structuralism'. For the development of this tradition has depended precisely upon the formulation and re-formulation of the topics with which we are concerned: on the one hand, the modalities of discursive meaning and the positioning of individual texts or statements within them, and on the other the manner in which subjectivity is implicated in this process. Clearly, an essay on comedy and humour is not the place to undertake a systematic study of the semiotic tradition, and what follows only deals with those features which are relevant to an understanding of the comic process.

There are clear reasons for drawing a close parallel between metaphor and comedy: in metaphor words are used in a way which deviates from their usual usage, in the sense that they are placed in contexts in which they apparently should not be used. Hamlet's 'slings and arrows of outrageous fortune' cannot *literally* be the weapons in question, for fortune is an immaterial entity incapable of manipulating the eminently physical entities in question. In this sense, to this extent, the metaphoric usage of a word is deviant, as the classical rhetorical tradition insisted. Similarly, the comic use of the word or the filmed event involves a contradiction of the word's normal use (Bob Hope's hypostasised 'pre-virginity', for example) or a contradiction of the audience's expectations concerning such an event, as we have seen *à propos* many examples. In both comic and metaphoric instances, what defines the situation as 'non-literal' is a deviation from a norm.

In both cases, furthermore, this deviation causes a surprise: we have already seen that the culminating point of a joke or gag – the punch line – consists, in one of its constitutive moments, of a surprise: the midget policeman, a pie in the face, pre-virginity, etc. Similarly, it is a commonplace of poetics that metaphors are surprising, in the sense that they make us see things in a fresh light; dead metaphors, metaphors which have become so conventional that they scarcely count as metaphors any more, are such precisely because they have lost the capacity for producing new insights: compare 'bored to death' with T.S. Eliot's 'The yellow fog that rubs its back upon the windowpanes'.

Finally, despite the surprise and the deviation, it is fundamental to both gag and metaphor that there is an element of similarity involved: a metaphor works by pointing out to us a similarity of which we were not previously aware; and the measure of plausibility which we have seen to be central to the structure of the gag involves some perception of an identity common to two things which are fundamentally incompatible, in other words a similarity. In the case of the midget policeman, the connection between squashing and reduction in size involves the perception of a logical identity in the same way as Hamlet's 'slings and arrows' involves recognising that fate can assault us in a way analogous to a human attack. Similarity means precisely the simultaneous presence in the same entity of both identity and difference with what it is being compared to.

Three reasons, therefore, for taking seriously the possibility of a comparison between metaphor and comedy. Clearly, such a comparison will run the risk of a conflation between two incompatibles in just the same way as the various studies quoted earlier; to anticipate somewhat, this risk will not prove insuperable.

The rhetorical tradition theorised the metaphor on the basis of a divergence between the normal sense of a word and the transferred, extended or deviant sense in which it was used when employed in a metaphor. Modern poetics insists that this is only partly correct: deviance does indeed occur, but it is not in the word that it is to be found, it is in the placing of the word in a context with which it is only partially compatible. The word in question is not used in a deviant sense: as Donald Davidson insists, in a metaphor words are used in their literal sense, and this is what creates the force of the metaphor. It is the context in which the word is placed which is responsible for the metaphor, or – to be more accurate – it is what is predicated of the word in question by placing it in a given context. T.S. Eliot's fog acquires a 'back' in *The Love Song of J. Alfred Prufrock*; the word 'back' is used in its literal sense, and it is because it is used in its literal sense that the line is striking, i.e. a metaphor, for this sense is incompatible with what is predicated of it in this context, that is, that it is the back of a fog. This process of predicating something which is only partially compatible with what it is predicated of, has been called 'predicative impertinence' by Jean Cohen, and is central to the theory of metaphor advanced by Max Black.

No doubt some further examples will be helpful. Corneille's *Horace* is based upon the story of Horatius defending the bridge. In this version Horatius' father learns at one point that two of his three sons have been killed, but that the third one has escaped alive; his father curses him for a coward, and the messenger who brought the news (which of course is false) excuses the survivor's behaviour:

Que vouliez-vous qu'il fît contre trois?
(What did you expect him to do against three?)

and the father replies:

Qu'il mourût
(To die)

This line was much admired in the classical period, and was widely commented on by rhetoricians, who cited it as an example of a forceful line that was not a figure of speech. Indeed, this is how it is still conceived generally today, as a line whose force derives from the psychological brutality (or extreme devotion to duty, depending upon the sense of morality of the commentator) of the speaker. However, this explanation confuses moral judgment of the line with analysis of it: one can judge the father in either of the ways indicated here, and probably more as well, but the force of the line does not derive from such psychological considerations: in fact, the exact opposite is true, for the father's state of mind is only imputable because of the force of the line. What father would condemn his son in such a brutal manner? Answer: a brutal one, or a very patriotic one. But it is the brutal manner that is responsible for this imputation, and the judgments that follow from it, and therefore it is the manner that needs to be explained.

Jean Cohen points out that this line is in fact a figure of speech, for to associate 'faire' (to do) with 'mourir' (to die) is an act of predicative impertinence: to die is not to do anything, it is to be the victim of somebody else's action; and therefore the line is striking, in just the same way as Eliot's daring assimilation of the fog to a cat on a window-sill. Using this model of metaphor, or of figures of speech, allows an explanation both of the intrinsic nature of this line and of the variety of moral and psychological judgments to which it can give rise. We will see an essentially identical process at work in the character of Basil Fawlty, despited the fact that *Horace* is a tragedy and *Fawlty Towers* a farce.

The basic structure of the process outlined above is therefore this: each term, or word, that is used has an associative field, or is drawn from a paradigm; this associative field or paradigm constitutes the set of connotations which the term is capable of evoking. This of course is not specific to metaphor: it is one basis of linguistic meaning in general. The term 'fog' derives from the associative field of terms to do with weather, but also of terms to do with winter, perhaps of melancholy, and – in the context in which Eliot places it – of terms to do with texture. Similarly 'back' derives from the associative set or paradigm of front, side, etc., but also of parts of the body. The term 'faire' inevitably connotes action, 'to die' derives from a set composed of the basics of life, and a set of terms to do with suffering, etc. What occurs in metaphor is that the connotations evoked by the placing of specific terms in a given context are contradictory: thus 'faire' connotes action, whereas 'mourir' connotes inaction, and placing the two terms together inevitably brings out this contradiction. Similarly, 'fog' connotes – beyond the associative field of weather and winter – the realm of the inanimate, whereas 'rubs its back' connotes the animate; the juxtaposition underlines the contradiction.

This process could be represented diagrammatically, using these conventional signs: $\rightarrow$ indicates predication, $//$ indicates incompatibility or contradiction. Thus, in the case of the line from Corneille's *Horace*:

$$\text{Mourir} \rightarrow \text{inaction} // \text{action}$$

Or in the case of the line from *Prufrock*:

$$\text{Rubs its back} \rightarrow \text{animate} // \text{inanimate}$$

This logical model of the process has its canonical form in the simplest form of predication:

$$X \text{ is } Q$$
$$\text{The table is brown}$$

What happens in the form of predication of the metaphor is that the predicate is reduplicated (X is Q and P), and the second term of the predicate is incompatible with the first (X is Q and not-Q, or: X is Q.#Q, where # indicates opposition.[2]

At this point the parallel between the metaphor and the joke/gag can be made more explicit. To use once more the example of the lift and the midget policeman: the midget connotes survival, that is, life, whereas squashing in a lift shaft connotes death. To phrase it in slightly different terms, squashing the policeman predicates his death, the emergence of the midget predicates his survival. Diagrammatically:

$$\text{Midget} \rightarrow \text{life} // \text{death}$$
$$X \text{ is } Q.\#Q$$

Or, in the case of Ollie and the collapsing porch, the porch connotes durability and its collapse indicates the opposite. Diagrammatically, therefore:

$$\text{Porch} \rightarrow \text{durability} // \text{frailty}$$
$$X \text{ is } Q.\#Q$$

As a final example, Bob Hope's comment on Doris Day:

$$\text{Virginity} \rightarrow \text{ab initio} \mathbin{/\!/} \text{preceded}$$
$$X \text{ is } Q.\#Q$$

Now it is obvious that this structure, common apparently to both the gag/joke and the metaphor, is also to be found in another form of statement, namely nonsense, the type of statement invented by logicians and linguists as the limit case of meaning, the point at which meaning collapses into non-meaning. Jean Cohen uses the example of 'Napoleon is a prime number', and one could also use Chomsky's famous 'Colourless green ideas sleep furiously'. In each case the failure of the sentence to have any meaning is imputable to the fact that what is predicated of the subject in each case is utterly incompatible with the subject in question.[3] Clearly this raises a problem, for if metaphors are sometimes obscure – and can even be perceived as meaningless by an inexperienced reader – and if gags are absurd, nonetheless the inexperienced reader can be taught to understand, and obscure metaphors and absurd gags do have meaning; whereas no such statement could be made about the nonsense statements quoted here. According to Jean Cohen, metaphors are saved from incomprehensibility by a process of decoding actively undertaken by the reader:

> Every figure of speech requires a two-stage process of decoding, of which the first is the perception of anomaly and the second its correction, by the exploration of the paradigmatic field, the nexus of relationships of resemblance, contiguity, etc., thanks to which a signified will be found which will give the statement an acceptable semantic interpretation (p.22).

This needs careful consideration, for in this remark several themes are bound together.

Firstly, Cohen conceives of the process of decoding the metaphor on the basis of two stages and implies that the articulation of these stages is chronological: 'the first ... the second'. Clearly, however, they are also logical steps which are semantically distinct, since one of them leads to incomprehensibility and the other to comprehensibility. This would seem to be more fundamental to the structure of metaphor than the question of chronology, since it is indispensable, whereas it would not matter if the steps were simultaneous or subsequent one to the other. In any event, the essential point here is that Jean Cohen indicates that metaphors are such because there are two paths through the associative field(s) surrounding any given term and not a single one.

Secondly, Jean Cohen says that 'a signified will be found' to resolve the anomaly; this use of the passive voice elides the question of the agency of this discovery: who or what is responsible for finding this signified? It is likely that Jean Cohen conceives of this process as being carried to fruition without an agent, as is commonly the case in structuralist theories; but we shall see that such a position is in fact impossible, since it is riddled with logical contradictions. Thus the theory of metaphor leads us to pose the question of the status of the speaking or reading subject.

Thirdly, this signified which 'will be found' achieves the result of providing an 'acceptable semantic interpretation'. This raises the question – although it does not answer it – of whether this new signified was in fact always already present, objectively, in the associative field surrounding the term or terms of the metaphor, or whether it is discovered and invented in the process of the second stage of the decoding. For, if the new signified is 'acceptable', this could be taken to imply that it pre-existed the metaphor on the grounds that it clearly fits in with some protocol of meaning that itself self-evidently pre-exists the metaphor in question. On the other hand, if this signified, which has to be looked for, did in fact pre-exist the metaphor, then why was it necessary to hunt for it, and how does it achieve surprise, or make the reader look at something in a new light which is the impact conventionally ascribed to metaphor? Jean Cohen's formulation does not allow us to decide between these two alternatives, and we shall see later that any attempt to do so implies recourse to or development of a theory of the speaking subject.[4]

However, leaving aside these implications of Jean Cohen's remarks, use of this framework enables us to clarify the distinction between metaphor and nonsense, and to understand the internal functioning of metaphor. In metaphor a 'second' reading of the statement provides a reconciling understanding of the terms involved. Thus, in the case of

Hamlet's slings and arrows, we can see that fate often appears to attack us in a way analogous to human assault. In the case of Horace's father's condemnation we can see that 'To die' is in fact an extreme ellipsis for some sentence such as 'To fight even in the knowledge of certain death'. In the case of T.S. Eliot's fog the evocation of texture is sufficient to make sense of the comparison. This 'reconciling reading' could be represented diagrammatically thus:

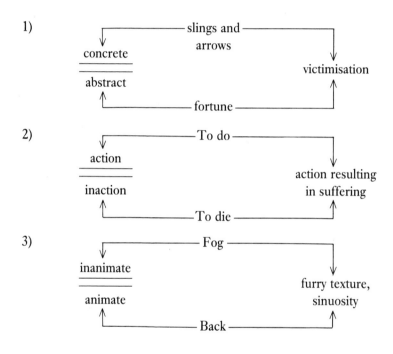

1)

concrete
—————
abstract

slings and arrows

victimisation

fortune

2)

action
—————
inaction

To do

action resulting in suffering

To die

3)

inanimate
—————
animate

Fog

furry texture, sinuosity

Back

Thus in each of these three cases the predicative incompatibility of one reading is balanced by the compatibility of another. Thus the single logical contradiction of X is Q.#Q is replaced by a reduplication, in which the metaphor would have to be represented by two equations:

The slings and arrows of outrageous fortune =
$$1)\ X\ is\ Q.\#Q$$
$$2)\ X\ is\ A$$

This can be formulated another way, using Paul Ricoeur's extension of Cohen's remarks. For Ricoeur, the tension conventionally associated with metaphor, and theorised by Cohen, is based less on the fact that there is a deviant predication in the statement than in the fact that there are two readings involved which contradict each other:

> In order that a metaphor obtains, one must continue to identify the previous incompatibility through the new compatibility. The predicative assimilation involves, in that way, a specific kind of tension which is not so much between a subject and a predicate as between semantic incongruence and congruences (p.146).

When Ricoeur speaks of a tension between congruence and incongruence as the basis of the semantics of metaphor, this remark is clearly an alternative formulation to the one proposed here.

We are now in a position to return to the question of the similarity between joke and metaphor, outlined in an informal manner above. For it is clear that the new two-part equation applied to the metaphor is equally applicable to the joke:

1) 'I knew Doris Day before she was a virgin'

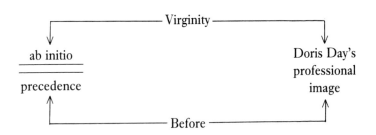

Here 'virginity' connotes something which is by definition from the beginning, whereas 'before' connotes the opposite. In logical terms then, the proposition of the joke takes the form 'X (Doris Day) is Q.#Q' (a virgin who has previously been a non-virgin, something logically impossible). This is Equation 1; Equation 2 shows us that 'virginity' is not a biological state, but a public relations image, which logically can be preceded; in this reading of the proposition, it takes the logical form 'X is A', where there is no contradiction involved at all.

2) The squashed policeman/dwarf

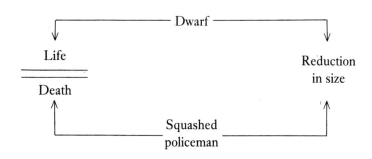

Here Equation 1 tells us that the dwarf/squashed policeman is both alive and dead, or in logical terms 'X (the man) is Q.#Q'. But Equation 2 tells us that a squashed man is smaller – 'X is A'. That is to say, in the structure of the joke, as in the structure of the metaphor, there is a moment of the perception of semantic anomaly and a moment of the perception of something which resolves this anomaly. However, if this is the case, it is clear that we are in danger of conflating the comic with the non-comic (the metaphoric, in this instance) in just the same way as the studies that were criticised on these grounds earlier; for it is clearly the case that metaphors demand a different response to jokes and gags: nobody roars with laughter at Hamlet's 'slings and arrows of outrageous fortune'. The solution to this problem is to return to the terminology used earlier in the analysis of jokes: the plausible and the implausible.

In the first place, it is clear that when Jean Cohen speaks of predicative impertinence and Paul Ricoeur talks of semantic congruence and incongruence, these terms cut across the notions of plausibility and its opposite. Any predicative impertinence, any semantic incongruence is inevitably implausible; and the 'second' reading, which resolves the impertinence and restores semantic congruence, is clearly plausible. What is it then that distinguishes the joke from the metaphor? The answer lies in the balance between plausibility and implausibility, for a certain stress has been laid upon the necessity, in analysing jokes, of seeing that implausibility massively dominates plausibility: that is what makes them absurd. What happens in metaphor is the opposite: plausibility dominates over implausibility, for when we come to see something in a new light, when a metaphor gives us a new 'insight' into something, what has happened is that the reading which makes the statement plausible dominates over the one that makes it implausible, or – in Ricoeur's terminology – semantic congruence dominates over semantic incongruence. This is not of course to say that congruence abolishes incongruence: Ricoeur is entirely right to insist that the 'previous incompatibility' must still be identified 'through the new compatibility'; it is only when metaphor is compared to joke that the necessity of talking about a balance between the two becomes visibly essential.

It was also stressed earlier that the allocation of plausibility and its opposite was not possible outside the context of particular discourses: if the highly determined effects of random causes appear implausible to us it is because our culture has a particular conception of causality, and in a culture with a different conception of causality this ascription of implausibility would not obtain. This analysis now needs to be refined, in the light of what we have discovered during the analysis of metaphor.

In the analysis of the relationship between jokes and the discourses which give meaning to the elements of jokes these discourses appeared in the form of something which was entirely external to the jokes themselves, something active in relation to the passivity of the joke statement which received meaning from them. It is this relationship which needs to be reformulated. In a metaphor or in a joke the terms which are in a relation of congruence or its opposite, and therefore seem plausible or otherwise, are capable, in abstraction from the context in question, of referring to a large number of different associative fields. T. S. Eliot's fog, for instance, could evoke the associative set referring to weather, the set denoting textures, and perhaps others; thus:

Fog 1) → sunshine/rain/storm/grey clouds/etc → weather

Fog 2) → cold/wet/furry/thick/ etc → texture
Fog 3): 'my mind befogged with confusion . . . '. Here: Fog → opacity/
clarity/etc → light.

In the case of Eliot's metaphor there is no question of the third set of
associations being evoked; in *Prufrock* it is only the literal meaning (a
state of the weather) and the notion of texture that are aroused: the
literal meaning because this is essential for the perception of anomaly,
the field of textures because this allows a semantically acceptable
interpretation. Thus which discourse the reader has recourse to is
specified by the structure of the metaphor in question, and therefore
the relationship of the statement to the discourse is not one of
passivity, as it appeared above, but one in which the statement itself
plays a determining role.

Clearly this is also the case where jokes are concerned. In the case of
the running gag involving Oliver Hardy and the collapsing porch,
everything turns on the fact that porches, as part of houses, evoke the
notion of sturdiness. But porches also are capable of activating other
associative fields, for instance that of neighbourliness, where the porch
is the place where people sit on rocking chairs, drink beer with their
feet on the rails and talk to their neighbours. In this running gag this
set of associations is irrelevant, that is, unactivated, because there is
nothing in the contiguity of the terms involved to activate it. The
concept of virginity is capable of arousing many associations –
everything from white weddings to patriarchy – but Bob Hope's one-
liner only activates one particular set, its chronological implications.

Therefore to say that a joke or a metaphor is simultaneously
plausible and implausible is in fact to make a statement which is
composed of several logically distinct stages. Firstly, the plausibility or
its opposite derives from reference to a particular set of discourses.
Secondly, the set to which reference is made is predicated upon the
syntagmatic structure of the statement, the contiguity between non-
congruent terms. Thirdly, plausibility and implausibility are always in
some sort of balance, and reference to this balance is necessarily
implied by referring to (im)plausibility. Lastly, that balance is very
different in the two cases of metaphor and joke.

No doubt this final assertion needs to be argued further, for it is not necessarily clear that a metaphor such as Eliot's yellow fog is more plausible than a joke such as pre-virginity. In the first place, it is important to stress that there are many statements where it is not necessarily clear whether we are in the presence of a joke or a figure of speech: this Marxist criticism of Hegel, for instance, in whom ideas have 'achieved a positively stratospheric autonomy from material life'.[5] It is equally possible to read this statement as a serious criticism using a measure of exaggeration in order to underline a point, or as a humorous attack which also has its serious side. Similarly with an ironical statement such as 'X is not exactly a genius', which is balanced right on the dividing line between the humorous and the non-humorous. That is to say, there are many occasions on which it appears that plausibility and implausibility are equally balanced, and if we wanted to go beyond this generalisation and to try to account for the reception of statements such as the ones quoted above, we would have to turn to the contexts in which they were made.

In the case of the criticism of Hegel, the fact that it is made in the context of an academic article in which recourse to metaphor and exaggeration is rare, as indeed it usually is in this form of writing, makes it seem incongruous, and if one is concentrating sufficiently strongly on the literal meaning of the terms which compose the argument Stuart Hall is proposing, it is likely that this incongruous exaggeration, or metaphor, will seem implausible and therefore witty. That is to say, context penetrates very thoroughly indeed the structure of the statement, for the impact of any term in a metaphor or a joke is totally inseparable from the links that tie it to the discourse in which it is situated as well as to the discourses that silently surround it and give it meaning. The same is true of a statement that is clearly a metaphor, such as Eliot's yellow fog. It is tempting to say, with Gerald Mast, that we interpret this line from *Prufrock* as metaphorical and not as comic because we know that Eliot is a serious poet; but we have already seen the infinite regression that such an argument involves. As we start to read *Prufrock* we observe that it involves a figurative use of language from the outset, and specifically that it opens with a simile – a weak form of metaphor where the plausibility of the comparison is strengthened by the use of 'like' or 'as' to underline the fact that this is a comparison, therefore the evocation of likeness, thus of dissimilarity as well as similarity. Thus in situations like this the use of figured language where plausibility clearly dominates over implausibility prepares the reader to stress the plausibility syllogism in a very strong metaphor such as this one. Moreover, in the case of *Prufrock* the fog fits in with the general evocation of night in the city which dominates the first stanza.

The conclusion that is to be drawn from these observations is that, provided we understand the relationship between statement and context in the way that has been outlined here, it is perfectly possible to provide an account of the difference between joke and metaphor which derives from the fundamental nature of both. Since the nature of metaphor is that the plausibility of the predication is greater than the implausibility, and that of the joke that the opposite is true, the distinction is necessarily intrinsic to their forms. By the same token, it is clear that both forms are productive of the type of meaning that they produce through the process of predicative impertinence and the tensions that results from it. These relationships can be summarised diagrammatically:

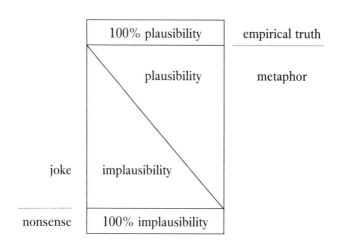

At the beginning of this chapter the question of the nature of expectations was raised, and its resolution in semiotic terms was anticipated. What this chapter has done is to demonstrate two things: firstly, how the concept of expectation can be reformulated in semiotic terms, as the play of associative fields surrounding words or cinematic images; secondly, how the notion of contradicting these expectations can also be reformulated in semiotic terms, as predicative impertinence. The value of this process of reformulation is that what were previously ungrounded concepts have now a firm grounding in semantics: the manner in which jokes and metaphors come to have meaning is thereby related to the manner in which meaning in general is produced. However, this leaves two major problems still unresolved: in the first place, the nature of predication in general, and thereby the associated question of 'normal' and 'deviant' predications; in the second place, the nature of the speaking subject, for on several occasions it has been necessary to say that such-and-such involves recourse to a theory of the speaking subject, and to defer discussion of it. These topics are the subject matter of the next chapter.

Notes

1. Hereafter, for the sake of convenience, any reference to joke or gag should be taken as referring to both.
2. I owe this model to Jean Cohen.
3. George Steiner pointed out once in a lecture that either example could also be considered as poetry. This is possible because the context of modernist poetry would lead us to look for a meaning.
4. See Chapter 4.
5. Stuart Hall, 'Culture, the Media and the Ideological Effect', in J. Curran *et al* (eds) *Mass Communications and Society*, 1977, p.321.

4

The Semiotics of Humour
Comic Utterance

The explanation of jokes and metaphors in the preceding pages is all based on a common procedure: explanation here consists of referring any given term back to the associative field from which it is drawn – or, to use the formal linguistic concept, the paradigm from which it is drawn – and this regardless of whether the term in question is a word or a visual image. Predicative impertinence works through reference back to paradigms: 'fog' and 'rubs its back' collectively constitute a metaphor because they refer back to incompatible entities, and that incompatibility is defined as such in the paradigms of ordinary speech. However, despite the fact that this method is traditional, it is fraught with problems which are especially pronounced in the case of the analysis of comedy.

These centre around a single feature of this analysis. We have already seen that each item in a joke or metaphor refers to a set of potential associations which is much more extended than the range of associations that are in fact evoked by any given joke or metaphor. That is to say, the fact of placing those items in conjunction has the result of excluding certain potential chains of meaning in the act of creating another set. This implies that the flow of the discourse, or the fact of placing these items in a discourse, plays an active role in relation to the paradigmatic sets from which items (words, images) apparently draw their meaning. This is most clearly seen by referring to the nature of the punch line in jokes: whatever the joke, the punch line must come at the end, it must follow the preparation stage, by definition, and it is obvious therefore that it is the placing of the punch line that gives it its meaning. Thus, to take a brief example, Bob Hope's crack about Doris

Day; here the comic meaning of the word 'virgin' depends entirely upon its placing in relation to the other words in the crack – there is nothing intrinsically comic about the word 'virgin' in itself. The significance of this point is this: in our previous explanations, comic meaning has appeared to derive entirely from the place of items within associative sets, or paradigms, and it is now clear that there is a further, entirely distinct source of comic meaning – the placing of items within the *mise-en-discours*, the setting-into-discourse.

The implication of this point which concerns us here is that such a placing implies an entity which has so far been absent from our analysis: the speaker, the humorist.[1] The reason why this implication is inevitable is that the form of placing which (in combination with predicative impertinence) results in humour necessarily involves two processes which can only be seen as referring to the person as well as to the signifying system: in the first place, introducing levity into a social situation of some sort, with whatever results this may have – including running the risk, analysed by Mary Douglas, of not being permitted to be humorous and causing offence. Secondly, as Freud says, overcoming the inhibitions against childishness and/or aggression which would clearly indicate the necessity of a form of analysis of meaning which goes beyond the concept of the static paradigm, which incorporates the dynamic process indicated here.

Modern linguistics makes a distinction between 'statement' and 'utterance', between what is said (statement) and the act of saying it (utterance), where the latter should be taken to include the circumstances in which it is said. The simplest example of this distinction would be any statement containing the word 'I', for its meaning can only be communicated by reference to the circumstances of its utterance, as the meaning of this word depends entirely upon the speaker: it has no meaning other than to refer to the speaker. There is in fact an entire category of words, labelled 'deictics' or 'shifters', whose meaning depends entirely on context – 'now' would be another obvious example. All of these words are such that their meaning can only be ascertained by referring them to the circumstances of their utterance: outside such a context they are merely empty vessels. But this notion has more interesting applications. Consider the phrase 'May I come in?' Spoken by a neighbour who has seen that your door is open it means one thing, it is a normal act of politeness; spoken by a prison officer at the door of a cell it is an act of derision: the meaning depends on the context. Another example would be an anodyne phrase such as 'Tom's coming tomorrow': is this a threat or a promise? It depends entirely on the relationship between speaker, addressee and Tom. The possibilities that this dimension of language open up have often been exploited in literature.

In Laclos' *Liaisons Dangereuses,* Valmont – the Don Juan-type hero – writes a letter to his established mistress while in bed with another woman (in the film version he writes it using her back as a desk), saying things such as 'Never have I taken so much pleasure in writing to you', and 'Already I can feel that I will have to break off this letter before I finish it'. This property of language can also be used for the purposes of tragic irony, as in a famous scene in Racine's *Britannicus,* where Nero forces the hero's mistress to break with him on pain of his death if she refuses, while he himself listens hidden behind a screen: the words that the girl uses have two entirely different meanings, one for her lover, and another for the audience.[2]

What the distinction statement/utterance implies is that meaning is dependent upon the situation in which the statement is uttered. Freud's late paper on 'Humour' (*Standard Edition,* v.21) distinguishes between 'jokes' and 'humour' on the basis of features of the situation of utterance. In a comic utterance in general, he says, there are three possible roles: the narrator, the recipient and the butt of the joke, and all three are people who have a real existence outside the framework of the joke – Bob Hope, his audience and Doris Day, for example. In a joke, says Freud, all three roles are present, although it is possible that the listener and the butt may in fact be the same person in some instances, as when a joke is made at the listener's expense, thus conflating the roles of recipient and butt. In humour, on the other hand, there is no butt: a condemned man being taken to the gallows on a fine Monday morning is overheard to comment, tongue in cheek: 'Well, the week's beginning nicely'. It is not relevant to our purposes to assess whether Freud's distinctions are valid or not: what is of interest for us is the concept of roles in the act of utterance, for here we have a concept which will enable us to think through the notion of comedy in a way that goes beyond the theory of paradigms.[3]

It is important to distinguish between roles in utterance and actual people. We have already seen that in one instance the roles of listener and butt may be conflated, and it is equally possible – if the joke is at the teller's expense – for the distinction between speaker and butt to be elided. Moreover, it is by no means necessary that the butt should be an actual person; consider this joke, current in the Soviet Union in the early 1980s:

Brezhnev's (or Gorbachev's, or Lenin's – it doesn't really matter) motorcade is driving along the privilege lane on the Moscow ring road, at its usual high speed, when suddenly a babushka (granny) throws herself in front of Brezhnev's car. The motorcade screeches to a halt, narrowly avoiding her and each other, and Brezhnev gets out in a fury.

'You stupid old . . . babushka!' he yells. 'What the hell do you mean by doing that? You nearly dented my car!'

'I just want to ask you a question, Leonid Alexeevich! Please! Just one question!'

'You? You want to ask me a question?'

'Yes! Just one question, Leonid Alexeevich!'

Brezhnev looks at her suspiciously for a moment. 'Alright. Just one question.'

'Oh thank you, Leonid Alexeevich! Oh thank you!'

'Yes, well, get on with it then.'

'Leonid Alexeevich, my question is this: is Marxism a science or a philosophy?'

Brezhnev looks at her in amazement: 'It's a philosophy, of course.'

'Oh Leonid Alexeevich, I can't tell you how happy you have made me. For I too, I believe it is a philosophy.' And she nods benignly, wreathed in smiles. Brezhnev too smiles down at her. 'Because you know, Leonid Alexeevich, if this was a science, they would have tried it on the animals first!'

In this joke, despite the prominent role played by Brezhnev, the butt is not really him but Marxism and its political pretensions, or misuse by the CPSU; the butt, that is to say, is an institution or a value, and that is commonly the case in what Freud calls 'cynical humour'. Similarly, in a comedy film, although a witticism may be spoken by one character, the teller is not really a person, but a narrative, the film itself, made by a team of people all of whom contribute in their different ways to the success of the joke. Of course, the witticism will also contribute to our picture of the character who utters it, and affect our perception of whoever, or whatever, is its butt within the narrative as a whole.

What we can learn from this is that the roles in the act of utterance are separable from the empirical individuals who incarnate them: what is important is that they should have some existence outside the framework of the statement itself, not that they should be actual biographical individuals. To preserve the distinction between these roles and the real individuals who may or may not incarnate them, we will call these roles 'actants', that is to say those people or values or institutions in so far as they are inscribed in the act of utterance. In the last joke they would be the teller, the audience, Brezhnev, the CPSU and Marxism (or: Soviet Marxism) in so far as they are implicated in this story. Now these roles must be distinguished from another set of roles with which it is very easy to confuse them: the actants of the statement. If we use the same joke as an example, it is clear that the actants of the utterance are largely different from the actants of the statement: the actants of the utterance are whoever is telling the joke (here: Jerry Palmer), whoever is listening/reading, and the butt: Soviet Marxism. The actants of the statement are the babushka, Brezhnev, and Soviet Marxism; an obvious way of demonstrating the pertinence of this distinction is to point out that if anybody is to be accused of anti-Soviet activities, it is not the babushka but the teller of the joke.[4]

We can see from the examples already given that the distinction between statement and utterance is crucial to the study of the attribution of meaning in general, and comic meaning in particular. To take yet again the example 'Tom's coming tomorrow': the meaning of the statement depends entirely on the situation of utterance, as we have seen, for here the actant of the statement, Tom, depends upon the actants of the utterance (the relationship between Tom, speaker and listener) for the meaning that he has.

At this point we are in a position to return to the question of comedy: the analysis of the inscription of the extra-linguistic, and especially of the speaking subject, into the syntagm allows us to ask what the utterance of a comic statement implies for an understanding of its utterer, the listener(s) and – where relevant – the butt. Whereas in the previous chapter all we could achieve was a semantic analysis of the internal structure of comic syntagms, we are now able to go beyond this position towards an account of the effectivity of comedy: the linguistics of the utterance enables us to trace a direct relationship between semic analysis and the group of people among whom the comic utterance is uttered. We have already seen the fundamental characteristic of the comic utterance: deviant usage, and the logic of the absurd; thus any account of the inscription of the speaker and the addressee into humour must be based on an analysis of how these features control that inscription.

Firstly, the question of deviant usage. We have already seen how this is common to jokes and to metaphor, and how they are nonetheless distinguishable, and we have already seen that the role of deviant usage in jokes is to create the moment of surprise, the peripeteia. In the light of the linguistics of the utterance, an obvious problem emerges: if meaning shifts in the flexible manner we have seen, according to the context of utterance, to what extent is it possible to talk of 'normal' usage? What is at stake is clear: no norm, no deviance. The answer lies in the observation that there is no boundary between linguistic competence and ideological competence, and thence no boundary between the 'purely linguistic' elements in the semic construction of words and ideological elements in their construction.

If we take the simplest case, nouns, it is clear that the concept which is the signified of any substantive signifier will be inseparable from the attributes that the cultural community in question attach to the class of objects that constitutes the referent of that sign. For instance, the noun 'pen': as well as the obvious attributes of the referent (writing), 'pen' necessarily also evokes all the attributes associated with writing, or more widely with culture. Hence the cartoon produced by a nameless left-wing French student in 1968 on the theme 'The pen is mightier than the sword', in which a puny student with a tiny broken sword is impaled on an enormous fountain pen wielded by a riot policeman. The success of this inversion underlines the degree to which the semic composition of a word (and its associated image) involves elements which cannot be isolated into any autonomous language system, components which are in fact ideological. Thus the deviant use (as in the case of this cartoon) of a word or image is deviant not in relation to some fixed lexical usage, but in relation to the terms in which the common sense of a particular culture defines it.

Two subsidiary points follow this. In the first place, as was suggested by the use of the cartoon example, to define signifiers in terms of the attributes of objects or other referential items elides any differences that may exist between verbal signifiers and cinemantic signifiers (see Metz, *Film Language*). As in the example of the cartoon, so in the case of Hardy's collapsing porch, analysed at length in Chapter 2: the conventional associations of porches are what defines the normal use of its cinematic image, and hence its deviant use. The same holds for referential items other than objects, and whose signifiers are therefore not substantives: the gag of the dwarf policeman depends upon the deviant use of an action, whose verbal signifier would be a verb, just as in a pun such as 'Run a company? He's not fit to run a bath!' Similarly with Rimbaud's 'Je est un autre' ('I is another person'), which is nonsense until referred either to its original context or to some implied psychoanalytic discourse: it is nonsense because of the deviant predication deriving from a pronoun; such a figure of course has no cinematic equivalent, as there is no cinematic equivalent of the pronouns.[5]

In the second place, nothing said here about common sense should be taken to imply that it is a unitary phenomenon, or that the semic composition of words or images is unified. As Chomsky said, in a well-known aphorism, a language is only a dialect with an army: all 'languages' are composed of a variety of dialects, sociolects and idiolects, and this implies a large measure of variation in semic composition. *Fawlty Towers* uses this wittily in an exchange between Basil Fawlty and the major, on the subject of women:

BASIL   Wasn't it Oscar Wilde who said they have minds like Swiss cheese?

MAJOR   Hard, you mean?

BASIL No! Full of holes!

It is possible to read this as another example of the major's stupidity, but given the wide possibilities of Basil's simile, and the major's curious relationship to women, the more likely reading would be based on the divergent possibilities of idiolect and sociolect. This is not of course to deny the existence of substantial agreement over semic composition, only to stress the alternative possibility of divergence.

Understanding deviant usage is further bedevilled by the problem of dead metaphors and jokes that fail because they are excessively obvious. Dead metaphors are metaphors that have become so standard that they are virtually lexicalised, virtually a dictionary item in their own right: 'bored to death', for example. In some cases they are literally lexicalised: 'to tantalise', for instance, was originally a daring metaphor, based on the legend of Tantalus: in the twentieth century, and probably before, it is an ordinary verb, with a literal meaning, and any sense that it was a metaphor, involving a deviant usage, has long since been lost. That is to say, it has lost the capacity to surprise the reader, and here there is a clear link with failed jokes: a joke which is excessively obvious, or a gag which seems to be nothing more than a worn-out convention (like many of the fights and chases of silent screen comedy seen nowadays) fail because they have lost the capacity to surprise us, to create a peripeteia: although they do literally still contravene the discourses of the social formation, this is neutralised by their conventional or obvious nature; that they are perceived as a comic convention removes the sting they once had, prevents their disruptive nature from being apparent.

Finally, a particularly complex example of deviant usage, and one which poses problems for the analysis of comedy: irony. The etymology of irony defines it immediately as a semantic figure: meaning something other than what is said, and in the canonical form at least, meaning the opposite of what is said – a figure which is also known as antiphrasis. In this form, there is a clear relationship between irony, metaphor and joke:

To identify a (metaphor) as such, it is necessary to:
1) simultaneously perceive two semantic levels (metaphor dies in

translation, literalisation)

2) put them in the correct hierarchy, using co(n)textual indications: properly speaking, it is impossible to speak of metaphor unless there are two semantic levels in hierarchy . . .[6]

Kerbrat-Orecchioni's case, which it is necessary to consider in some detail, is that irony is one form of metaphor among others, and that the semantic structure of all of them conforms to this description, whose essence is that of the two semantic levels only one is the actual meaning – and the other is to be discarded.

Clearly this description is an accurate account of antiphrasis, but it is incompatible with the analysis of jokes and metaphors in the previous chapter. Here the two semantic levels (or paradigmatic references) were maintained in balance, a balance which differed between joke and metaphor but where both semantic levels were maintained and neither discarded. Not that this criticism affects our assessment of her account of irony in so far as it takes the form of antiphrasis, since it is an adequate account of that figure; however, irony also takes other forms, she claims: litotes, for instance, where once again the apparent meaning is not discarded but maintained in balance as in the case of metaphor.[7] Thus to that extent her theory is threatened by an over-simplification. However, the main thrust of her argument lies in a somewhat different direction: observing that irony can consist of figures that also have non-ironical applications, such as litotes and hyperbole, and observing that irony is on many occasions entirely devoid of any semantic markers, she concludes that the specificity of irony is not semantic at all, but pragmatic – it is defined by its purpose, namely mockery. The details of this argument and its general adequacy need not detain us here, for it is its implications that are of relevance for our purposes.

To define irony on the basis of mockery clearly raises another problem, which she does not confront: the forms of mockery (Freud's 'tendentious wit') which involve no recourse to irony, such as the Doris Day joke quoted earlier. By the same token, there are undoubtedly forms of irony which involve no mockery: the scene from Racine's *Britannicus*, described above, is intensely ironical in that there are clearly two semantic levels involved: the meanings of words that the

lover is capable of understanding on the basis of his inadequate information, and the meanings that the heroine and the audience are
able to attach to what she says, armed with a true knowledge of the
situation she is in. Kerbrat-Orecchioni excludes from consideration all
units larger than the sentence, no doubt for perfectly valid operational,
heuristic reasons (p.108); however, the result in this instance is to produce an awkward anomaly. In both the cases alleged here the problem
is essentially the same: what sort of statements are to be admitted as
ironical? Kerbrat-Orecchioni's solution is to accept popular usage as
her guideline: any statement that someone has called ironical will be
regarded as such, and its properties investigated; correlatively she dis-
misses the linguists' pretensions to construct an object that is theoretically coherent, but different from popular usage (p.120). Her discussion is therefore inconclusive, by her own admission (p.122 – which
is not to deny it considerable value as an exploratory analysis), and we
are left with a series of categories that overlap with each other and
whose relationships are unclear.

The reason for considering this analysis of irony at some length is
this: we can see immediately that irony is often used in a manner that is
intensely funny (Basil Fawlty, for example, in Chapter 6), but it is
equally clear that not all irony is used in this way – Racine's *Britannicus*,
for example. Kerbrat-Orecchioni's analysis would lead us to discard
the relevance of semantic markers as a distinguishing feature of irony,
whereas all the examples of humour that have been discussed in these
pages have been strongly semantically marked: the basis of the last
chapter's distinction between joke and metaphor was based on semantic markers that permitted an attribution of different balances of
plausibility and implausibility. If Kerbrat-Orecchioni's analysis is correct, it would be difficult, in appearance at least, to maintain this basis
for distinctions. Appearances, however, are misleading: the ascription
of plausibility and its opposite does not in fact depend upon semantic
markers, but upon either semantic or pragmatic markers. A pragmatic
marker consists of something in the context of the utterance that enables the listener and/or any third party to ascribe to a given statement
a meaning that the text of that statement alone would not permit: thus
the phrase 'What lovely weather' changes its meaning dramatically in
England according to the conditions referred to; if it is a sunny day, we

judge it is meant literally; if we are confronted with a panorama of solid rain, we judge it is meant ironically; it is the pragmatic marker that enables us to make sense of the statement. But this example reveals with all the clarity necessary that the balance of plausibility is precisely the distinguishing feature involved: it is highly improbable that any Englishman would look at a sheet of rain and say 'What lovely weather' sincerely.[8] The concept of plausibility and its opposite is triggered as easily by situation (pragmatic markers) as by semic incongruities (semantic markers), and the fact that most of our examples so far have been strongly semantically marked is due to heuristic values: they are easier to discuss in isolation from their fictional or real contexts.

We are left with one final problem: how can the model of the logic of the absurd account for the difference between funny and unfunny irony? In principle, the answer is clear: in unfunny irony, as in metaphor, some element either in the semantic or the pragmatic marking of the statement must assert that the statement is more plausible than implausible. However, this excessively abstract and schematic consideration scarcely constitutes an adequate answer: what is needed is an example, and a clearly privileged one is Mark Antony's 'Friends, Romans, countrymen' speech, and especially its refrain: 'Brutus is an honourable man'.

Let us recall the locus of the problem: according to the model developed here, and in Kerbrat-Orecchioni's study of irony, it is far easier to account for funny irony than for unfunny irony; in fact, it may be taken as axiomatic now – despite the ambiguities of Kerbrat-Orecchioni's study – that funny irony does not constitute a problem: its function will be amply analysed in *Fawlty Towers*. Therefore, what has to be accounted for is the apparently anomalous fact that some irony is not funny, and Mark Antony's speech clearly is not. Further, according to the logic of our model, it ought to be some increase in plausibility that is responsible for its seriousness.

Two features of the speech seem to be responsible for this particular aspect of its impact.[9] In the first place, it is not in fact clearly apparent from the outset of his speech that he is being ironical. It is true that we know, before the speech begins, that his supposed acquiescence in the new state of affairs defined by Caesar's death is faked: his soliloquy in Act III, Scene 1 promises civil war; and it is true that Cassius has repeatedly warned Brutus of the dangers of letting Mark Antony speak. Thus we can be certain, as he starts to speak, that he will use the occasion in some way that will be unfavourable to Brutus and the other conspirators; but what his rhetorical strategy will be is completely undefined at this moment. Indeed, as he starts he appears to concede ground to Brutus, admitting the possibility of Caesar's ambition, stating with apparent unambiguity that Brutus is honourable; in the whole of the first section of his speech the references to Brutus' honour are at most paradoxical, rather than clearly ironic, and it is only subsequently that the level of irony becomes apparent with the rapid repetition of 'honourable' in the second section of his speech. Further, we know, from the earlier parts of the play, that Brutus is indeed honourable, that his motives are not suspect. In combination, the chains of literal meaning lead us to place considerable stress on the reading of Mark Antony's refrain that would make it plausible.

In the second place, our perception of Mark Antony's speech is filtered through our perception of the effect that it is having on the onstage audience, the crowd of citizens he so successfully manipulates. They only clearly perceive the irony of Mark Antony's repetition after the third section of his speech, when the fourth citizen says 'They were traitors: honourable men!' Thus, as we respond to the various semantic levels of Mark Antony's speech, we judge them both in terms of what we understand his intentions to be, with the foreknowledge gleaned from the previous scene, and what we understand their effects to be upon the citizens who have no such foreknowledge: but these effects are predicated upon the fact that the citizens fail to see that Mark Antony is being ironical, for it is central to his rhetorical strategy that he appears to be genuinely well disposed to Brutus until nearly the end of his speech. If the citizens were to perceive that Mark Antony was being ironical then they would be aware that he was manipulating their emotions, and the outcome of the scene might be very different.

This schematic account allows us to see the difference between funny and unfunny irony. In unfunny irony such as this scene from *Julius Caesar*, various elements in the situation lead us to stress those elements in the reading that indicate plausibility: the chains that bind the ironical use of 'honourable' to early non-ironical use, and the manner in which the citizens' lack of perception of irony is responsible for the effectiveness of that irony. Since they do not perceive it as such, but as proof of Mark Antony's sincerity and concern for the public good, our own perception of it is intrinsically bound up with this other perception, and the effects of his cynical abuse of language colour our reading of it.

At this point our discussion of the question of deviant usage is complete. Its purpose has been twofold: firstly, to show that the linguistics of utterance is capable of generating an account of all forms of deviant usage, through the notions of ideological competence and pragmatic markers (a by-product of this version of semantics is to show that at this level there is no difference between verbal and visual signs, that is, that such differences as there are are not relevant to the subject under discussion). Secondly, it was to demonstrate that all the various forms of deviant usage can be described within the framework of the logic of the absurd. This discussion of deviant usage was prefaced with the stated intention of using it to analyse the specificity of comic utterance, and that apparently has not been achieved; however, the point was to demonstrate the extent to which conceptions of linguistic deviancy are imbricated into the logic of the absurd, for it is here that we shall be able to locate the specificity of comic utterance.

There is a brief passage in Kerbrat-Orecchioni's *Enonciation* (pp.188–90) which considers the topic of the linguistic effectivity of jokes, and which constitutes a convenient starting point. Jokes, in common with all statements are marked, inter alia, by the intention to produce some change of attitude on the part of the addressee; they do this by a mechanism that is internal to them: presupposition.

> Prague, 1968, during the Soviet intervention. A Czech and a Russian soldier are on patrol together at night, in the deserted streets. They come upon a case of German beer – full. Checking there is no one to see them, they drag it into the shadows. The Russian soldier says to his Czech colleague: 'Comrade, I propose that we divide this case of beer in a fraternal fashion.' 'No!' says the Czech, 'No! Not fraternal, I insist! Fifty-fifty instead!'

The presupposition of this joke is clear: minimally, that the Czech soldier believes that Soviet political rhetoric is a mask for rampant exploitation; maximally, that this is objectively so. Without this framework the joke is not even comprehensible, let alone funny. Thus to find it funny is to concede the possibility – not to put it any more forcefully – that this might indeed be so.[10] The essence of Kerbrat-Orecchioni's case about the persuasive power of jokes is that the presupposition is hidden, buried behind the joke; as a result anyone who wants to challenge it is forced to change the mode of discourse and to confront the joker polemically, at which point he is probably accused of 'not being able to take a joke'.

No doubt Kerbrat-Orecchioni is right to point to hidden presuppositions in jokes. However, to do so is to conflate humorous and non-humorous statements, for the role ascribed to presupposition here is the same as the role it demonstrably plays elsewhere. The traditional name for this form of presupposition is enthymeme, which is defined in logic as a syllogism with one premiss unexpressed, and in rhetoric as implicitly basing arguments on some belief that the audience is known to hold.[11] To phrase it thus is to indicate an obvious parallel with Althusser's theory of ideology in *Reading Capital*[12]: 'It was not only in the reply that there was mystification, but in the question itself' (vol.1, p.63). In all of these instances the role of enthymeme is clear: an appeal, by various rhetorical strategies, to some presupposed notion hidden within the individual statement or text. But it is equally clear that the texts discussed by Barthes and Althusser are not characterised by humour: serials and news reporting (Barthes) and classical English political economy (Althusser). Moreover, Kerbrat-Orecchioni's observations on jokes are explicitly based on what are asserted to be the properties of all statements (p.188). Thus while the role of enthymeme in jokes is clear, it is still necessary to place it in relation to the logic of the absurd, for that will give it a dimension that is specific to comic utterance.

In jokes the appeal to enthymeme is absurd. The Czech soldier is funny, and not polemical in the usual serious sense, for two reasons. In the first place, his interpretation of 'fraternal' is inconsistent with the normal meaning of the word. In the second place, his naivety is excessive, for he has only seen one meaning of the word 'fraternal', and if he was really able to see the connection between the two meanings of the word upon which the joke depends, he would be unlikely to take the

Russian's proposal sufficiently seriously to respond angrily. That is to say, the Czech soldier's interpretation is implausible; yet it is given a measure of plausibility by the Soviet Union's use of the word – or perhaps its abuse, especially in relation to Eastern Europe. Thus – to use Kerbrat-Orecchioni's terms – the surreptitious evocation of presuppositions is done in an absurd way; although the presupposition is indeed evoked, just as it is in non-humorous enthymemetic statements, it is evoked on a different modality.

At this point we have returned to the question asked, but not answered, in the introduction: what is the relationship between a joke and the object of that joke? Or to use the more formal terms introduced during the discussion of the linguistics of the utterance: what is the nature of the actants of a comic utterance? What are the positions implied by the play of such actants? In what way are they different from the actants and positions of other types of utterance? Much of the discussion of this topic must be deferred until the analysis of further themes and more examples can allow firmer conclusions, but it is already possible to deduce something from the form of analysis allowed by the linguistics of the utterance.

Central to the logic of the absurd is the construction of a surprise (the peripeteia); implicit in this is the primacy of two enunciative roles, the speaker who wishes to surprise his audience, and the audience who is/are to be surprised. But it is equally central to the logic of the absurd that this surprise is more implausible than plausible, and clearly the function of this aspect of the surprise is to construct the butt of the joke, the third enunciative role, as Freud asserts. Everything in the statement – the arrangement of the dramatis personae, the various attributes they are given, the careful structuring around the moment of the punch line – is subordinate to these enunciative roles, and it is clear therefore that it is the actants of the utterance and not the actants of the statement that must be the focal point of the analysis.

What distinguishes the actants of comic utterance is that they are inextricably caught up in the logic of the absurd:

– the butt is rendered absurd because he/she/it is made to do or say something that is more implausible than plausible.

– the audience is made to find the butt absurd, made to accept that this butt does something more implausible than plausible.

– the narrator/subject of the utterance posits himself as someone who finds the butt absurd, by ascribing to him/her/it some attribute that is more implausible than plausible.

Thus, for example: a TV interviewer asks Ronald Reagan: 'How would the USA respond to an imminent Soviet nuclear attack?' – 'Waal,' says Reagan, 'the first thing you gotta do is put the wagons in a circle.' Reagan's 'reply' is more implausible than plausible because his intelligence has not been that much affected by years of Hollywood, but is nonetheless plausible because of his past and because of his belligerence on international issues. Anyone who laughs is accepting that Reagan may do something more implausible than plausible, and the narrator implicates himself as someone who finds it appropriate to attach such an attribute to Reagan.

It is in the process of constructing absurd actants that the effectivity of humour lies. What this effectivity is we shall see subsequently. However, it is clear that it is because the actants in question are actants of the utterance that humour can have whatever this effectivity is: for the actants of the utterance, inscribed in the statement in their various ways, are also features of the real world – Reagan is both an actant in the joke-statement, an actant of the absurd utterance (its butt) and President of the USA; the Soviet soldier of the 'fraternal' joke is simultaneously an actant in the joke statement, an actant in the utterance (by metonymy, he incarnates the butt) and since he uses actual Soviet rhetoric, the USSR is implicated too. If the absurd actants were only actants of the statement, the links between them and the real world would be considerably more tenuous; it is because the butt of the absurd is always, inherently, a feature of the real social world in some form or another – a person, an institution, a value, a discourse – that it/he/she is also an actant of the utterance, or – put in another form – it is its pragmatic inscription in the absurd utterance that marks such-and-such a feature of the real world as the butt of the joke. The actant of the statement, on the contrary, need have no connection with the world outside the statement: he/she/it may be pure fiction. But the actants of the utterance are necessarily also features of the world outside the statement.

The speaker too is an actant of the utterance, the constructor of the absurd peripeteia; by inscribing himself in the utterance in this way, he marks himself as the joker. To tell a joke about X is not a neutral activity: it is to adopt the position of (a) someone who finds the butt ridiculous, and (b) someone who finds that moment in a conversation appropriate for the evocation of the absurd (obviously this second consideration does not apply to professional, scheduled comedy). To make a joke is a particular (if limited) form of commitment, both in terms of the implication of levity towards a particular feature of the real world, and in terms of levity towards an occasion. J. Emerson finds (in a study of joking among medical personnel in formal meetings) that senior personnel devote a far higher percentage of their speaking time to jokes than do juniors, whose few jokes are usually self-disparaging; the implication clearly is that to adopt a tone of levity implies a particular attitude towards the circumstances in which one is speaking, an attitude that is sufficiently controversial to involve risk and to demand the assurance given by hierarchical position. Once again, it is because the speaker is an actant of the utterance that these implications follow: by postulating a situation subject to the logic of the absurd he necessarily implicates himself as the locus of the absurd, as the person who introduces the absurd into a situation (or re-introduces it) and the person who attaches absurdity to the butt in question.

What we have seen in this application of the linguistics of utterance to the logic of the absurd is how comedy and humour are located within the general process of the production of meaning. All meaning must pass through the circuit of utterance; in the previous chapter we saw the roots of the comic in paradigms, and we have now seen that the activation of these paradigms in the act of utterance (comic or otherwise) necessarily implies a speaking subject, a subject who in the case of comic utterances adopts a particular profile defined by the logic of the absurd. Finally, this leads us to specify a particular relationship between the instance of comic utterance and its speaker, butt and audience, a relationship also defined by the logic of the absurd.

This is also the point to return to a topic raised in the introduction: the conflation of the verbal and the visual.

It has often been pointed out that verbal and visual signifiers convey meaning in significantly different ways: the word refers not to an actual empirical object but to a concept, whereas the visual image refers to an actual individual object. The result of the word's mode of functioning is that words can be assigned meanings independent of the contexts in which they are used – that is how dictionaries are possible; but by the same token visual images cannot have generalisable meanings, and therefore there cannot be a visual equivalent of a dictionary. Now the process by which words and objects are given meaning in humour – if the arguments of the preceding pages are correct – is apparently dependent upon the process of lexicalisation, upon the possibility of creating a dictionary of the signs in question, for the process of humorous meaning derives from connotation, or predication (see Chapter 3), and the semiotic tradition has in general insisted that connotation is a secondary phenomenon, deriving from and supported by denotation. Put more simply, this means that the literal meaning of a sign is the starting point for the set of derived meanings that constitute connotative codes, of the variety analysed in the preceding chapter. But whereas there is no problem in assigning meaning to words in this manner, it is less obvious how the same process can be applied to visual images, since the two types of image do not have 'literal' meanings in quite the same way: the literal meaning of a word is a concept whereas the literal meaning of a visual image is an actual object, an individual object rather than something generic like a concept.

The resolution of this problem lies in shifting the focus of analysis from how individual signs have meaning independent of contexts to how signs are mobilised in discourse, in particular contexts. The knowledge of the meaning of a sign involves, inevitably, a certain 'ideological' or 'cultural competence' which is inextricably part of linguistic competence in general: to know that a sign refers to a concept ('table' refers to the set of tables) necessarily means also being able to associate it with the relevant range of real objects in the real world, having relevant knowledge of the functions of such objects and in general their 'place' in the cultural map of a particular civilisation or ideological formation. Such a conception of meaning is based not upon the static model of reference to paradigms, as was apparently the case in Chapter 3, but upon the dynamic model of the mobilisation of signs in discourse, in sets of statements about the world, where meaning is settled not only by reference to a paradigm but also to a context of utterance, in which some meanings are actualised and other are ignored, as we have seen. Crucially, if meaning is conceived in this way the distinction between verbal and visual signs disappears, for clearly the capacity to recognise a visual sign presupposes the same relationship between meaning and cultural competence as the one outlined here; therefore the differences between forms of denotation lose their significance when applied to the forms of meaning under analysis. In passing, we may note that this is essentially why the theory of meaning applied in this essay is largely of linguistic origin, even though many of the examples used are non-linguistic in nature.

At this point we have enough theoretical tools at our disposal to allow us to consider a wider range of comic phenomena than has been possible up to this point. Ultimately, the intention of this essay is to ascribe a particular effectivity, a particular form of impact, to the comic or the humorous. In the meantime, two other matters will retain our attention: firstly, the relationships between the individual gag and the larger narrative framework in which it is set; secondly, the relationship between what jokes are about and the identity of the teller, or of the narrative in which they are told.

Notes

1. This point is in fact controversial within linguistics and semiotic theory, but this is not the place to try and resolve such difficulties, which revolve around the relationship between the speaker and the rules of discourse, as well as around the nature of the speaking subject, whether (s)he is to be considered as the locus of difference (Derrida), of desire in language (Kristeva), or of the play of power relationships (Foucault). Fortunately, it is unnecessary to resolve these disagreements (even if it were possible) for our current purposes, since no one disputes the necessity of referring to the speaking subject when theorising discourse.
2. These remarks indicate the site of another series of controversies in recent linguistics, surrounding the relationship between signified and referent in the pragmatics of language. For a general introduction to this area of debate, see Smith and Wilson, especially Chapter 8.

3. See T. Todorov, 'Freud sur l'Enonciation', in *Theories du Symbole*, Paris, Editions du Seuil, 1976, for a detailed discussion of the implications of these points for linguistic theory in general.

4. I have derived the term 'actant' from A.J. Greimas; however, my usage is not quite the same as his. For both of us, 'actant' refers to an entity whose identity derives from its role in narrative. Thus for example, the narrative role of the ghost of Hamlet's father is to give Hamlet the mission of avenging his death; it is also to confuse him, in the sense that the origin of the evidence is such as to render it suspect. For Greimas, his role would be no more than what is dictated by the place that he occupies in narrative structure in general, in other words a combination of the two narrative roles that could be played by different 'characters' in different narratives: the 'mission-giver' – a role presented as basic to narrative structure in Propp – and the source of (potential) red herrings, a role well established in the detective story, for example. What is excluded from this account is what derives from the fact that Hamlet's father is a ghost, with all the ambiguities this entails. This is excluded because it has no place in the structure of narrative as such, since it derives from the field of ideology, which is external to narrative. That is to say, for Greimas, 'actant' is defined as such entirely within the structure of narrative (this is logically entailed, since otherwise narrative structure cannot be the object of autonomous analysis). In my usage, on the other hand, actant is defined both within narrative and within utterance too.

5. With the possible exception of extended use of the point of view shot, which is approximately analogous to the first person singular; see, for example, *The Lady in the Lake* (1946), shot entirely in point of view to approximate first person narrative. By common consent, it is a failure.

6. C. Kerbrat-Orecchioni, 'L'Ironie comme Trope', in *Poetique*, vol.11, February 1980, p.111. She in fact uses the word 'trope' where I have used 'metaphor'. No doubt her terminology is more correct; I have preferred the more commonly used word, especially since the definitions of both are in a state of constant renegotiation in essays such as hers and mine.

7. Jean Cohen provides an account of both similarities and differences between the various figures of speech. See J. Cohen, 'Théorie de la Figure', *Communications*, 16, 1970.

8. It is also clear that such figures cross cultural boundaries with difficulty. One summer in Paxos, where the only water supply is rainfall, during a rare cloudburst I made the mistake of saying to a Greek friend 'What lovely weather', to which he replied 'Yes! It's saved me 10,000 drachmae' (to buy water from a tanker).

9. These comments are not intended as a full analysis of the speech: they are only intended to illuminate the relationship between irony and comedy.

10. I used this example in a lecture on humour in France in 1982. A member of the audience, a member of the French Communist Party and a supporter of Soviet interventions in Eastern Europe, walked out at that point. But we should not imagine that such a joke – or the one about Brezhnev used earlier – is necessarily oppositional: they are as often told in self-mockery by Communists too. We shall return to this point.

11. R. Barthes, 'L'Ancienne Rhétorique', *Communications*, 16, 1970; cf. my 'Damp Stones of Positivism', *Philosophy of Social Sciences*, vol.9, no.2, June 1979.

12. It is often held that this theory is discredited by Althusser's own later theory, in 'Ideological State Apparatuses'; in my opinion the earlier theory is incorporated in the later one as one possibility; it is therefore inadequate, not incorrect.

5

Comic Articulation

The Silent Screen

▬▬

The preceding chapters have been concerned with the structure of the single gag, for the reason argued in the first chapter: the structure of the minimum unit of comic narrative seemed a necessary basis for the analysis of both comedy and humour. However, even the slightest and most informal acquaintance with comic texts tells us that comedy which consists only of single gags is the exception rather than the rule, virtually restricted to stand-up comics who specialise in gags and one-liners in the manner made famous by Bob Hope – and, of course, to the everyday situation of telling jokes. Well-established though this form of comedy is, it is only one form and the other well-known forms such as television sitcom, cinematic comedy, theatrical farce and the variety show all use forms of narrative that operate at a qualitatively greater level of complexity than the stand-up comic's series of gags and one-liners. That is the topic of the following four chapters.

More exactly, those chapters are devoted to a range of interconnected topics all focusing on this question. The first of those topics is the way in which jokes are arranged together in sequences, thus creating two things which have not so far been mentioned:

a) an escalation of comic effect through a sequence;
b) a miniature narrative which consists of nothing more than a sequence of jokes.

The second topic is the relationship between comic and non-comic narrative – or, to use other words – between jokes and narrative in general; to this extent, this book is intended to make a contribution to narratological theory. The third topic is the relationship between jokes

97

and one particular narrative category which intuitively is very important in the more developed forms of comedy: the category of character.
Here the essential question to be asked is 'What is comic character?'
The first two chapters are devoted to the subject of the articulation of
gags together into gag sequences – to comic articulation, in fact; narrative in general and character are the topics of the following chapters.

It is becoming more and more difficult to satisfy the public for cin-
ematographic comedy. Yesterday's slapstick no longer satisfies the
spectator's needs. There was a time in the theatre, and especially in
the cinema, when all an actor needed to make the public laugh every
time was particularly grotesque make-up. Those times are past.

Spoken by an unimpeachable witness, Mack Sennett, these lines have
two elements of surprise for us: firstly, that they were spoken in 1916;
secondly, that there ever was a time when comedy was simpler and
more basic than it was in the 1920s.[1] And yet the films that have been
quoted earlier, especially the Laurel and Hardy films, date from the
very last years of the silent cinema – *The Finishing Touch*, for instance,
was made in the last winter before sound was introduced. Implied,
therefore, is a long 'pre-history' of the silent screen farce, and a specific
type of continuity linking it to the examples we have already seen: the
augmentation of complexity.

One of the simplest of film comedies is to be found in the British
Film Institute's compilation, *Beginnings of Cinema*. A miller dressed in
white and carrying a sack of flour, bumps into a sweep, carrying a sack
of soot; they proceed to belabour each other with their respective sacks,
and each change colour as a result. A rather more complex version is to
be found in an early Buster Keaton/Fatty Arbuckle feature called *The
Butcher Boy* (1917). Buster goes to the store to buy molasses. At the
counter he tosses a quarter piece in the air, catches it and kisses it and
drops it in the tin he has brought to carry the molasses in. He slaps
the tin down on the counter, startling Fatty, who starts to fill the tin with
molasses while Buster 'helps' some irritated old men with their game
of checkers. Fatty holds out the full tin and demands payment: all in-
nocence, Buster points to the coin in the tin. Unable to retrieve the coin
from the bottom of the tin, Fatty pours the molasses into Buster's hat

while he is looking the other way. Buster puts on the hat, and gradually realises, with mounting anxiety, that something is amiss. Trying to pull off his hat he drops the tin on the floor, spilling all the molasses. Fatty tries to pull off the hat and Buster steps in the molasses. To get him out of the sticky puddle Fatty pours a kettle of boiling water over his feet and then gives him a mighty kick which sends him somersaulting down the front steps and into the road. Buster re-enters the store just in time to get a sack of flour in the face, and the first reel ends with a general mêlée of flour flinging.

Nor should we imagine that this style of humour was specifically Anglo-Saxon: in both France and Italy there were flourishing schools of farce production creating a style of humour that was essentially similar to the examples we have just seen. For example, David Robinson quotes films by André Deed, whose stage names were first Boireau (in French films) and then Cretinetti (in Italian). In *Boireau a mangé de l'ail* (*Boireau's Been Eating Garlic*, c.1908):

> The hero wanders the streets of Belle Epoque Paris, blissfully un-aware that passers-by are collapsing, unconscious at the mere whiff of his garlicky breath. Only a stalwart carthorse maintains his feet in face of Boireau's exhalations, but even he is driven to gallop backwards (in reverse motion) taking the cart with him ('The Italian Comedy', p.106).

In general, Robinson demonstrates that both Italian and French schools of pre-World War One created a form of humour essentially similar to the more sophisticated American form that developed a few years later.

Clearly these examples of very early cinematic comedy demonstrate an almost total reliance on the discourses of the social formation: the comedy derives almost entirely from the contradiction of various commonsense expectations to do with respect for the human body and in-hibitions against aggression. By the later 1920s such things were only good for opening more complex and extended sequences of gags, as we saw in the example of the running gag of the ramp and the porch in Laurel and Hardy's *Finishing Touch*. Ollie's opening pratfall is only in-tended to start things moving, and while it may well have got a laugh, it would certainly not have been a very big one. But the whole sequence

of pratfalls on the ramp is intended primarily to build up to the unfore-
seeable moment when the entire porch collapses, and they are absolutely essential to prepare it.

The second way in which the comedy of the late 1920s was more
complex than the examples of early comedy we have just seen lay in the
development of psychologically consistent characters. All of the major
comedians developed consistent personae. Chaplin's tramp, the 'little
fellow', is no doubt the most famous, but Keaton's is at least as much
appreciated by latter-day aficionados. That this was a very conscious
manoeuvre on their part is well-attested in interviews: Keaton often
talked about how he distinguished his 'little man' from Chaplin's, and
Harold Lloyd has described how he and Keaton swapped gags which
did not fit in with their own personae.[2]

This is the aspect of silent screen comedy which has attracted most
critical comment, and there is no need to retread such a well worn path.
However, two comments are worth making. In the first place, a certain
amount of the film space devoted to the distinctive elements of the
clowns' personae is non-comic, in the sense of being non-funny, that is
being ordinary realist narrative (assuming, of course, that the original
audience found these moments as unfunny as modern audiences – we
shall return to this question at the end of the chapter), and the focus
of the present chapter is intended to be on the way gag sequences are
built up.

Secondly, despite the clowns' insistence on the distinction between
their personae and the incompatibility of certain gags with their personae, there are clear overlaps. A good example is to be found in
Chaplin's *The Gold Rush*, in a gag sequence which is reminiscent both
of Keaton and Laurel and Hardy. At an early stage of the story the
'little fellow' is marooned in a snow-bound cabin with two large men,
both of whom are going mad with hunger, and a shotgun. They start
to fight, wrestling with the gun, and wherever – and however fast –
Chaplin tries to avoid the muzzle, it is always pointing straight at him.
This is very reminiscent of a Buster Keaton gag in *The General*, which
involves a giant mortar loaded and pointing straight at Keaton's cab,
and is reminiscent of many Laurel and Hardy gags which involve
desperate repeated attempts to avoid a situation which always recurs.
Not that this should be taken to indicate a rejection of the traditional

view of the silent screen clowns as distinct personae: clearly this view is basically correct, but it would be an exaggeration to imagine that there were no overlaps.

The organisation of sequences of gags was equally a conscious technique on the part of the silent clowns, as James Agee clearly shows. The silent comedians distinguished, he demonstrates, between different types of laughter and the different stages of a gag or a gag sequence that were intended to produce them. They divided laughter into four categories, in ascending order of hilarity: the titter, the yowl, the belly laugh and the boffo. The titter was exactly what the term means in ordinary English; the yowl was a kind of short isolated yelp which indicates considerably more amusement than a mere titter, but not enough for extended laughter; the belly laugh was both more profound and more extended than the yowl, and corresponds again to ordinary English usage; the boffo was the kind of laugh that kills, leaving the audience in helpless pain on the floor. In any sequence of gags, the beginning would probably only raise a titter, and the succeeding stages would gradually escalate the laughter. They also distinguished between the stages of a gag, talking about 'milking' the gag and 'topping' it. To use Agee's example of the large number of large men getting out of a small car, already discussed: the sequence of large men is milking the gag, the midget is topping it, and the car collapsing is 'topping the topper'.

This is clear evidence of a high degree of conscious planning on the part of the comedians. Yet Petr Kral, in a recent book on silent comedy, insists (pp.61ff) that their films were largely improvised, quoting remarks by leading comedians – for example, this from Harold Lloyd: 'It was the location that inspired the comedy and as we filmed we looked for new gags to fill the reel.' No doubt this is true, for there is plenty of evidence that the silent clowns placed a very low degree of emphasis on narrative in the usual sense – as Kral insists, it is action that is king in these films, as opposed to narrative or character. Does this contradict the assertion, derived from Agee, that there was a high degree of planning in silent screen comedy? Not necessarily, for the planning that Agee refers to is internal to the structure of gags, and does not refer to narrative in the wider sense. Indeed, what we can begin to see now is that the articulation of gags in sequences to a large extent replaces narrative in the conventional sense in silent screen farce, and provides the link between the careful planning of the gag and the apparent disinclination to take narrative seriously.

This is not to assert that the categories Agee reports constitute a theory of gags and gag articulation. In the first place, the stages (milking, etc.) do not necessarily correspond to the degree of laughter aroused: in Agee's example it is far from clear where the process of milking and topping laughter was intended to ascend from one level to another. In the second place, this terminology tells us nothing about how the different stages of a gag are related to each other: why – to use Agee's example again – is the midget topping the gag? What is it about the relationship between his appearance and what has preceded it that makes it capable of providing a sudden increment of comic affect, as the term 'topping' implies? What is it about the collapse of the car that makes it 'top the topper'? The reduplication of the term both implies that this stage of the gag marks another qualitative shift in comic effect, and that it is incapable of theorising that shift: mere repetition hides the nature of the shift rather than reveal it. Nonetheless, comedians' terminology is a precious indication of where we should look to explain the augmentation of comic effect: to the manner in which gags are articulated together into a gag sequence.

This is not to suggest that all gags are necessarily in sequences, or that articulated sequences are necessary in order to multiply comic effect. The lift/cop gag which opened our discussion is isolated from the gags that surround it, and there is an excellent example of an isolated sight gag in Chaplin's *The Great Dictator* (1940): when he learns that the police are at the door, the previously unafraid, even somewhat boastful, Chaplin dashes across the room and in literally a single movement leaps at a closed chest, opens it while (apparently, at least) still in the air, lands in it already horizontal and closes it on itself. The sudden shift from braggart to coward certainly starts the process of laughter, but it is the positively galvanic activity that achieves an immediate yowl or belly laugh. But it is empirically clear that in the 1920s there was an increasing trend towards gags that were organised together in sequences. This short sequence from Buster Keaton's *Cops* is a good example: a man calling a cab drops his wallet, which Keaton (who happens to be passing) picks up and returns; the man, visibly in a bad mood, pushes Keaton out of the way but takes the wallet; as he gets into the cab he slips and falls. Keaton, ever helpful, gives him a hand up; as the cab pulls away we see Buster counting money in his hand. The cab does a fast U-turn and as it comes past, the man grabs the wallet from Keaton's hand; but the money is in the other hand. Another U-turn and the cab stops in front of Buster, hiding him from us; the man gets out on our side and goes round the cab; after a brief delay the cab leaves with Buster in it.

Here the impact of the gags is incomprehensible without giving an account of how they are related to each other. Buster's goodwill is appallingly rewarded, and thus his theft becomes plausible, but still less plausible than implausible – after all, it is still theft, and therefore a contradiction of our expectations, perhaps especially when disguised as a second act of charity. His opponent's first attempt to retrieve his money is implausibly neat (leaning out of the window of a moving cab), but is given a measure of plausibility by (a) his bad mood (b) the fact that he is in the cab (c) the fact that it is possible, which is proved by the fact that we see it. The coincidence of timing which ensures that the money is in the other hand is also implausible, but possible, therefore a little plausible. Finally, the coincidence of timing and place which makes it possible for Buster to escape in the cab is implausible, but possible; and the neatness of the reversal of the situation – the impeccable symmetry – is also highly implausible, but possible. In all of these cases, the implausibility and plausibility of the various actions derives from the way in which they are linked to what precedes them: the coincidence of timing which separates the money and the wallet at exactly the right moment (from Buster's point of view, that is!) derives from the previous shot of Buster counting the money; the fact that his opponent is obliged to pull up in front of him is explained by his previous failure to retrieve his money, and Buster's success in escaping is motivated by his opponent getting out of the other side of the cab. Finally, the main humour of the escape derives from the neatness with which Buster reverses a situation, and the symmetry is only apparent on the basis of what has gone before.

Here, therefore, we have a brief gag sequence in which each stage is both a gag in its own right, and at the same time the preparation stage for the next gag: this is what was meant by the articulation of gag sequences. In the two examples to which the rest of this chapter is devoted, we shall see how this principle can be applied to more extended sequences.

But this principle has a further application which is of even wider significance. We have already seen that the silent clowns carefully developed consistent personae for their screen performances: an examination of gag sequences will demonstrate that it is out of their articulation that comic character grows, in other words that comic character is a product of gag rather than the opposite.

In the opening sequence of Laurel and Hardy's *Wrong Again* (1929) we see a groom and a client standing in front of a stable door talking; a forkful of hay flies through the door and covers the smartly dressed client, and stable lad Ollie slowly emerges, looking bashful, but failing to repress a smile. Ollie and the groom then try to back a horse into the stable, apparently encountering an obstacle, which turns out to be Stan and a bucket trying to get out; the look he directs at the others clearly means 'What do you mean by trying to get that horse in while I'm on my way out?' As gags go, these are rather feeble, but they are only intended as an opener, to put the audience in the mood; this introductory sequence finishes with a well-milked version of one of the oldest gags in film farce, the 'arroseur arrosé'.

Stan goes to fill his bucket with water and as soon as he turns the tap receives a jet of water on his backside from the hose. He takes some time to realise his mistake, and turns the tap off again. Ollie strides up with his customary efficiency and takes over, picking up the bucket and hose and ordering Stan to turn the tap on again. As Stan obeys, Ollie is looking in his direction cursing him and fails to notice that the bucket has no bottom. The jet of water passes straight through. In pique Ollie hurls the bucket away, out of the frame, and it knocks the wheel off the trap a client is getting into, perhaps the client he had just covered in hay.

Simple though this gag is, it is of a very different nature both to the opening gags and to the lift-cop gag in *Liberty*: none of these have successive stages with an articulated relationship between the stages, whereas here both the peripeteia and the syllogisms refer back to the earlier stages of the gag. Even the lift-cop gag, boff though it is, is strictly once off, virtually isolated from the structure of what surrounds it.

The opening is as simple as what precedes. The peripeteia consists of the contradiction between dignity, connoted by the human body in general, and the indignity connoted by a wet backside. The first syllogism is the same as the first syllogism in the hay gag – randomness commonly produces no result. The second says that since the hose is not being controlled it is equally likely to be pointing at Stan as in any other direction, in other words that it is not impossible. Of course, Stan's carelessness emphasises the implausibility – any normal person would have checked the nozzle before turning on the tap – but then we already know that Stan's capacity for foreseeing consequences is limited, and – which should not be underestimated – lack of foresight is a convention in slapstick.

Ollie's arrival complicates matters. His inadequate attempt to better Stan's efforts releases a series of peripeteia. Ollie's manner connotes efficiency, but he is in fact highly inefficient:

Peripeteia I   Ollie   Ollie
Efficiency | | Inefficiency

A bucket and hose are an obviously complementary pair, but in Ollie's hands the complementarity is destroyed:

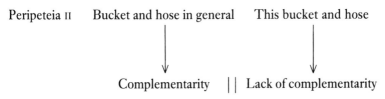

Peripeteia II   Bucket and hose in general   This bucket and hose
Complementarity | | Lack of complementarity

Finally, the parallelism of their action – one tries, then the other – connotes contrast, whereas in fact there is none:

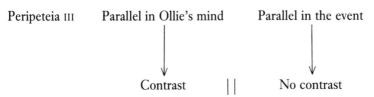

Peripeteia III   Parallel in Ollie's mind   Parallel in the event
Contrast | | No contrast

105

The two syllogisms run thus:

1) A bucket without a bottom is obvious, therefore it is implausible that Ollie should not notice it.
2) Ollie has no reason to think it is anything other than an ordinary bucket, and is looking the other way; ergo, it is plausible.

The internal articulation of the gag at this point turns on the parallelism. Ollie sets out to provide a contrast and fails, thus creating a peripeteia; but from another point of view – that of general connotation, rather than the specific connotations of Ollie's behaviour – parallel suggests similarity, which is what in fact occurs. In other words, the audience remembers Stan's blunder with the hose, which is equally plausible/implausible, and Ollie's blunder so to speak echoes Stan's. But since we have already accepted the plausibility of Stan's, the plausibility of Ollie's is reinforced, because in general we expect parallel actions to be similar. This is not a strong internal articulation, but it demonstrates what is meant by the notion.

In a rage, Ollie throws the bucket away, with disastrous results. Traps connote a kind of solidity, and rapid collapse connotes exactly the opposite. But there is a second, more subtle peripeteia. The simultaneous parallel and contrast of Ollie's blunder, which milked the gag, connotes the end of a sequence, since the actions that are contrasted and compared form – apparently – a closed unit, whose components face only inwards towards each other. The collapse of the trap, on the other hand, shows that the sequence of events is open-ended after all, or at any rate longer than expected. In fact, any lengthily milked gag will get laughter partly from the fact that at each stage the audience expects it to have finished.

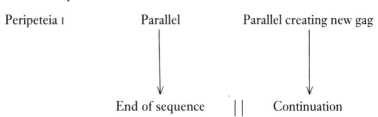

Peripeteia I   Parallel   Parallel creating new gag

End of sequence || Continuation

Similarly, there is more than one pair of syllogisms involved. The first pair concerns the results of randomness, and is identical to the pair evoked by the hay gag that opens the movie, or by Stan's wet backside.

The second concerns the collapse of the trap, regardless of whether the destruction was intentional or not. It is implausible that a trap should collapse under such a minor impact, but looked at from another point of view, if a wheel is knocked out from under it (as in fact happens), collapse is plausible. The plausibility syllogism is weak, undeniably. But it is strengthened by what precedes: we know by now that we are in a sequence of unforeseen consequences resulting from ill thought-out actions, and therefore the acceptance of previous plausibility syllogisms makes it easier for us to accept this one.

If the opening of *Wrong Again* is weak in its reliance upon highly conventional gags, it is considerably strengthened by the internal articulation of milking and topping: clearly the organisation of gags into sequences, in such a way that gags serve as the preparatory stages for further gags, is a way of increasing comic impact as the viewer is caught in the hallucinatory progress of a process that is simultaneously logical and absurd. There is a short, beautifully articulated sequence of gags in *Wrong Again* that will serve as a demonstration of how laughter accumulates in this way.

Stan and Ollie find out there is a reward for the stolen Blue Boy, and Blue Boy is in their stable. Unfortunately, the stolen one is a painting, not a horse, but they only find that out at the end of the film, by which time they have obeyed the unwitting owner's instructions to 'take Blue Boy inside and put him on the piano'. The first indignity they inflict on the chic decor involves Ollie tripping over a nude statue and breaking it in three pieces. Ollie does not merely knock the statue over: as he trips he embraces it and falls with it, managing to rescue his bowler on the way down. This protracted collapse is an example of a common source of silent screen humour: exaggeration (here mixed with indignity). According to Freud, exaggeration is always funny because it involves an effort that is disproportionate to the results achieved (*Jokes*, pp.249ff). The types of exaggeration typical of silent comedy were in fact extreme, as James Agee attests: the silent comedian hit on the head would never just fall down, he would

> make a cadenza out of it – look vague, smile like an angel, roll up his eyes, lace his fingers, thrust his hands palms downwards as far as they would go, hunch his shoulders, rise on tiptoe, prance ecstatically

in narrowing circles until, with tallow knees, he sank down the vortex of his dizziness to the floor and there signified nirvana by kicking his heels twice, like a swimming frog (p.439).

Nonetheless, this does not contradict Freud's principle, which is easily translated into the logic of the absurd: the disproportion is both surprising and implausible, but plausibility is given both – minimally – by the fact that such a thing is possible, and seen to be done, and maximally by some feature of the actual situation; in the case Agee cites, by the disorienting effect of a blow on the head.

Ollie's pratfall with the statue gets a laugh, no doubt, but probably only a titter. He then sets about repairing the statue, presumably in the hope that the cracks will not show. This too should get a titter, since the idea of 'repair' implies return to functionality, but since the only function of the statue is ornament, there is an obvious contradiction here:

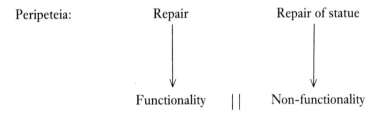

Peripeteia: Repair Repair of statue

Functionality || Non-functionality

The repair is therefore implausible, but the implausibility is not in fact very strong, since people do in fact live with battered ornaments. The plausibility derives from the commonplace short-sightedness associated with the clowns of the silent screen.

This gag is weak. But it is only the introduction to a beautifully articulated pair of gags. Ollie puts the feet and legs of the statue back in place and goes to lift up the trunk. As he does so he realises that his right hand is firmly planted on the statue's buttocks. A look of shocked modesty passes over his face, and he takes off his jacket to veil these outrageous organs. This is silly, since modesty refers primarily to animate objects, and a thoroughly respectable nude is scarcely appropriate for such a principled reaction. On the other hand, sexual taboos are sufficiently strong for Ollie's transference to make sense.

108

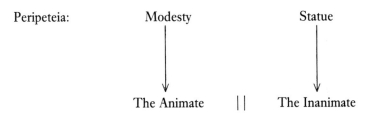

Peripeteia: Modesty   Statue

The Animate || The Inanimate

Syllogism I: It is difficult to confuse the animate and inanimate and the distance is sufficiently great to make transference unlikely.

Syllogism II: Sexual taboos are so strong that anything even remotely sexual comes under their ban, and therefore Ollie's reaction is plausible.

As Ollie lifts the decently swathed torso, there is a cut-away shot to Stan nodding satisfied approval, which probably gets a titter since it shows he is victim to the same illusions as Ollie. Back to Ollie, who has re-assembled the three components and is delicately removing the jacket. As he steps back, the statue is revealed: the buttocks point in the same direction as the knees and the face.

This is worth a solid belly laugh. It is to be decoded through a series of peripeteias, and a particularly strongly articulated pair of syllogisms.

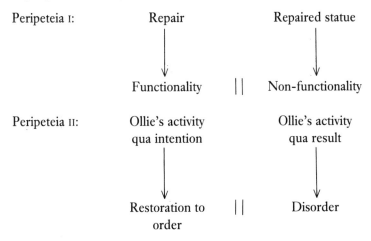

Peripeteia I: Repair   Repaired statue

Functionality || Non-functionality

Peripeteia II: Ollie's activity   Ollie's activity
qua intention   qua result

Restoration to || Disorder
order

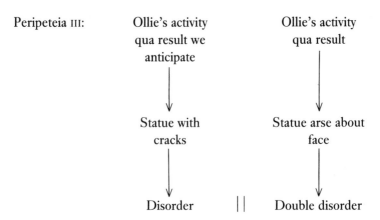

Peripeteia III:

Ollie's activity qua result we anticipate → Statue with cracks → Disorder

|| Ollie's activity qua result → Statue arse about face → Double disorder

Finally, we expect the three parts of the statue to connect up with each other, in the purely formal geometric sense: the function of the middle section is to link the two outside sections. But in the event, because of the dysfunctionality of the repair, the 'link' becomes a form of disconnection, or dislocation. The contradiction of anticipated symmetry is a further peripeteia:

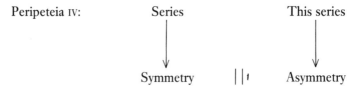

Peripeteia IV:

Series → Symmetry

|| ⫽ This series → Asymmetry

The multiple peripeteia derive from the process of decoding. When the spectator decodes a gag (a syntagm), he does so by seeking a paradigm, or paradigms, that 'make sense' of the syntagm. The richer the syntagm, the more paradigms there are to be found as referents. Thus the dislocated statue can be 'read' in various different ways. From the point of view of aesthetic and hedonistic judgment, the number of paradigms which are evoked in the reading is probably a measure of how good a gag is.

The other measure is the rigorousness of the articulation of the two syllogisms. Here the implausibility is effectively monstrous: it would be very difficult to make Ollie's mistake. But on the other hand, since he was so embarrassed, and wrapped his coat around the torso, it is also plausible.

This is a perfect example of rigorous internal articulation: the plausibility of Ollie's final blunder depends entirely on the plausibility of the previous stage of the gag: we accept his modesty and find his solution to shock a natural one. We follow his reasoning, thus as usual emphasising the plausibility syllogism; this emphasis carries us forward into his final blunder and helps us to emphasise this plausibility syllogism in its turn.

At this point we are in a position to return to the question – raised earlier – of the relationship of comic character to gag. As we saw, traditional accounts of the major comedians of the silent era have tended, with noteworthy exceptions, to focus on their screen personae, whereas the account given here insists that it is the gag that is the central feature of this comedy, and therefore that comic character is to be understood on this basis. Our example is Laurel and Hardy, whose screen personae are very well-known, even though no brief description will ever correspond entirely to anyone's experience of them: Hardy's pomposity, his aggressive insistence on his right to run their joint affairs, his incapacity to do so, his conviction that he is a real lady-killer; Laurel's child-like qualities – bursting into tears, tantrums, incapacity to avoid being side-tracked by the smallest distraction in the immediate environment – and his genius for making the most elementary blunders, his equally developed genius for really inspired solutions and his feyness. How are these characters built up?

In *The Finishing Touch* Stan and Ollie are assaulted by Nurse Dorothy Coburn, who is so incensed by the noise they are making that she punches them both in the stomach, hard. Manners being what they are – or were – they are unable to retaliate in kind, though Ollie has to re-strain Stan from doing so; Dorothy sees a hammer lying on the floor and bends down to pick it up, clearly with offensive intent; as she bends over Stanley tears a piece of sandpaper in half and Dorothy assumes her skirt has split down the rear; Ollie indicates that the split is indeed of huge and embarrassing proportions and she retires in confusion.

At the beginning of this sequence Dorothy demands to know who is in charge. Ollie takes off his hat with his most unctuous, lip-pursing, piggy-faced smile, clearly convinced that he can easily handle the situation, whereupon Dorothy belts him in the guts and Stanley laughs. Dorothy crosses to Stan and gives him one too, making his hat fly in the air. He retrieves it, and puts it on again with a mildly aggrieved air; suddenly his face puckers, he bursts into tears and he says (clearly!) 'I'll tell my mummy of you!'; then he switches to anger and has to be prevented from attacking Dorothy. Stanley's reactions here are perfect examples of his childishness, and it is in the development of the gag, in the way in which the basic gag situation of a woman punching two men is milked, that his character is revealed. Similarly with his inspired solutions to awkward situations (perhaps the most famous is the combustible thumb in *Way Out West*): the sandpaper that routs Dorothy is typical of his improvisational genius and it is given to us in the development – specifically, the topping – of the same gag.

Ollie's lady-killing pomposity too is given to us in the process of gag creation. Dorothy enters, asking who is in charge, and Ollie's unctuous response is an indication of his character; of course there is nothing funny about Dorothy's entrance, though an audience of connoisseurs may anticipate what is about to happen, but Ollie's response is already caricaturally exaggerated. No doubt to a modern audience, this is not especially funny: these forms of exaggeration have become part of the clichés of the past. In any event, amusing or not, this caricatural behaviour is clearly part of the process of the gag, for it is his sense of dignity which is so directly controverted by Dorothy's punch in the guts. This too, of course, is only the opening stage of a well-milked gag, as we have seen.

What these comments on Laurel and Hardy indicate is that comic character is produced in the process of gag creation. Now this should not be taken to imply that all comic character creation is reducible to the process of the gag in this manner. Laurel and Hardy are among the most plausible examples it is possible to find, and it would not be difficult to allege instances from Chaplin, Keaton or Harold Lloyd films where character creation is apparently pursued by non-comic means. Now it is true that this argument could be counteracted by reference to Mack Sennett's comments on growing audience sophistication. Many of what might be considered non-comic aspects of the performance of these clowns – Chaplin's walk, Keaton's mask-like face and impassive glance – on the grounds that they no longer make us laugh, may well have seemed hilarious at the time (James Agee implies this throughout 'Comedy's Greatest Era'), for they are all abnormal or exaggerated behaviour traits, comparable to, if more subtle than, something like Fatty Arbuckle's grotesque parodies of young love – compare Arbuckle and Keaton playing together in an Arbuckle vehicle called *The Hayseed* (1919), for example. If contemporary audience reaction was what we have guessed, then the reduction of character to gag would be more plausible. However, we shall see in subsequent chapters that there is no shortage of comic characters who are also developed in a non-comic manner as well, by conventional realist narrative. To anticipate later discussion, the range of comic forms, from the broadest farce to the subtlest 'social-realist' or 'romantic' comedy, includes both comic characters who are no more than a series of gags attached to the same face and make-up, and also characters who are given much more psychological depth. Indeed, this is probably the main element distinguishing different sub-types of comedy in the way just indicated.

Notes

1. Quoted in J-P Coursodon, *Keaton et Cie*, Paris, Seghers, pp. 15–16. I have been unable to find the original and have retranslated from the French.
2. See F. Mars, *Le Gag*, Paris, Editions du Cerf, 1964, p.38.

6

Comic Articulation

Fawlty Towers

━━━

This chapter is devoted to an extended example of comic articulation, taken from what is by common consent one of the best British television farce series, *Fawlty Towers*. Indeed, the point will be made that it is *because* it is so well articulated that it has been so successful.

As is commonly the case with sitcoms, each episode of *Fawlty Towers* uses the same characters, in the same relationship to each other, in situations which have recognisable similarities. At the centre of each episode is the character of Basil Fawlty, played by one of the co-authors of the series, John Cleese. We have already seen, *à propos* Laurel and Hardy, how it is possible for comic character to be built up out of gags and gag sequences, and we will see something essentially similar about the character of Basil in the following chapter, which is devoted to comic narrative and the place of character within it. In the meantime, it is important to stress one theoretical point about the relationship between the logic of the absurd and comic character, and to introduce our main topic: the articulation of gags into sequences.

In an early episode of *Fawlty Towers*, Basil is the victim of a conman who finds it remarkably easy to play on his snobbery by pretending to be a peer of the realm. When his naivety is finally beyond doubt Basil loses control, knocking the man down and kicking him repeatedly, yelling 'Bastard! Bastard!'. No doubt anyone who has been the victim of a con feels like doing this, but Basil's lack of inhibition is hilariously implausible, especially since his capacity for boot-licking self-delusion about the man was equally implausible. Such a swing from one extreme to the other is a great exaggeration of what we would expect from any normally constituted human being (it is important to remember that the concept of plausibility is as much a normative concept as a stochastic one – things seem implausible because they *ought not* to happen as much as because we think they are *unlikely* to happen). Now this action must also be plausible – if it was not it would be nonsensical – and the question therefore arises: what is the source of its plausibility? One potential answer is clearly that it is plausible because Basil Fawlty is likely to behave in such a fashion, and we could frame a general notion of plausibility in which character would be responsible for actions – as Hugo von Hofmannsthal said, 'Character is destiny' – and therefore the source of plausibility.

However, we must reject this answer, on several grounds: firstly, because it is not in fact the individual character which figures in our reasoning here – our reasoning is based upon what that sort of character is likely to do, not what that individual is likely to do. Secondly, because if individual character actually was the basis of plausibility then any action that was in conformity with the norms of that character would be totally plausible; and yet we know that Basil's action is relatively implausible – that is why it is so surprising. Thirdly, because if we were to accept this reasoning we would have difficulty in distinguishing between a comic action and a tragic one. Consider Othello's murder of Desdemona: it is monstrously implausible on both normative and stochastic grounds, and yet comprehensible (that is, plausible) by referring to his obsessive jealousy. Now while it is of course true that in Othello's case as in any other we make judgments about what this sort of person is likely to do, judgments about what jealousy is likely to do to people, nonetheless the narrative form of tragedy (or indeed, the realist novel or film narrative) leads us to look for chains of motivation that are internal to the character in question, and to this extent it is the plausibility of such behaviour that is stressed rather than its implausibility. We shall return to the question of the narrative organisation of comedy in the next chapter.[1]

What these considerations establish is what we already know: that both the implausibility and plausibility of actions and events stem from the discourses of the social formation, not from individual character – though it is certainly true that *generalisations* about character are part of these discourses. We are now in a position to consider the way in which gag sequences are built up in *Fawlty Towers*; three examples will be used to demonstrate how they work, in different degrees of detail, and for convenience's sake all three are taken from the same programme – the moose's head/fire drill/German tourist episode.

Here Basil's wife Sybil, who usually rescues their hotel from Basil's attempts at efficiency, is in hospital having an ingrowing toenail removed, and Basil is made responsible for the safe conduct of the three events referred to above: mounting a moose's head in the lobby, conducting a fire drill and dealing with a group of German tourists. At the beginning Basil visits Sybil in hospital and has a brief confrontation with Sister, who walks in and peremptorily orders him out of the room. Basil's response is heavy irony: 'Are you talking to me? I'm sorry, I thought there was a dog in here' (looking under the bed); as a concession to Basil's desire to be treated as more than a minor adjunct to Sybil's toenail, and to have an explanation for being ordered out, Sister says 'Doctor's coming', which attracts the withering sarcasm 'My God! Not a doctor! Here? In the hospital?'. Basil then expresses a desire, rhetorical no doubt, to say goodbye to his wife as she is 'under the knife in the morning', which Sister ridicules: 'It's only an ingrowing toenail'; Basil: 'Oh, you know, do you? That'll be a help'; and when finally forced out his parting shot is: 'Ingrowing toenail, right foot. You'll find it on the end of the leg'.

The structure of all these gags is the same. Sister's peremptoriness initiates a sequence in which feigned, sarcastic misunderstanding is to be considered sympathetically, and it is tempting to see our sympathy for Basil as part of the process of the absurd, part of the process of reasoning that enables us to see these insults as humour. In general, we might say, it is plausible that someone might behave this way given this degree of provocation. This is true, of course, and it is one reason why we often find Basil sympathetic as well as finding him appalling and/or ridiculous. But we must be careful to distinguish between humorous aggression and aggression in general: what Sister's peremptoriness makes plausible here is not a humorous response but an aggressive one, which here happens to take the form of humour. We are back with the problem that we had with Freud (see Chapter 1), where the pleasure of humour allows the lowering of inhibitory barriers against aggression, but where the nature of humour is not specified semiotically; cracks such as Basil's are not funny because they are aggressive: they are a permitted form of aggression because they are funny. But it is also true that the general tenor of the fiction in which we find them ensures that we will find them funny rather than embarrassing, and this is the point at which we may reconsider the question of comic cues that was mentioned in Chapter 1. There the argument that comedy was a question of context was rejected on the grounds that it involved an infinite regression with no possibility of grounding the experience of the comic, and that argument is logically true. However, once it is established that a given text is in fact comic – by making us laugh – then it is possible to turn things into humour that it might not be possible to without that context being already secured.

A certain section of the British public found Basil Fawlty embarrassing rather than funny (we shall return to this question later), and we may intuitively guess that this was because much of the humour was 'a bit close to the bone'; starting an episode with relatively gentle humour, then building to the more problematic forms, is a way of trying to avoid this, and it is possible to use this tactic precisely because of the way in which comic context works: finding a given sequence of events funny predisposes us to seek similar chains of meaning in subsequent events. But the essential grounding experience is still the logic of the absurd: there must be something external to us in which humour is immanent and which has the impact upon us of producing a humorous frame of mind.

Each of Basil's sarcastic remarks forms a peripeteia in the same way. In each case the information contained in the line is incomprehensible if taken at face value: to believe in the presence of a dog, in the unlikeliness of a doctor's visit, in the necessity of pointing out the location of the foot, all these statements common sense tells us are excessively naive; to use linguistic terminology, each of these sallies of Basil's is pragmatically marked as ironic, a form of marking which is inseparable from ideological competence. Since not even the most grotesque simpleton could actually be surprised that a doctor was coming to a hospital room, etc., it is clear that the naivety is false: there is a clear predicative incompatibility between the statement and the context in which it is made. This predicative incompatibility interrupts the flow of the discourse in the same way as predicative incompatibility sets up the tension internal to the metaphor or a one-liner joke where there is no context. In each case the flow of the discourse is restored, in an alternative circuit, by another reading of the syntagm: Sister is indeed treating Basil like a dog; she has used the doctor's visit as an excuse for doing so, which implies it is an event of some importance, and thus in some sense of some scarcity value; and feet are indeed to be found on the end of legs so Basil's parting shot is, literally, true. But the interruption of the flow of the discourse by predicative incompatibility is in each case far stronger than its restoration, and therefore in each case we judge that the syntagm is more implausible than plausible, thus distinguishing comic irony such as this from non-comic irony such as Mark Antony's 'Friends, Romans, countrymen' speech.

Basil uses this humour for aggressive purposes: his reference to the dog implies that Sister's manners are defective, his reference to the doctor implies that both her reasoning and her manners are defective, and his parting shot implies that her medical competence is unspeakable. Although these acts of sarcasm certainly require the overcoming of certain social inhibitions, they probably require less than the direct insults they replace, and this would indicate that Freud's conception of humour is right. Additionally, cracks like this are a much more satisfactory expression of aggression than mere insults because they are unanswerable; we shall return to this property of humour in a subsequent chapter. It is also significant that these three lines are organised in a sequence. Although there is no tight logical connection between them, in the way that there was in the Hardy gag of the nude statue, for instance, nonetheless it is clear that the final line gains much of its impact from the fact that it is at the end of this sequence, built up to therefore by the rest of the sequence. What is the nature of this build-up?

An approximate way of describing it would be to say that the level of sarcasm increases as the sequence develops: Basil's first sarcasm ('dog in here') is less so than the direct insult of 'You'll find it on the end of the leg'. But the essential question, from our point of view, is to find a way of rephrasing this observation in terms of the semiotic model of the absurd. This is to be done in two ways. In the first place, the increasing level of rudeness means that the peripeteia quantitively increase: the peripeteia of 'end of leg' is bigger than the peripeteia of 'dog in here'. In the second place, because the peripeteia is bigger, the implausibility is greater, and therefore the plausibility has to be increased as well. The plausibility of 'dog in here' is relatively weak, but the plausibility of 'end of leg' is enormously strong because it is, literally, a true statement. However, this still does not fully explain the development of this sequence of gags, for development must consist of some relationship between the various stages of what is developing, a relationship of articulation rather than a relationship of mere contrast. The articulation takes this form: Basil's response to Sister's peremptoriness creates a situation of conflict; with each stage, represented not only by the two later gags, but also by the aggressive but non-comic lines in between, the conflict intensifies, and the intensity of the conflict serves to reinforce the plausibility of Basil's sarcasm. This is to say, in each case the internal nature of Basil's statements has its own plausibility – Sister treats him like a dog, she uses doctor's visit as an excuse, his medical advice is true – but this plausibility does not explain why Basil says it, it only explains why, once said, it is in fact plausible; but the new plausibility given by intensifying conflict also explains why it is said.

These two forms of plausibility are equally significant: the internal plausibility of each statement makes each funny in itself, and the external plausibility of intensifying conflict articulates them together so as to provide for an increase in comic effect over and above the comic impact of each individual line. Moreover, the existence of the second, external form of plausibility provides a further clear link between gag and character. If a single gag already indicates Basil's character as being the kind of person who responds to the situation in such-and-such a way, the sequence of gags does so with increased clarity. Basil's aggressiveness is such that he continues to respond in this way, and even intensifies conflict rather than seeking a compromise. That is to say, the gags are comprehensible in terms of how people may respond to such situations; the fact that Basil does so leads us to judge that he is of an aggressive nature.

The second sequence to consider is the fire drill and the fire that is its sequel. Basil has agreed with the fire brigade that the annual fire drill will take place at midday. Just before he is due to start it, Sybil rings from hospital to check he has remembered and that he knows where the key to the fire alarm is; he doesn't, and it's in the safe; when he opens the safe, the burglar alarm rings because he had forgotten to switch it off beforehand, and the guests assume it is the fire bell. Basil insists that it isn't, and that they must wait for the right bell. With various interruptions, the drill takes place, but one of the interruptions is Manuel the Spanish waiter, whose English is apparently inadequate for the task of differentiating between a fire and a fire drill. Basil testily solves the problem by telling him to start cooking the chips for lunch, and Manuel promptly starts a real fire. Such a coincidence, a basic element of farce organisation, is clearly comprehensible in terms of the logic of the absurd: it is a remarkable coincidence that Basil's actions should result in a fire starting at exactly the time that a fire drill has just finished, and that coincidence (reinforced by a series of other features of this plot that we will come to shortly) is highly implausible. On the other hand, Murphy's law – as Terry Lovell pointed out – makes it plausible, for Murphy's law states that 'if it can go wrong, it will'.[2] Such coincidences are a commonplace in farce: for example, in the traditional version associated with Feydeau, if a man arranges to meet his mistress in a certain hotel, it is almost certain that his wife will arrange to meet her lover in the same hotel at the same time, and that the management will have confused the names in the room booking. Thus the basic organisation of this sequence is clearly rooted in the logic of the absurd: Basil's actions when confronted with a real fire are comprehensible, as we shall see, because it is so implausible that there should be a real fire at exactly this moment. The syllogism of one gag sequence is used to launch the syllogisms of the following sequence.

   The opening part of this long gag sequence introduces one of its key elements: Basil's obsessiveness. Confronted with the wrong bell ringing, and the guests' natural mistake, any sane man would conduct the fire drill as if all was normal; but Basil decides to be correct, and from this basic premiss all the subsequent confusion stems. That is to say, his decision is in itself perfectly comprehensible, not even really implausible – if there is implausibility, it is that the wrong bell should ring (Murphy's law again) at just this moment – but the results it produces are highly implausible if only because they are so exaggerated and devastating. On the other hand, they are plausible because the chain of coincidences actually does happen, right before our eyes. The guests assume that the bell is the fire drill bell and start leaving the hotel; Basil informs them, with acid, self-righteous politeness, that it isn't and that anyway it isn't twelve o'clock, the scheduled time. The guests argue back by pointing out that it's nearly twelve, the major says he can't hear a drill, and anyway how were they to know the difference between two bells. As they come in one by one, advancing different arguments, misunderstanding the situation, Basil becomes more and more irritated by having to explain to each one in sequence what has happened, including Manuel whose English does not allow him to grasp the fine distinction between the two bells. This sequence is funny in its own right, but serves also to prepare the climax: as one of the guests points out, 'It *is* twelve o'clock'; pause, while Basil looks at his watch, then, almost hysterically 'Well, it is *now*, but that's because we've been standing here arguing about it!'

This superb moment depends upon the preparation stages that lead up to it, and the skill of the writing of *Fawlty Towers*, as against run-of-the-mill sitcom, is that the preparation stage is itself hilarious. The implausibility of the situation derives from two sources: firstly, the emotional frustration of an obsessive confronted with such a situation; secondly, the perverted logic of the situation itself – and certainly the two are connected. This perverted logic is essentially the fact that all Basil's arguments were designed to justify not conflating the two bells, but they have resulted in destroying one of the main reasons for this refusal; it is indeed monstrously implausible that such correct arguments should self-destruct in such an incontrovertible way. The emotional frustration derives from the structure of self-righteousness: we can guess what it is like to be proved wrong under these circumstances, and it is monstrously implausible (in the normative sense more than the stochastic one here) that it should occur. On the other hand, it does, visibly. Basil could afford this little ego satisfaction because he was technically correct: suddenly he no longer is, and thus the logical trap is also an emotional one by the same token, for his self-righteousness was premissed upon the correctness of his arguments.

Situations of this nature are relatively frequent in *Fawlty Towers*: in fact it is probably one of the series' hallmarks that so much of the humour should derive from frustrated, positively squashed self-righteousness. In each case the structure is basically the same: Basil's obsessiveness puts him in a situation where it is inevitable (given the circumstances) that he will suffer, and this situation contains elements which are very easily convertible into the logic of the absurd. It is implausible that someone should always be put in a situation where exactly the thing that he needs like a hole in the head should occur with a regularity that would be monotonous if it was not hilarious; and yet on each occasion the concatenation of circumstances is such that the course of events is also plausible.

The sequence continues with Basil's demonstration of the second reason for his insistence that the fire drill could not be started by the alarm bell – the two bells are totally different, for the fire bell is a 'semitone higher, at least'. With some asperity he rings both, and the guests now assume that this really is the fire drill and start to leave the hotel. But for Basil this was only a demonstration, not the real drill, and he is sufficiently incensed to insult them and make them come back in. During all this time the fire bell has been ringing, and Basil switches it off: blessed silence; but within two seconds the telephone rings. Basil grabs it, jumps in the air in a paroxysm of rage, bellows something incomprehensible down it and slams the receiver back on to the base as hard as he can. This is a superb moment, and one which demands detailed consideration. At the simplest level, it is a coincidence that the telephone bell should follow the fire bell at such a precise interval, and coincidence – as we have already seen – is one of the basic laws of farce precisely because it inherently involves implausibility; here then is one element in the construction of this gag. But beyond this is a logic which refers to Basil's obsessiveness: the audience is intuitively certain – on the grounds of previous evidence – that this is Sybil phoning to make sure the fire drill is all right, and the coincidence that she should phone at just the moment that it is going wrong is yet another input into this event that Basil will find excruciatingly difficult to cope with, especially after all the other ego blows he has just received. To this we should add two elements of comic performance: firstly, the timing of the bell; secondly, Cleese's acting.

Timing, any comedian will insist, is essential to successful comedy, in the sense that the worst joke can be made to succeed if timed right, and the best can be ruined by bad timing. In this context, timing probably has two meanings: in the first place, it refers to placing the joke in the right context. At an earlier stage in this episode of *Fawlty Towers* there is an atrocious pun: when Basil insists on the difference between the alarm bell and the fire drill the major says 'Drill? I can't hear any drill!' In any other context this would probably be awful, but here it works because it is motivated by the major's well-established stupidity (this is not its plausibility which derives, as always in puns, from double meanings) and, centrally, because it is another element in Basil's calvary of frustration. This is intended as a single example of a widely used principle. In the second place, timing refers to details of delivery. Here, it is important that exactly the right interval should elapse between the end of the fire bell and the telephone ringing: it must be long enough for the audience to appreciate the blessed silence, but short enough for the contrast/connection between the two bells to be obvious. If the interval is miscalculated, the telephone bell ceases to be felt as implausible, for it loses its emotional force, and the bell's implausibility is not primarily a matter of reason but of our sense that nobody on screen (and ourselves) wants a bell to ring at this moment, and especially not Basil. Its implausibility, in other words, is the same as that of all the elements in Basil's misfortunes: he needs it like a hole in the head.

Secondly, the question of John Cleese's acting. Much of the impact of this moment derives from Cleese's exaggerated behaviour: jumping in the air, bellowing, etc. – in general giving a convincing portrait of somebody on the edge in comic circumstances, and it is this reaction to the bell that indicates to us just how implausible it is, in the way indicated above. In other words, what we are responding to here is the combination of the bell and Basil's reaction to it, and it is clear therefore that the performance skills involved in an incident like this are directly related to the logic of the absurd: they directly incarnate one of its central elements. The exaggerated movements of the traditional clown, as described by James Agee, for example, are no different in this respect.

It is at this point that Manuel starts the real fire, and Basil refuses to believe him – despite smudges all over his white waiter's jacket – and locks him in the kitchen, Manuel bouncing up and down in an agony of failed communication at the same time. This is milking the gag very thoroughly. The coincidence of Manuel starting a fire at exactly this moment is considerable and constitutes a peripeteia in itself, but the key moment is Basil's refusal to admit that Manuel may be right: this is a peripeteia because Basil is denying what looks to us like clear evidence, and is therefore implausible; but it is plausible in so far as Manuel has already failed to understand the situation before, thus angering Basil. This new development is itself milked by Manuel's anguished bouncing up and down and Basil's forcible imprisonment of him: exaggerated movements are always potentially humorous, as the tradition of clowning shows, because they are both surprising and implausible. Here they are plausible because of the impossible situation Manuel is in and his need to emphasise his point.

Having locked Manuel in the kitchen, Basil goes outside and tells the guests they can return. Manuel is shouting and hammering on the inside of the kitchen door, which leads the guests to complain of the noise. Basil agrees to open it, with characteristic sourness, and is confronted with billowing smoke and Manuel collapsing at his feet, pan still in hand, gasping 'You saved my life, Mr Fawlty!' This is funny in itself, but it is Basil's reaction to the discovery of a real fire that constitutes the next section of this gag sequence. He stares, unbelieving, into the smoke then closes the kitchen door, firmly muzzles the collapsed Manuel with one hand, clears his throat nervously and begins: 'May I have your attention, please, ladies and gentlemen . . . I don't know quite how to say this but . . . shall I put it this way . . .er' and in a very thin, high-pitched voice 'fire', and then he starts bellowing 'FIRE! FIRE!', leaning over the uncomprehending guests and shouting in their faces.

A hilarious reaction: his disbelief is surprising and implausible because of the weight of the evidence, plausible because of the coincidence and the fact that Manuel, of all people, was right, especially given that Basil had locked him in the fire which was enough to arouse anyone's disbelief. His subsequent attempt to preserve his calm and to maintain an appearance of polite normality is surprising and implausible because inappropriate to the urgency of the situation, but plausible as an attempt to stem the tide of panic. Which in fact soon takes over: he dashes around trying to find the fire alarm key, which he has misplaced during the drill, yelling his ever-increasing disbelief, which culminates in 'Thank you, God, thank you so bloody much!' and shaking his fist at the heavens. His panic is surprising and implausible because of its exaggeration and its contrast with the previous calm, plausible because of the difficulty of the situation. The main function, however, is to prepare for his imprecation against fate: at this point, the sequences of coincidences, the panic they have provoked, the mauling that such events inflict on the ego, all are synthesised into a plausible vision of malignant supernatural intervention, rendered in sarcasm. Basil's curse is also surprising and implausible because the sequence of events is perfectly comprehensible without recourse to the notion of divine interference. It is all the funnier because sarcastic, for the form of sarcasm and irony is itself always potentially absurd, as we have seen.

This gag is articulated on to the previous one, in a manner deliberately designed to increase its impact. The fact that the real fire occurs at exactly the moment that a fire drill – a mismanaged one, at that – is taking place is an implausible coincidence (the logic of the aleatory) but it is made plausible by Basil's partial responsibility: it is he who orders the incompetent Manuel to start cooking the chips, which causes the fire. Secondly, it is the havoc of the misunderstandings about the two bells which leads Basil to mislay the fire alarm key, thus giving plausibility to his paranoid sense of divine persecution.

Deprived of the key, Basil decides to break the glass of the fire alarm. He punches it, only succeeding in hurting his fist; casting around for something harder, he lights on the typewriter, which he throws at it, but misses; at that precise moment the phone rings, Basil grabs the receiver, yells 'hello', smashes the fire alarm glass with the ear piece, shouts 'thank you' down the phone and throws it on the floor.

This little sequence of gags is articulated on to his panic, then internally articulated. To try to break a piece of glass by punching it is surprising and implausible, but made a little plausible by panic; it is also a peripeteia because of the indignity of pain and failure. The choice of the typewriter is surprising and implausible because of its unsuitability, plausible because it is after all harder than flesh and bone. The coincidence of the phone ringing again at an inappropriate moment is a peripeteia and absurd, but even more absurd is the way Basil turns it into something appropriate. This novel use of the phone, especially in combination with its normal use, is surprising and implausible, plausible both because it is after all more suitable than hands or typewriters, and because it offers an opportunity for revenge on an instrument that has been the chosen vehicle for Sybil's persecutions.

Having started the fire alarm, Basil turns his attention to the fire. Still panicky, he gets the fire-extinguisher, gets Polly to open the kitchen door, gets Manuel to pull the safety tube off the extinguisher, starts it and gets the full squirt in his face. He doubles up in anguish with Manuel hovering solicitously over him and when he straightens up bangs his head hard on the frying pan Manuel is still carrying. He then tries to punch Manuel in the face, but just as he does so he loses consciousness and collapses backwards in a magnificent pratfall.

The fire extinguisher in the face is surprising and implausible because it is obvious how fire extinguishers are meant to be used; it is plausible because people make mistakes with machinery all the time, and especially when in a state of panic. It is also an infliction of indignity, which constitutes a second peripeteia. The crack over the head with the frying pan is an indignity too, but also a coincidence, since the position in which Manuel is holding it is randomly chosen. For both these reasons it is implausible, but is plausible because Basil is doubled up with his hands over his face and can't see where the pan is; and since the position of the pan is random, there is no reason why it shouldn't be in the way of his head; moreover, Manuel's solicitude motivates its proximity. Thus these two stages of this gag sequence are well articulated together. In the final stage, Basil's attempted assault on Manuel is surprising and implausible because unjustified, plausible because anyone might feel it justified in the heat of the moment. His collapse is surprising and implausible because of the exaggeration of the movement and the coincidence of its timing; it is plausible because of the short time lapse after the crack on the head.

Throughout the analysis of the fire drill sequence two features have received special attention: one is the role of coincidence, the other is the role of Basil's obsessiveness. The reason for this stress is that they play a key role in the articulation of this sequence: for the central point of this analysis is to show how the gags that constitute it are organised into a sequence and do not merely follow each other in passive contiguity.

The organising principle of the sequence is that a series of coincidences creates a set of circumstances that someone as obsessively correct and self-righteous as Basil cannot possibly cope with. Each of these coincidences constitutes a gag in its own right, and each one at the same time prepares the next one. Thus, Basil's explanations of why the fire drill cannot be started by the burglar alarm at two minutes before the scheduled time lead ineluctably to the situation where the two minute gap has disappeared: it is because of this sequence of events that the new situation is both plausible and implausible. At the same time, the loss of one element of his justification is what leads Basil to demonstrate the difference between the two bells, which leads into the next gag, and it is the frustration he experiences which leads him to tell Manuel to start cooking the chips – this, incidentally, is one of the few key moments in a gag sequence in *Fawlty Towers* which is not in itself funny. The principle which underlies the whole sequence is no doubt clear enough without further examples. At the same time as the sequence of events consists basically of a series of coincidences, Basil's reaction to each of them helps to constitute their implausibility, and – especially – to make this implausibility something with emotional power. Thus, in tandem with the series of coincidences is the recurrent fact of Basil's inability to cope with what he is confronted with, which also operates, on each occasion, to tie the event into the logic of the absurd. Although in general his incapacity and obsessiveness do not cause the sequence of events (they only do so on occasions), nonetheless they are one of the two principles that underlie the structure of the whole sequence. Most importantly, it is this incapacity that accounts for the mounting hysteria of his behaviour, which is in its turn an integral part of the comic crescendo that gives the episode its impact.

In short, it is because the episode is so tightly articulated that it has the impact that it has, and we should not underestimate the importance of this point, both in terms of being able to account for the difference between good comedy and average or poor comedy, and – more fundamentally, perhaps – in terms of its implication for aesthetic theory. It has always been basic to the aesthetic theory of the post-Romantic period that the truth of artistic vision is an integral part of the difference between great art and the rest. But here we have clearly seen that what distinguishes *Fawlty Towers* is not at all the truth of what is portrayed – Basil is a grotesque caricature, from this point of view – but on the contrary the purely aesthetic dimension of the text: its fictional organisation, and specifically the tightness which links every element so closely to the basic enunciative mechanism which is responsible for the type of pleasure that this category of text sets out to offer its audience. A genre, says Aristotle, 'does not produce any chance pleasure, but the pleasure which is proper to it' (*Poetics,* Chapter 14).

The final section of this episode finds Basil, concussed from the blow on the head from Manuel's frying pan, trying to cope with an influx of German tourists. Just as the previous gag sequence was based, in part, on one of Basil's obsessions (being in the right) leading him into situations where the outcome was inevitably the opposite, so here another of his obsessions will provide the thread that links together the entire sequence.

The first set of gags with the Germans involve Basil's limited command both of German and of the niceties of manners towards those who don't speak English. There is no articulation internal to the sequence, but in it is laid the foundation of the following sequence: in an aside to Polly Basil says 'Whatever you do, don't mention the war', and from this point on the war will constantly obtrude itself into virtually the entirety of his conversation, quite without his wanting it to. It is this piece of pathology which serves as the foundation of the internal articulation of the sequence.

That it is quite literally a piece of pathology is made clear in Basil's speech of welcome to his guests, some of whom turn out to speak English: 'Please let me introduce myself, I am the proprietor of Fawlty Towers and I should like to welcome your war . . . your wall . . . you all'. This piece of linguistic deformation deserves a place in clinical literature as a classic instance of a Freudian slip in the most literal sense. Basil's subconscious has taken over at the most crucial moment and left its typically indelible mark upon the flow of his speech, and once this stain is there we understand the accumulation of such references as his speech continues: ' . . . sorry! Would you like a drink before the war? Sorry! Before your meal? That is, trespassers will be . . . tied up with piano wire . . . sorry! . . . a bit of pain in the old leg . . . piece of shrapnel from the war . . . Korean! Korean war!'

What occurs here is that each of Basil's references to the war is highly implausible, since he is apparently trying hard to avoid embarrassing his guests by talking about the war but nonetheless is constantly doing so. For a psychoanalyst, no doubt, the process would be better described thus: Basil is trying hard to avoid talking about the war and *therefore* constantly does so; for a psychoanalyst, indeed, Basil's constant slips of the tongue are all too plausible, and perhaps would not be funny as a result. Each remark (for non-psychoanalysts) is thus highly implausible in its own right, both because it is rude, and because Basil is trying to avoid it. We feel that people ought to be able to avoid such catastrophic lapses, but it is plausible because we all know about such embarrassing slips of the tongue even if we don't think of them as pathological, and because Basil is after all suffering from concussion. The plausibility of Basil's behaviour is therefore rather high, and as the speech continues it becomes even higher, for these slips of the tongue are self-reinforcing. When Basil seeks an excuse for them he embroils himself still deeper by alleging pain caused by 'a piece of shrapnel from the war' and has to extricate himself by shouting 'Korean'. That is to say, the plausibility of each reference to the war is based on the previous one: this is clearest in the case of his anguished yell of 'Korean', for here it is implausible because it is obviously a lie and spoken in such a manner as to make this obvious; and yet it is plausible because there was such a war, and it is therefore a viable interpretation of his previous statement. As in his insult to Sister, the lines are strongly linked to each other.

The sequence continues with a series of minor punning lapses on Basil's part that turns into a horrendous catalogue of references to the war. The logic of this sequence is not essentially different from that of his speech of welcome (a series of references that are mutually self-reinforcing) but it is a more complex set. One of the Germans orders a prawn cocktail and Basil, at his most genial, says 'Certainly, why not indeed, we're all friends now, all in the Market together, old differences forgotten and no need at all to mention the war. Sorry! [Pause] What was it you ordered?' – 'A prawn cocktail' – 'Oh yes, that's it, when you said prawn I thought you said war.' His first mention of the war here is motivated in just the same way as his previous ones (obsession), except that the sheer fact of repetition adds to its plausibility: if it is always implausible for the same reasons – people ought to be able to avoid such embarrassing lapses – it is extra-plausible because his temporary pathology is now well-established. Secondly, Basil is here trying to establish just how well-disposed towards Germans he is now, and this involves – precisely – not mentioning the war: a well-known double-bind situation, how to stress that one is refraining from something – how can he point out that he is not mentioning the war? Thus the plausibility of this comment is high indeed, for it refers back to the structure of what he has been saying up till now.

Basil continues: ' . . . thought you said war. [Pause] Oh . . . the war . . . oh yes, completely slipped my mind . . . forgotten all about it. Himmler and that lot. Completely forgotten it. [Pause] What was it you ordered?' Monstrously implausible, because manifestly untrue as well as rude, plausible because he is still trying to demonstrate that he is not obsessed by the war, thus plausible because of continued internal reference to the flow of his speech. The guest replies: 'A prawn cocktail' – 'Oh yes', says Basil, 'Eva prawn . . . Goebbels too'. – 'And a pickled herring' – 'Yes', says Basil, 'A Hermann Goering, yes'. Again repetition increases plausibility, reinforced by the assonance of 'prawn – Braun', and once the list of Nazi personnel is initiated it makes sense to say 'Goebbels too': plausibility is again due to internal self-reference. Now that the list is well-established it is easy to turn 'a pickled herring' into 'Hermann Goering', and the internal articulation continues. The guest's order finishes with 'four cold meat salads', and Basil concludes 'Certainly; well I'll just get your orders . . . ORDERS . . . which must be obeyed at all times', which uses a pun to justify the continued series of references to the war.

At this point a brief conversation with Polly acts as a diversion, but then Basil returns to check he's got the orders right. 'Two egg mayonnaise, a prawn Goebbels, a Hermann Goering and four Colditz Salads. Sorry! I got a bit confused there . . . got a bit confused because everybody keeps mentioning the war.' The plausibility of this unpalatable menu is given by the earlier list of names, of course, thus developing the self-reference that is the basic organising principle of this sequence. Blaming it on somebody else is plausible not only to the extent that trying to shift the burden of guilt is understandable, but also because in a real sense it is someone else's voice that Basil keeps hearing mentioning the war: the voice of the awful other person in his subconscious who is now largely out of control. This too involves the system of self-reference.

At this point one of the German women bursts into tears and her husband shouts at Basil to stop talking about the war. 'Me?' says an indignant Basil. 'You started it' – 'We didn't!' – 'Yes, you did, you invaded Poland!' This monstrous perversion of his own and their meaning is plausible both because of the ambiguity of 'started it', and because of the series of constant references that make up the conversation thus far: the punning ambiguity is thus articulated on to the entirety of the conversation.

To cheer up the distraught guest Basil starts to tell a joke, unfortunately involving a bomber over Berlin, and then tries to do an impression of Hitler, interrupted by Polly, which he then combines with Cleese's 'silly walk' from the Monty Python 'Ministry of Silly Walks' sketch, which bears more than a passing resemblance to the goose step. The 'silly walk' is funny enough in itself – any actions involving a disproportionate effort for the results obtained is funny, as Freud points out (*Jokes*, pp.248ff) – but is all the funnier here because both its implausibility and plausibility are heightened by the resemblance to the goose step. The more deeply embroiled Basil becomes in the set of references to the war, the more difficult it is for him to break out of it and the more plausible his actions become; at the same time the embarrassment of watching someone increasingly out of control of his own obsessions increases too, thus making his actions increasingly implausible. Perhaps the inter-textual reference to Cleese's own earlier performance also increases the comedy: any inter-textual reference is implausible to the extent that texts are meant to be self-contained, plausible here because of Cleese's own presence.

This exhibition provokes the Germans into telling him just how rude he is being, and just how unfunny. Basil responds: 'You have absolutely no sense of humour, do you' and 'Who won the bloody war, anyway?' Immediately after this the doctor's arrival brings this segment to a close. Basil's responses are the final and most direct representation of his obsession: to accuse Germans of lacking a sense of humour is a well-established English theme, which makes Basil's accusation plausible, in conjunction with his interpretation of his efforts to cheer up his distraught guests: given this perspective – his understanding of the preceding minutes – it is reasonable to see their current reaction as proof of a well-known theory about Germans. Therefore the Germans are exactly what he always knew they were, and therefore his obsession is justified. In the same way this justifies his final assertion, whose implication is that since he was on the winning side, anything he has to say about Germans must be justified. To understand why he says something so apparently irrelevant, as well as signally rude, is to look back over the entire obsessive performance: he is obsessed by the war because in it is to be found the clearest proof of the intrinsic superiority of the English race, of whom Basil thinks himself an eminent member, and this is what justifies his reference to the outcome of the war.

This analysis of the final segment of the episode amply justifies the commonsense perception – if it needed justifying – of its impact. The German tourists produce genuine boffos, to use 1920s terminology. It also gives added strength to the semiotic model, for it shows this model is capable of producing a coherent analysis of another clearly important aspect of comedy: the crescendo effect sought by every comedian. The manner in which a gag serves as the basis of the plausibility of the next gag necessarily involves an increase in comic effect, it seems reasonable to assert: the comedy of moment A (the first gag) is maintained and subsumed into the comedy of moment B, and thus laughter feeds on itself, reduplicates itself.

These comments on *Fawlty Towers* have been based on the assumption that it is an unequivocal success, as indeed have all the comments on comedies so far, with the exception of a brief reference to unfavourable reactions to Laurel and Hardy. This is the point to consider the question of comic success and comic failure.

Criticisms of *Fawlty Towers* have commonly fallen into two categories. Firstly, it is excessively aggressive, and therefore ceases to be funny; Jack Waterman quotes another reviewer:

The trouble is that (Cleese) cannot see beyond himself. The only character who exists in his scenario is his alter ego, Fawlty. Until he can acquire a less egotistic view of the world and see some humanity in those people who at present he thinks are merely put on earth to drive him up the wall, Cleese will never make me laugh . . .

and Christopher Price MP commented that 'jokes about dagoes and wops horrified some Americans who were watching with me'.

Secondly, it is excessively close to the truth, so that while absurd it is nonetheless embarrassing. I have been told, verbally, of various people who found sections of the series embarrassing because 'too close to the bone', and hence difficult or impossible to watch.

Essentially, there is little difference between these criticisms and contemporary critics' to Laurel and Hardy's *Block-Heads*, who found their comedy too 'black'. Clearly, such critics are 'taking things too seriously': for some reason they are unable, or unwilling, to see that what they are watching is absurd, and can only perceive in it something to be taken 'at face value'. In other words – the words of the logic of the absurd – they are placing upon the plausibility syllogism a weight that it is not meant to bear: to find Basil's antics embarrassing is to see them as excessively plausible (excessively in relation to the process of the absurd), as something that is not sufficiently implausible to be absurd.

Indeed, it is easy to see how such a reaction is possible. Much of Basil's discomfiture derives from the illusion that he is super-competent at his chosen profession, whereas the reality is the opposite; to be revealed as incompetent is probably one of the more common and deep-seated fears to which we are prone, and Basil's antics are especially well-suited to evoke it for it is his capacity for obsessive attention to the wrong detail – an eminently rational process that has the misfortune to be based on an irrational foundation – that is often the basis for his downfall (witness his obsessive distinction between the alarm bell attached to the safe and the fire bell). Given the desire to distinguish them, what he does is eminently rational; it is the premiss that is stupid. Similarly with his obsessive reference to the war: this degree of loss of control over one's obsessions is potentially extremely worrying, perhaps especially when the obsession in question happens to be the Germans, to whom many English still have ambivalent attitudes, to say the least. It is not difficult to see how someone to whom this form of behaviour was worrying, either in him/herself or others, could place excessive stress on the plausibility of Basil's actions.

This is not to suggest that this is the only form of comic failure that is possible. No doubt the commonest form is to produce only boredom, but this by no means exhausts the repertoire of comic failure: comedy may be boring because it is predictable, or because it is silly; it may be offensive because it is a total abomination, or because it is embarrassingly close to the bone; it may appear to be no more than the literal portrayal of a possible, if not normal, situation; and it may be literally incomprehensible. No doubt these commonsense reactions to comedy are easily recognisable, cast in this form; the problem in the present context is to articulate them in the terms of the logic of the absurd. We shall see that doing so is the key to understanding not only comic failure, but comic success too.

It is clear from the presentation of the logic of the absurd that it can only come into play on the condition that there is in fact a peripeteia, that there is a surprise, a punch line; for it is the peripeteia that unleashes the two syllogisms of the absurd. If there is no peripeteia – or rather, if what was intended as the peripeteia fails to surprise a given audience – then the syllogisms will never come into play, and the joke will not seem absurd at all. There are two reasons why the peripeteia may fail: it may be excessive, or it may be inadequate. That is to say: just as a given event is only plausible or the opposite in terms dictated by given discourses, so a peripeteia is only surprising in such terms too. Nothing is *naturally* surprising, it is only surprising in relation to the norms and values of a given culture. And in relation to such norms a given attempted peripeteia may be either excessive or inadequate. If it is excessive, the would-be joke will be offensively unfunny: a blue joke at a church social, an anti-semitic joke in front of a Jewish audience. Under these circumstances the degree of shock involved will obliterate the potential balance between plausibility and implausibility, and the joke will not get as far as appearing absurd. The opposite possibility is that the shock will be inadequate, it will not in fact be shocking at all: the situation will merely appear normal. A cartoon in the *Guardian* (28 November 1983) showed a mother explaining to her indignant children why they had to put up with inviting children they did not like back to their house to play: she had no other way of repaying their parents for looking after her children. To me this situation was excessively plausible, a situation I could easily imagine happening absolutely literally in everyday life, and therefore it was totally unfunny. My expectations were not contradicted and there was no peripeteia.

Since peripeteia can be either inadequate or excessive, it is logically necessary that even when they are adequate they may be more or less surprising. This may be represented diagrammatically:

excessive	high peripeteia	low peripeteia	inadequate
shocking	very surprising	a little surprising	serious

limit
of joke

limit
of joke

That is to say, the shocks that unleash jokes constitute a continuum. Within the limits of the joke, surprise does occur, and therefore the syllogisms of plausibility and implausibility come into play: the logic of the absurd demands, indeed, that they should be combined, that any event – in order to be funny – should be simultaneously surprising, implausible and plausible. What possibilities of comic failure are built into the operations of the syllogisms? Clearly they would derive from the wrong balance between plausibility and implausibility: either the implausibility of the item would be excessive, and therefore the plausibility inadequate; or the opposite: excessive plausibility, inadequate implausibility. Schematically, one could say that excessive implausibility would tip comedy in the direction of nonsense, make it appear merely silly; and excessive plausibility would tip it in the direction of seriousness, make it appear mere literal truth. However, because peripeteia may be more or less surprising, it is necessary to combine the calculation of the balance of plausibility and its opposite with the degree of surprise evoked by the punch line, to give a matrix of possible forms of comic failure for what would nonetheless be recognised as a joke.

1) a high level of surprise and excess implausibility: at least one viewer of the *Fawlty Towers* fire drill has said to me that it is just silly: no rational person would allow the misunderstandings to develop to this extent. This is no doubt the reaction of someone with a very literal-minded view of the world.

2) a high level of surprise and excess plausibility: the TV comic series *The Young Ones* featured a hippy who was constantly victimised by all the other characters. My personal reaction was to feel that this was simultaneously surprising and also very plausible: I could not see that it was absurd, and it seemed only cruel and therefore unfunny. Conceptions of plausibility, it should be stressed, are as much normative as stochastic: things are (im)plausible on the axis of right/ wrong as much as on the axis likely/unlikely. Comedy which affects a lot of people in this way is often called 'over the top'.

3) a low level of surprise and excess implausibility: this is typically the reaction to a joke or comic episode which is excessively predictable because a well-known comic routine. The contradiction of everyday discursive expectations is visible and clear, but because it is so well known it is hardly surprising; the events are highly implausible – say, exaggerated pratfalls – but their comic impact is neutralised by their conventional nature.

4) a low level of surprise and excess plausibility: this situation is little different from the case of inadequate surprise, discussed earlier. The TV sitcom *Butterflies* regularly featured situations which were only very slight exaggerations of normal everyday situations, which were therefore highly plausible and only a little surprising. For many viewers this must have seemed more like happy soap opera than sitcom.

This matrix of possibilities of comic failure can also be summarised diagrammatically:

	excess implausibility	excess plausibility
high peripeteia	silly	over the top
low peripeteia	boring, conventional	serious

There is one further form of comic failure: total incomprehension. C.P. Wilson quotes American surveys that find that in excess of 50 per cent of respondents failed to identify the theme of a cartoon, and failed to find it funny (pp.193ff). T. Cohen's thesis that jokes create intimacy is based on the supposition that all jokes mobilise shared knowledge, and he quotes a joke that can only be understood by a tiny minority.

- What is a goy?
- If examined before time T, it is a girl; if examined after time T, it is a boy.

To understand this joke, one needs to know a) the Yiddish word *goy* ('gentile') and b) certain features of information technology. Information is processed by dividing it up into bits, and machines reach conclusions on the basis of each bit. Thus 'goy' is divided into two bits, 'g' and 'oy'; at time T, the only information the machine has available is 'g' and it assumes it is a girl; then it is fed 'oy' as a separate piece of information, with no connection with 'g': it comes to the conclusion that it is a boy. Naturally, the explanation kills the joke, as I found out when it was explained to me. Nonetheless, when one appreciates the reasoning behind it, it is possible to see that it is indeed absurd in the way defined here; but devoid of any surprise, any reversal of expectations, the syllogisms of the absurd never come into play.[3]

What the example of this joke does is to transfer the focus of our explanation to the audience for the joke: its incomprehensibility forces us to recognise that the moment of the reception of a joke is an integral part of the joke process, that reference to 'the discourses of the social formation' as the source of the comprehensibility of jokes should not be taken to be unproblematic. For those discourses are not spread evenly across a social formation, they have different impacts upon different sections of the population, difference which may or may not be isomorphic with traditional notions of stratification. We shall return to various implications of this principle in the final chapter.

The purpose of these pages has been to demonstrate that the logic of the absurd is capable of providing a framework within which comic failure can be described. It would be incongruous to finish a chapter devoted to one of the most successful of British comedies with an account of comic failure, and thus what follows is an attempt to show how the logic of the absurd can also generate a description of comic success. In a sense this is not necessary, since the premiss of the logic of the absurd is that it is to explain successful attempts to arouse laughter. But it is clearly the case that some attempts are more successful than others, in the sense that they arouse more laughter than others, or a laugh of greater intensity – the 'boffo' of the silent screen clowns, for instance. We have already seen that this is to be explained in part by the notion of comic articulation: the way in which one stage of a gag sequence prepares another (the fire drill and the real fire, for instance). However, this cannot be the total explanation, for everyone has had the experience of being told a joke, in isolation from other comic artefacts, that is much funnier than the average run of jokes: is it possible for the logic of the absurd to provide an explanation?

All jokes create comic impact in the first instance by the contradiction of discursively defined expectations – the peripeteia; but not all discourses are of equal weight and some are more contentious than others, at any given point in time and space, and therefore to contradict them is more contentious than to contradict less contentious discourses. Thus the discourses that define permissible levels of rudeness and aggression towards others – and especially towards wives, perhaps – is highly contentious, in the sense that breaches of it are deeply felt. Here may lie an explanation of the success of *Fawlty Towers*, whose abrasive quality was much appreciated by those who liked it (it is not of course the only explanation). It is also possible that seeing a discourse contradicted for the first time may well create more surprise than a contradiction of a discourse which every one is very used to serving as the basis of jokes. In any event, it is intuitively clear that the choice of discourse to contradict, or the incongruous intersection of discourses, is one way of distinguishing between degrees of comic success. This may be taken one stage further: the more incongruous the intersection of discourses, or the contradiction of discourses, the more implausible – *mutatis mutandis* – the peripeteia will seem; to counter-balance this increase in implausibility an increase of plausibility will also be needed. Take Basil's obsessive references to the war: his lack of control is monstrously implausible, especially normatively – such a collapse is felt to be extremely threatening. To counter-balance such gross implausibility, some massive countervailing plausibility is essential: Basil is concussed. If he was not concussed, this sequence would be entirely threatening, and unlikely to arouse laughter. Not only is he concussed, but on top of that all the linguistic resources of the pun are mobilised to make his obsessive reference even more comprehensible. Here, therefore, is a second way in which the contentiousness of the discourse that is contradicted may contribute to the degree of comic success.

Comedy is thus always treading a very narrow dividing line. In order to produce laughter it must be genuinely surprising, and preferably a little shocking: the contradiction of discursively defined expectations must be as sharp as it possibly can be. But if the shock is too great, it risks either (or both) giving offence or creating embarrassment. On the other hand, playing safe and making sure that no offence is given runs the opposite risk: a comedy so anodyne that no one is amused. To use Mary Douglas' insight: in the first case a joke will be perceived but not permitted, in the second it will be permitted but not perceived as funny. *Fawlty Towers* treads this line with remarkable success, and this is probably one of the reasons for its ecstatic reception; it is hardly surprising that on the way it should also have trodden on a few toes.

The purpose of the pages devoted to *Fawlty Towers* has been to demonstrate that the model of the logic of the absurd is capable of generating an analysis of an extended comic narrative as well as of shorter comic units. On the way it has also been shown capable of accounting for the notion of comic character, and of providing a framework for and the analysis of comic failure and comic success.

Notes

1. It is no accident that historically the question of plausibility came to the forefront of narrative aesthetics at just the time when literature came to be concerned primarily with exceptional actions, i.e. heroic ones. See my 'Function of "le vraisemblable" in French classical aesthetics', *French Studies*, vol.29, no.1, January 1975, pp.15–26.
2. T. Lovell, 'A Genre of Social Disruption?', in BFI Dossier no.17, *Television Sitcom.*
3. T. Cohen, 'Metaphor and the Cultivation of Intimacy', in S. Sacks (ed), *On Metaphor*, University of Chicago Press, 1979, p.9.

7
Comedy and Narrative

The basic modality of the organisation of a sequence of gags is that one gag is incorporated into the next in the form either of the basis for the peripeteia of the succeeding gag, or as the basis for one part or another of its syllogisms. Now the result of this form of organisation is that any given sequence of gags is in fact a narrative in itself, albeit a miniature one; indeed, the very form of organisation of the single gag on the basis of two chronologically distinct stages – preparation and punch line – implies that the single gag itself is already a narrative, albeit a narrative of a single event. However, it is clear that frequently gags are incorporated into larger-scale narratives that are not themselves organised in the way that we have just seen to be typical of the gag sequence: what form of relationship is it possible to trace between gags and non-comic narrative, or between gags and narrative in general? And especially, what form of relationship is it possible to trace between gags and that fundamental narrative category, the character?

In the situation of telling jokes in everyday life, or of the stand-up comedian telling strings of jokes, there is no narrative, and therefore these situations need no consideration here. Where comedy which does contain narrative is concerned, we may postulate that the relationship will take one of two forms, either:

a) the narrative will in fact consist of nothing more than the articulation of jokes together into a joke sequence, in which case the narrative conforms to the description given in the previous chapter; or

b) jokes will be linked by something which is not in itself comic, in other words some form of non-comic narrative; in this case we need to theorise the relationship between the comic moments and the non-comic narrative; this relationship in its turn will necessarily take one of two forms, either:

b i) the non-comic narrative is no more than a series of links between jokes; or

b ii) the narrative serves some further purpose, such as the delineation of character, or of a sequence of events which has some aesthetic purpose above and beyond that of merely linking some jokes together – and obvious example of this would be a Dickens novel such as *Martin Chuzzlewit* or *David Copperfield*, where the comic episodes and grotesque characters such as Sairey Gamp and Mr Micawber are inserted into a narrative framework which has a purpose beyond that of linking jokes or comic episodes.

However, although narrative which does no more than link comic episodes is theoretically possible, in practice it is probably never to be found: in comic forms where we might expect it such as the revue, vaudeville or variety sketch, comedians take care to make the linking elements between jokes funny themselves if possible, even if only by way of speaking in an unusual accent or tone of voice, or by accompanying their dialogue with exaggerated gestures or caricatural clothing and make-up. Apparent exceptions to this rule are illusory. Take, for example, a sketch in the British TV variety show *The Two Ronnies*, in which a farm-hand with a caricaturally red face and 'country bumpkin' clothes tries to quit a job because he cannot stand cowdung. This sketch is launched by an establishing shot of the farmer sitting at an office desk reading a magazine, followed by a close-up emphasising the magazine, followed by a shot of the farm-hand entering the room. If the caricatural clothing of the farm-hand gives an element of comedy to this shot, the two previous shots have nothing comic at all about them, for although it subsequently becomes clear that the farmer is in fact a kind of manager who knows nothing about farming, and this is central to the humour of the sketch, the opening shots show us nothing more than a farmer sitting at a desk reading. These shots are the beginning of a narrative that could be either funny or serious, and thus apparently this is a piece of non-comic narrative articulated on to a gag sequence. But in reality this is what we find in many gag sequences, for the preparation stage of most gags is not in itself funny – it is only the punch line which converts it into comedy. Therefore apparent exceptions of this nature are in fact no more than examples of comic articulation, and not examples of the mixture of comedy with non-comic narrative.

So it is that the relationship between comedy and non-comic narrative necessarily takes certain alternative forms: either A or B, if not A then necessarily B; and we have now seen that all the forms of this relationship are either comic articulation as analysed above or the type where comic episodes are inserted into a narrative which has some aesthetic function beyond the creation of humour. Therefore we can say that the problem of the relationship between humour and narrative is effectively located here.

That this relationship is indeed problematic can be shown by considering recent theorising on the subject. One set of theories is of course excluded – the traditional literary theory which insists that the defining feature of comedy is its specific narrative rhythm and not its humorous qualities. By effectively ignoring the question of how humour is produced, any problems that might arise from the relationship between this form of aesthetic production and narrative can be relegated to silence. But any theory which owes a debt to formalist or psychoanalytic thought, and which refuses the easy option of silence, is obliged to tackle this area of debate. The essays in the BFI's *Sitcom Dossier*, and especially those by Jim Cook and Terry Lovell, are an example.

The thrust of Jim Cook's argument here is that there is a divergence between two ways of reading a text, one of which bases reading on an appreciation of aesthetic structure, the other of which bases it on an appreciation of what the narrative refers to – the discourses of the social world that are outside the text; this form of appreciation of narrative is essentially the one that realist narrative invites. The nature of comedy is such that it inevitably makes us read structurally, because 'we read and assess each element (of the narrative) separately in terms of its differential success in producing laughter' (p.16); yet it is also 'quite possible to respond quite consciously to comedy in two distinct ways: one assessing skills of performance, writing, etc.; one following the narrative', and this 'double response' is normal because:

most film comedy and virtually all television sitcoms fall into a category broadly classifiable as *social* comedy – i.e. finally all the conventions and all the skills, clowning, etc., are at the service of the narrative's discourses about the social world and offer some perspective on it (p.17).

Cook concludes that this 'dual reading focus' is responsible for the particular type of aesthetic and ideological impact that 'social comedy' has (p.18), where the structural reading constantly interrupts the realist, narrative reading.

Now it should be stressed that none of this is wrong, as this is indeed how comedy works; but the question is: *how* is it possible for this to happen? For there is an unresolved tension in what Cook says, for if comedy foregrounds performance and enunciation and by the same token backgrounds narrative, what process is it that controls the relationship between the two? On the basis of what aesthetic cues does the reader/spectator switch from one mode of appreciation to the other? On the basis of what aesthetic process is such a 'dual reading' possible? And what is the effect – the *ideological* effect – of a reading which is a dual reading, an interrupted reading? These questions remain unanswered, unsurprisingly, thanks to their objective difficulty.

Terry Lovell's 'A Genre of Social Disruption?' is an attempt to go beyond these impasses by relating different types of comedy to different types of plausibility.[1] Different narrative genres, she notes, have different rules of plausibility. What constitutes plausibility in fantasy narratives (say, *Lord of the Rings*) is not the same as what constitutes plausibility in a realist novel (say, in the work of Balzac). Since there is no such thing as a specifically comic plot – we have already seen this in our discussion of Mast's *Comic Mind* – it follows that all comic narrative is composed of some genre plot schema or other turned into the comic mode through the inclusion of comic material. But – and this is central to her arguments:

The central conventions of different genres provide certain constraints on the way in which jokes, wit, gags, etc., can be used, and the comic mode of these genres may highlight or strain those conventions in turn. Formal comic disruption, a play with language and with generic conventions, would be inappropriate to comedies of social realism, because it would interfere with the goal of realism (p.22).

The way in which this is achieved, says Lovell, is through respect for the conventions of the genres in question. In realist comedy, the comic devices are naturalised in such ways as placing jokes in the mouths of witty characters, so that the play with language that they are composed of is presented as a feature of personality, rather than as a formal device which is laid bare in the course of the narrative by its interruption of the narrative. But in fantasy genres in the comic mode – crazy comedy, or as she calls it, comedy governed by Murphy's law (if it can go wrong, it will) – this is not necessary, since the rules of plausibility of fantasy are such that Murphy's law is normal.

Clearly this goes some way to resolving the tensions we saw in Cook's argument, for it specifies the narrative process which is responsible for the relationship between comic device and narrative, realist or otherwise. This process is the law of plausibility appropriate to any given genre. In between the two genres mentioned so far lies the 'mixed type' of comedy, which explicity includes 'the majority of television sitcoms' (p.24). Lovell's example is *Porridge*, where Fletch's wit and Ronnie Barker's comic performance 'create distance between character and performance which weakens identification with the character'. On the other hand, these comic features do not really interrupt the narrative as they are features of Fletch's character, and therefore part of the narrative. Clearly this is true; and clearly it is not unreasonable to claim that this represents a mixed type of comedy, where the performance elements disrupt the narrative and derive from fantasy genre plausibility, and where their naturalisation derives from realist plausibility. However, it is equally reasonable to claim the opposite, to argue that in a comedy of this type (the 'majority of television sitcom', we should remember) neither type of plausibility is operating, precisely because the performance elements do contradict the norms of realist narrative. Both Fletch's wit and the absurd way he manipulates the prison system are implausible by the standards of realist narrative, and only plausible by the standards of fantasy narrative – but there is no element of fantasy narrative present other than the humour, and norms of plausibility only operate, *ex hypothesi*, within a generic framework. Similarly, the norms of realist narrative are constantly disrupted, constantly shown not to apply or to be a relevant way of judging events, by the absurd elements of both plot and performance.

Now it must be admitted that this way of interpreting Lovell's arguments is no more cogent than her own. However, there is a further problem, which is directly related to the question of the mixture of genres: there is much more in common between realist and anti-realist comedy than this model allows, and what they have in common is precisely the logic of the absurd. The reason why Fletch's caustic, subversive wit is funny is exactly the same as the reason why Basil Fawlty's misfortunes are funny; we have already seen how the latter are analysable on the basis of the model proposed here, and Fletch's wit is equally amenable. When confronted with repressive prison guard McKay's insistence on the military orderliness of his domestic life, as opposed to the disorder of the inmates', Fletch undermines it by using McKay's language back at him in an ironically inappropriate way: 'Do everything by numbers, did you? Stand by your bed . . . Wait for it, wait for it . . . Two, three . . . knickers down!' The peripeteia derives from the inappropriateness of military discipline terminology to sexuality, which makes it implausible; the plausibility derives from McKay's boasting about the virtues of a military organisation of everyday life. What this example indicates, therefore, is that the basis of the comic process is the same in both genres, and indeed this was Lovell's starting point, for in her model each non-comic genre is turned into comedy by the inclusion of comic material; the problem is that the nature of the comic material is such as to undermine the distinctions between genres that is the other basis of her argument.

In these arguments much turns upon whether comedy interrupts narrative. For Cook this is necessarily so because comedy is seen as a form of enunciation, where the telling is privileged over the told, and narrative is seen as realist narrative, where the signified or the referent is privileged over the signifier; under these circumstances comedy will inevitably interrupt narrative. For Lovell, narrative is primarily a question of convention rather than of the discourses of the social formation, since plausibility derives from narrative convention. Under these circumstances narrative meaning must derive ultimately from the formal structure of narrative, whether this is conceived in terms such as

Propp's – a narrative grammar, where meaning is derived from place in the narrative flow – or in terms such as Greimas', where meaning comes from a deep structure which by means as yet unspecified 'generates' the flow of the text.[2] Here too it is inevitable that comedy will appear to disrupt narrative, since in both of these cases – the Propp model or the Greimas model – meaning ultimately derives from place, whether place in a flow or place in a matrix, and the structure of comedy owes nothing to place but everything to the prime relevant feature of enunciation, the intention to amuse; hence the judgment made by both Lovell and Cook that Freud's book on jokes has little to offer a theory of comic narrative (pp.15,19).

The advantage of the logic of the absurd as an explanatory model is that because it insists on the relevance of the semiotic level in the mechanism of enunciation (see especially the remarks on Freud in Chapter 1) it offers a way out of the aporias that a radical separation between an enunciative model and a narrative model inflict upon those who try to use them in combination. In this perspective, the essential point about the logic of the absurd is that its insistence upon the relationship between plausibility and implausibility necessarily involves placing the comic moment in a specifiable relationship with a narrative which has criteria of plausibility, and yet at the same time uses the element of implausibility, which also derives from the same narrative structure, to show how the enunciative mechanism emerges within the flow of the narrative. This is perhaps easier to appreciate on the basis of examples.

Woody Allen's *Hannah and her Sisters* (1986) is a film composed of a series of only partially connected narrative strands concerning the three women of the title and the range of characters – mostly lovers – with whom they are linked. Much of the film is non-comic, and only one of the narrative strands – the one concerning the Woody Allen character himself – is more or less consistently funny. One strand of the narrative concerns Hannah's husband, played by Michael Caine, who is in love with his younger sister-in-law, played by Barbara Hershey. In an attempt to create an opportunity to talk to her about his feelings he takes a client to the studio apartment where she is living with her current lover, an artist. As artist and client go to look at paintings, Michael Caine says in voice-over that now that he has the opportunity to speak he is terribly embarrassed and that whatever happens he must be extremely circumspect. Immediately after saying this he grabs her, kisses her passionately and then says he loves her madly, all to her evident bewilderment. At this point the artist and client return. This careful, hilarious juxtaposition of intended circumspection and actual crassness is moreover central to the way in which the Michael Caine character develops, for although at this stage of the story we have no reason to doubt the genuineness of his feelings for his sister-in-law, it becomes obvious by the end of the film that he is in fact in love with his wife and that his relationship with his sister-in-law was primarily a matter of infatuated desire – the traditional 'bit on the side'. Thus his comically inconsistent behaviour at one moment is at a deeper level an indication of a fundamental element in both his character and the narrative pattern of the whole film. Moreover, in general, the mixture of comedy and non-comedy is what is responsible for the emotional 'tone' of the movie as a whole. What is important for our purposes is to translate this commonsense perception – and no doubt professional concern on the part of the director – into formal terms which relate comedy to the overall narrative flow.

If we approach this moment in the film in terms of the logic of the absurd, this is the account that would result: Michael Caine's clumsy pass at his sister-in-law is surprising and hilarious because of the overt and exaggerated contrast between his action and his intentions. The action is also highly implausible because of this contrast – people like this, with these intentions, are not meant to behave in this way, to say the least. Yet, at the same time, his action is a little bit plausible because we know that desire is apt to paralyse intelligence. But this easy application of the logic of the absurd is not in fact what is most important here: what is most significant is that the very mechanism that explains the humour of this incident also relates it directly to the flow of the narrative as a whole. It is implausible because Michael Caine is trying to be a careful, calculating seducer and it is plausible because of the nature of the psychological circumstances he is in – the force of the desire that he has been repressing for months. His clumsiness indicates that he is far from the careful calculating seducer that he partially wants to be, while simultaneously indicating the extent of his desire and lack of self-control.

More generally, it is because he behaves in this (hilarious) way that their love affair (or lust affair) takes the course that it does, the banal sequence of demands that he quit his wife, the temporisations and equivocations, her final realisation that he is never going to divorce, etc. That is to say, the play of motives that structures the character's behaviour is closely related to the mechanism of comedy. In short, the very form that comedy takes, the balance between plausibility and implausibility, inevitably links the hilarious action with the sequence of preceding and succeeding actions in some manner or other.

In this instance it is clear that so far from interrupting the narrative, the moment of hilarity makes a specifiable contribution to it, and one which could not be made by non-comic means. The absurdity of Michael Caine's action at this moment both indicates what we are to make of his motives, and on what level we are to respond to his course of action. Because it is funny we are not invited to condemn his behaviour with the same rigour that we might if his clumsy attempt at seduction was portrayed seriously, or if his attempt at seduction was in fact carried off smoothly on the basis of a pre-arranged plan of some sort. In other words, the presence of comic moments in the film – throughout the film, for this is only one small example – is responsible for the lighter emotional tone that the film has, lighter than if the same range of subject matter was treated in a non-comic mode. This, of course, is a very obvious point; what is less obvious, perhaps, is that comic moments are able to have this effect precisely because they are articulated on to the narrative in the way that they are, according to the logic of the absurd: the balance between plausibility and implausibility is simultaneously responsible for the comic impact *and* for the way in which the incident contributes to the overall structure of the narrative.

A second example will reinforce this point: later in the same film Woody meets (for the second time) the other of Hannah's sisters (played by Diane Wiest), who is portrayed as an ineffective, feckless, ex-addict depressive who drifts from half-hearted occupation to half-hearted occupation without any commitment. At this point she has decided to become a TV script writer, and has written a script which she is showing to Woody (who plays a TV producer). Visibly the script is based upon her own recent experiences, which includes the fact that one of her girlfriends has just snatched her boyfriend, an architect, and Woody's appreciation of the script includes the line 'I *loved* the moment when she jumped out from behind the garbage cans and knifed the architect's girlfriend!' – which gets a solid yowl from the audience. This gag is complicated because in it several narrative strands are gathered together: in the first place, the reference to the sister's experiences and life-style; in the second, to Woody's experience as a TV producer. Is he being ironical or sincere? The third consideration is to the future – at the end of the film they are married. This bringing together of several narrative strands affects the play of plausibility and implausibility, as we would expect. The implausibility of Woody's statement derives from three sources: firstly, from the idea that anyone, especially a TV producer, should like such a moment in a script; secondly, from the fact that he would be much less impressed if he knew it was pure wish-fulfilment, as we do; thirdly, from the sheer unlikeliness that a writer would in fact utilise her own fantasies in quite such a caricatural manner. The counterveiling plausibility derives from the facts of her experience and the desperation that we know accompanied them, and from commonsense knowledge about the nature of TV narrative – it is not difficult to project this moment on to a *Dallas*-type script. The significance of this moment in the narrative as a whole, however, is based on a further element: up until this moment the relationship between Woody and this sister has been presented as a total disaster, for they have appeared to be entirely incompatible, but in a hilarious manner.

As we know (but of course do not when watching the film) by the end they are married: somehow the transition from one level of relationship to the other has to be stage-managed in a way that is plausible – for this is not a Murphy's law type of story, basically – and this scene, which is simultaneously humorous and indicates a form of rapport between them, is a way of achieving this stage-management without the bones of the plot creaking too audibly. Making this moment comic achieves this because the chains of plausibility and implausibility bring them together in a way that fits both their pasts and plausibly gives them the basis for a rapport. Thus here again the logic of the absurd demonstrates how a comic moment makes its own contribution to narrative as a whole.

These points should not be taken to imply that the relationship between comic moment and non-comic narrative is always of the precise nature described here: another example from the same film will point us in a rather different direction. In a flashback in the middle of the film the Woody Allen character and his then wife are told by his doctor that they cannot have children because he is infertile. As they walk away from the clinic the conversation turns a little acrimonious and his wife suggests that maybe he is responsible for his state, perhaps as a result of excessive masturbation. Woody replies, 'Hey! Don't knock my hobbies.' Clearly this remark can be explained in terms of the logic of the absurd: surprisingly because of the inappropriateness of the term 'hobby' under the circumstances, therefore implausible, plausible both because in a sense 'excessive' masturbation would be a hobby and also because marital disagreements over hobbies are a well-known form of domestic discord. But it is also clear that this gag is an interruption of the narrative, in exactly the way that is postulated by Cook's and Lovell's analyses. It leads nowhere in the story and is even mildly out of character, since the Woody Allen character is more given to wittily concise but anguished introspection than this kind of crack. But we should note that in the first place it is an interruption and out of place precisely because of the way the logic of the absurd is functioning in this instance. The implausibility does not refer us to any zone of the Woody Allen character in such a way as to illuminate his character – whereas the implausibility of the Michael Caine character's clumsiness *is* revealing – nor does it point the way forward in the narrative in the way that Michael Caine's behaviour does. Nor does the plausibility of 'hobbies' refer us to any element of either Woody's character or the story. Thus this gag is a genuine interruption of the narrative, and it is clear that comic moments may well constitute such an interruption, and this also on the basis of the way in which the logic of the absurd functions within narrative.

However, since the presence of comic moments in a realist narrative will always have some effect on the overall tonality of the story, even if only the obvious function of lightening it or of making such-and-such a character appear witty or ridiculous, even a comic interruption will inevitably have some relationship with the rest of the narrative. The nature of realist narrative is such that everything is always connected, in some way or another, to everything else.

A review of these examples and the associated theoretical arguments reveals this: the problem that we found in recent theorising was that the notions of comic enunciation and of narrative made it exceedingly difficult to show how comic moments and narrative flow were articulated together; but once the logic of the absurd is specified as the normal mode of comic enunciation this problem disappears, for the logic of the absurd is based on the notion that humour is essentially a process in which various discourses are brought into contact with each other in a particular way. What the examples we have seen have shown us is that humour can be articulated on to non-humorous narrative in a variety of ways, and that these ways are describable in the terms set up by the logic of the absurd. To this extent our model of comic enunciation may be said to provide the basis for an analysis of comic narrative.

Notes

1. T. Lovell, 'A Genre of Social Disruption?', in BFI Dossier no.17, *Television Sitcom*, 1982.
2. See Shlomith Rimmon Kenan, *Narrative Fiction: Contemporary Poetics*, London, Methuen, 1983, pp.10–28.

8

Comic Identity

In the last chapter we saw how the model of the logic of the absurd was able to generate descriptions of the relationship between comic moments and non-comic narrative: the basis of this method lay in the way in which the chains of plausibility and implausibility in each gag reach backwards and forwards into the narrative. This principle, as we shall now see, is capable of further application: because the relationship between humour and narrative takes this form, we can see how different comic forms are built up, how different comedies have different identities and how different comic characters differ from each other.

At the minimum level of comic narrative are those forms of humour with no narrative at all: the string of disconnected jokes, whether told professionally or by amateurs. At the next level of narrative complexity are various forms of comic monologue, farce, revue or vaudeville sketch. The typical form of narrative organisation here is comic articulation, in which each gag launches the next in the way we have seen. At the highest level of narrative complexity we have the forms of comedy found in canonical literature: Restoration comedy or Dickens, for example. Here the logic of the absurd mostly functions to articulate comic moments on to the narrative in such a way as to serve the non-comic intentions of the narrative as a whole, as we saw *à propos* examples drawn from a Woody Allen film; however – as we saw in another example from the same film – there is no reason in principle why such narratives should not be interrupted by comic moments which add little to the non-comic meanings achieved by the narrative at a whole. In between farce and canonical realist comic narrative are all the intermediate forms of which the television sitcom is probably the best known nowadays – that form which (as Sir Denis Forman remarked in a lecture) is often little more than an extended revue sketch, and yet which at its best is capable of producing major comic documents such as *Fawlty Towers*. In sitcom the logic of the absurd equally frequently articulates gags together into farce sequences, articulates gags on to non-comic narrative in the form of interruptions, and articulates them on to each other in the way typical of canonical realist narrative. This situation could be summarised in a diagram, thus:

Type of comic narrative	Role of logic of the absurd
none: jokes in daily life, stand-up comedian	internal structure of the single gag
comic monologue, farce, revue sketch	articulation of gag sequences
intermediate forms such as TV sitcom	articulates either as above or as below
social realist comedy	articulates onto narrative predominantly in such a way as to serve the purposes of realist narrative

The purpose of this schematic typology is less to provide a watertight account of all conceivable types of comedy – it has certainly failed in this – than to indicate how the model of the logic of the absurd may be used to generate an account of the differences between different types of comedy. Thus for example commonsense accounts of television comedy often point out that one TV sitcom is more realistic than another, which is more farcical: *Butterflies* and *Fawlty Towers* are examples that spring readily to mind. What our schema does is to explain *how* they are different in this respect: the more often the logic of the

154

absurd is used to articulate gags on to realist narrative in order to serve realist purposes, the more realist the narrative as a whole will seem; the more often it is used for the purposes of farce, the more farcical the narrative as a whole will seem. Thus the capacity of the logic of the absurd to describe the relationship between comedy and realist non-comic narrative has the further benefit of providing the ground for a description of the emotional tone of different styles of comedy.

However, despite what has been said about the lack of narrative linking revue or vaudeville sketches, we should not imagine that there is no connection at all between the comic episodes that compose a variety show, for it is well known that different variety or vaudeville shows have distinct identities, and perhaps distinct audiences to go with these identities, although it is impossible to be sure of this since audience research is purely quantitative and tells us little about the identities of the different audiences for different broadcast outputs. In any event, the identity of a show derives from two main sources: firstly, from the identity of the main comedian or comedians in the show – Rowan and Martin, Benny Hill, for example – and secondly from the type of jokes that are told, the type of sketches that are performed. The identity of the comedian(s) works on two levels: firstly, in terms of their identity in the simplest sense – a name and a face; secondly, in terms of the type of material that is associated with them and the style of delivery that they (usually consistently) adopt. Clearly this second level overlaps with the second feature of a show's identity, indeed in the case of a show with only the main performers it may be co-terminous with it. However, many variety shows feature a large number of other performers as well as the headliners, and under these circumstances the type of material that is performed by these other performers will contribute to the identity of the show as a whole.

Now the applicability of the logic of the absurd to this feature of TV variety and vaudeville shows is this: any gag works by contradicting discursively defined expectations, in other words by disrupting some discourse or other, as we have seen. It follows that the emotional 'tone' of any gag or gag sequence will be given by the nature of the discourses that it disrupts and the manner in which it does so. Thus we talk about styles of humour being 'dirty' (sexual innuendo) or 'sick' – evoking death or other 'unpleasant' features of the world – or 'alternative' because addressed to a range of concerns which are novel to comedy and perhaps only of interest to a counter-culture. Because it is intrinsic to 'joke-work', to use Freud's term, to evoke some discourse or discourses, it necessarily follows that if a series of jokes or sketches is based around a certain limited range of discourses and ways of disrupting them, then these jokes or sketches will have a common identity, which if pursued consistently will become the basis of the identity of a show or a comedian.

The long-standing British TV variety show *The Two Ronnies* exemplifies these traits. The show's identity derives in the first place from obvious repeated features of format, of which the most obvious is the identity of the two leading performers, Ronnie Barker and Ronnie Corbett, and certain of their attributes: one is large, the other small, both wear heavy horn-rimmed glasses, for example. Beyond this, the show's format is based on repeated situations: it opens and closes with a series of one-liners or three-liners spoken to camera by the lead pair, in a mock TV newscast format; it always features a monologue by Ronnie Corbett sitting in a large armchair, full of self-deprecating jokes about his size; it usually features a doggerel duet, frequently a sketch featuring the lead players as tramps. As a last concession to the tradition whereby variety shows actually featured a variety of forms of entertainment, it usually has a musical interlude. But beneath these obvious devices of format lies a deeper identity based upon their style of humour, upon the type of jokes and sketches they use; an exhaustive analysis would be tedious, and probably unnecessary, but a series of examples will give the flavour of the show.

A typical three-liner in the opening segment involves a group of Midlands drivers sacked for not knowing the geography of the area: they resolve to send the boss to Daventry! The obvious joke mechanisms here involve the use of a pun and the attribution of stupidity to a non-controversial butt (a largely anonymous group of workers) – puns and stupidity are both implausible, in ways we have already seen; but beneath this is a recurring theme in their humour, and in British humour in general: the mismatch between individual and social roles. Here the mismatch consists of lack of knowledge; in the farm-hand sketch referred to earlier it consists of unwillingness to accept normal features of farming life – the farm-hand cannot accept that cows produce cowdung, the farmer cannot accept that he has to sack useless workers. A sketch about bikers (done as a pseudo-heavy metal rock number) is based in part upon their pretentions to being super-bad – when their mothers let them out. A crack about open-plan living ('they knocked the goldfish bowl and the budgerigar cage into one') is aimed at rich intellectuals, and thus becomes a mild attack upon pretentiousness. A three-liner involves crossing an aborigine with a plumber – the result is a boomerang that says it will come back in the morning – a reference to the legendary (in both senses) unco-operativeness of plumbers. In each case the relationship to the logic of the absurd is sufficiently clear not to require detailed exposition; the result is to create jokes whose common reference point is the interminable British discourse about knowing your place, doing your job properly and not sticking out.

Another favourite theme is scatology: the farm-hand's intolerance is for cowdung, not early mornings, or haymaking; the bikers like eating baked beans, with results comparable to their machines; the risk of breaking a monocle by sitting on it is dismissed on the grounds that 'that's not where you wear it'; a cupboard full of toilet paper has served that purpose 'ever since the time of Ethelred the Unready', etc. The British stand-by of the pun is a steady resort, usually in combination with some other source of humour, whether scatology, stupidity, satirical references to public figures, etc. Topical references are common: Sir Keith Joseph and the teachers' strike ('likes whisky, hates t/Teachers'); topless model Samantha Fox's anatomy; actor Oliver Reed's supposed rudeness and the BBC's legendary meanness are but a few examples.

The Two Ronnies usually features a longer sketch with both the headliners and a supporting cast, sometimes done as part of a mock serial. In the episode on which this analysis is based it consisted of a visit by a businessman and his secretary to a village where everyone is called Smith, done as a spoof of a Hammer horror movie – slightly eerie camera angles, jangling music on the soundtrack at appropriate moments. The story which holds the sketch together is based around the idea that the village hotel owner sends out pretty girls to seduce businessmen and bring them to the hotel, where they are baffled to find that the secretary disappears, the hotel owner has apparently been dead for years, etc. Many of the jokes are in fact relatively unrelated to the 'plot': the village bobby is directing invisible traffic – 'unpredictable stuff, traffic, sir'; a visit to the village doctor gets the offer of a cure which unfortunately has a side effect – 'it doesn't work'. Much of the humour derives from the incongruity of a small, elderly randy business-man with an obvious toupee with a glamorous young lady, and is thus a further version of the theme of mismatch between role and individual, interspersed with innuendo.

The logic of the absurd accounts for the functioning of each individual gag in the usual way, but beyond that it demonstrates how the gags are grouped together into thematic units: all the scatological jokes are implausible because they mention the unmentionable, the social misfit jokes are implausible because laziness, or excessive sexual desire, or pretentions produce bizarre behaviour – knocking the goldfish bowl and the budgie's cage together, for instance – and are plausible because we know, as a matter of stereotype, that such features of personality are apt to produce such results. Thus what the operation of comic enunciation produces is a series of ways of referring to, or incarnating, discourses of the social formation, and it is the selection of a limited range of possibilities from among such discourses that is responsible for the comic identity of the show or comedian in question.

In the case of *The Two Ronnies*, most of the dominant characteristics are negative: if a joke is bawdy, it is only mildly so; if it is directed at a butt, it is either at a more or less anonymous one, or the attack is mild, or it is at a category which is conventionally considered fair game – tramps or gays, for instance; if it is satirical, it is at the expense of well-established targets, such as the BBC or the Post Office. Above all, it is gentle humour – it lacks the punch of, say, *Fawlty Towers* or the murderous precision of someone like Alexei Sayle: 'Recession is just a rumour put around by four million people without jobs.' It is, in short, consensual humour: fairly entertaining, non-controversial, guaranteed to cause no offence to anyone with any clout, bland, anodyne – all in all, harmless, except in so far as the overall message which comes across is that people who don't fit their prescribed roles are ridiculous.

Thus the identity of this show derives from a combination of the factors listed here: in the first place, the actual identities (in the legal sense) of the headliners, and their individual performance skills; in the second place, the format of the show, designed to deliver the maximum number of gags in the allotted time and to showcase the performance skills of the headliners; in the third place, the themes that are commonplace in the jokes themselves.

This form of analysis can also be applied to the notion of a comic character: that is to say, schematically, a comic character is defined on the basis of the type of jokes that are associated with him or her. A simple example is the type of character in a sitcom who is witty: say, Jane in *Agony* or the eponymous Shelley. Clearly, and obviously, they seem witty to us because they make lots of witty remarks, that is, remarks that function according to the logic of the absurd. However, because wit can be used in a variety of different ways, the emotional tone of these two shows is rather different. A comparison of typical episodes of the two series will show how this is achieved.

In the opening sequence of the episode of *Shelley* entitled 'Moving In', we see Shelley and his girlfriend having breakfast in a café, and looking through advertisements for flats. The sequence opens with a series of gags which are all put-downs: Shelley cannot tell the difference between the tea and the coffee, despite careful slow drinking; he asks the waitress if she's wearing 'real Terylene' and makes a series of derogatory comments about advertising and his ex-girlfriends. Later, viewing a very grubby bedsit he comments 'I've seen a lot of places today, but this is by far the worst. Mind you, competition has been fierce but you've almost achieved uninhabitability.' Jokes such as these, directed at all and sundry, regardless of whether they in any way deserve them, are a frequent feature of the series. Not that this is the only way in which wit is used: in another sequence, Shelley confronts a particularly oily estate agent, who asks if he and his girlfriend are intending to start a family; 'No', says Shelley; 'Jolly good' comes the drawled, unctuous reply. 'Perhaps I'd better go and have the operation straight away', says Shelley, 'just to make sure. I'm surprised you haven't got facilities right here on the premises.' Of course, this is just as much of a put-down as the previous examples, but it is different from them in two significant ways: in the first place, the estate agent has been clearly shown to deserve what he gets – he's a greedy, racist liar with appalling manners, whereas the previous victims have merely been ordinary – and in the second the logic of the joke relates it directly to what he

159

says. His pleasure that they are not going to start a family is motivated solely by the knowledge that it is easier to get a flat without a baby than with one, and this increases his chance of a commission; this selfish pleasure is the starting point of Shelley's exaggerated but logical extrapolation from the situation, which ridicules his attitude. Thus not only does the victim clearly deserve what he gets, but sows the seeds of his own ridicule into the bargain.

Elsewhere, Shelley uses his wit to talk his way out of difficult situations, either by telling preposterous lies (his mother's wooden leg, for instance) or by ingenious use of logic: confronted with an unemployment office clerk who reproaches him for being wilfully unemployed when he is so well qualified and there are millions on the dole, Shelley replies 'You wouldn't want me to take a job away from one of them, would you?' Here again he is turning the logic of his opponent's position against him: in reality, the number of other people on the dole is irrelevant to the fact that Shelley is a 'freelance layabout', as he calls it; but because the clerk has made the mistake of mentioning it, Shelley can use the situation to create a rhetorically unanswerable way out for himself, by pretending to see things from the point of view of the other unemployed rather than his own. In a way this is a put-down of the clerk (there are plenty more of them), but it is also a survival skill on Shelley's part, a way of using wit to avoid difficulties not of his making (in the sense that unemployment is a fact of life in a recession). Similarly, when the clerk reveals he knows a lot about Shelley's past, Shelley asks 'Working on my biography, are you?'

Another series of jokes in the episode turns around sexual innuendo – jokes about toad in the hole with the rather dumb working-class waitress in the café and about the fact that he and his girlfriend are sleeping on a friend's floor and they suspect that he is only pretending to be asleep when they make love. The innuendo is mostly at the expense of the waitress: typically, she fails to understand what Shelley is saying and replies in an absurdly irrelevant way – when he suggests troilism she says food isn't served till later, for example. Here it is not Shelley who is doing the putting-down, but the situation, and thus Shelley's wit is integrated with the series' identity in general.

The identity of the series thus depends upon the type of jokes that are made: 'real Terylene', for instance, is funny because of the implausible linking of 'real' with an artificial fabric; it is a put-down because it is unanswerable and because it implies lack of taste. To say 'Ugh! You're wearing Terylene!' makes the same charge, but is answerable by saying 'What's wrong with Terylene?' or some such, but 'real Terylene' is not answerable in the same way. The only adequate response would be another joke – 'Is that a real sense of humour you've got there' would be a possibility; we will return to the reasons for this property of humour at a later stage. If the entire series consisted of nothing but put-downs such as this, its tonality would be unrelieved aggression, but we have seen that other put-downs are articulated on to the story or on to previous gags in such a way as to show that they are deserved, and other witty lines – 'stealing a job', for instance – are not only put-downs, they are also ways of justifiably avoiding unpleasant situations. If these features of the show are combined with the frequent use of sexual innuendo of a rather traditional kind, we can see how the show has the identity that it has.

In the first place, we should note that all the jokes are either spoken by Shelley or are unintentionally made by other characters in such a way as to support Shelley's view of them. There is an apparent exception here: when Shelley asks Fran, his girlfriend, whether she has told their future landlady about him, she replies 'I never tell anyone about you', which is in a sense a put-down of Shelley; but because his persona is that of a smart-ass terror, what from her point of view may be a put-down is from his a compliment. In the second place, it is easy to list the topics which produce the majority of jokes – sexuality and the inadequacies of others: the show's identity is therefore based on aggressive male-centred banter. As a result, Shelley easily seems supercilious in a rather unpleasant way because most of his jokes are easy triumphs at the expense of others, especially those less educated than himself. On the other hand, he may be admired as someone whose easy superiority makes sense in a world full of mediocrities out to get him, and his wilful unemployment no more than an expression of this. But whichever way he is evaluated (which is dependent upon the world-view of the evaluator) the starting point of the evaluation is the way in which the jokes he makes at other people's expense are constructed.

Agony presents a real contrast in comic identity, despite the fact that both shows have at their centre someone who is forceful and witty.

161

Part of the reason for this is that in *Agony* there are serious moments – usually brief – which indicate that Jane is indeed a very caring person, as her job as 'agony aunt' implies, moments for which there is no equivalent in *Shelley*. In the episode 'From Here to Maternity', which launched a new series, the basic situation, from which most the laughter derives, is that Jane is massively pregnant, and that despite spending all of her pregnancy adamant that she would be a working mother who took the situation in her stride, she has decided to resign her job and be a full-time housewife and mother – or 'h . . h . . h . . hhousewife', as she calls it, announcing her decision to the press conference at which she is to receive an award for her oustanding contributions to the cause of avoiding unwanted pregnancies! Not that hers was unwanted, she insists: she really wanted it once she found she'd got it. This joke, which is a self put-down, is typical of one form that jokes in the series take: wry, rueful admission that self is not the centre of the known universe. When her boss asks why there are so many people inquiring about her job, she replies 'I'm glad you're here so I can tell you in person . . .' (to her secretary) 'tell her, Val'. At the end of the episode her secretary – now her successor – needs information about an association for the colour-blind; 'it's in the red book', says Jane, 'or is it the green one?' This of course could be either a self put-down or inadvertent naivety: in either case the central character is the butt of the joke. In all of these jokes the implausibility derives from the fact that self should not have to face these onslaughts as well as obvious features of the situation such as coincidence; but circumstances make them plausible.

Most of the other jokes derive from role reversal, in some form or other, particularly gender roles: the men take on supposedly 'feminine' traits, such as domesticity, fainting, etc. Thus, in the middle of the first half, Jane announces to her baby's father that she has decided to be a wife and mother, and Lawrence's reaction is to look in the pregnancy advice book and seek an explanation under 'irregular behaviour in pregnancy': if the reaction is typically male, what it seeks to explain is not. Jane's response is 'Does it say anything about an overwhelming urge to stick a toasting fork up a patronising husband's nose?' Here the joke derives of course from aggression, always implausible because of social sanctions against it, here doubly implausible because of the proposed mode of assault; the choice of instrument is also responsible for holding the aggression at an appropriate emotional level, reducing the aggressiveness through the monstrously implausible scenario it evokes. This is milking the gag, and the process continues, for Lawrence takes her literally and checks the book – 'No, it doesn't'. Jane's reaction is to fall kneeling on the floor screaming just as her mother, a stereotypical scheming Jewish matriarch, comes in: 'Oy veh! My daughter's a Muslim!' This way of topping the gag introduces a new comic sequence based on the Jewish matriarch stereotype, and the first half ends with the revelation that the new German au pair is also heavily pregnant.

The pregnancy of the au pair continues the theme of rueful recognition of the waywardness of fate, and the Jewish matriarch is an often inserted segment into the series, to which we shall return shortly. The important point for our purposes is the use of role reversal in this excellent little sequence: it is Lawrence who is being the worrying mother here, and Jane the aggressive one. The implausibility of looking in the pregnancy book to explain Jane's behaviour derives from the feature of behaviour that is being explained: stereotypically, there is nothing unusual about giving up your job days before labour is due; deriving from this is the implausibility of Jane's aggressive reaction and the naivety of Lawrence's response to it. In each case, role reversal combines with some other incongruous feature to create a gag, and this is a frequent source of humour in the series. The final element of humour that marks the series is something that it apparently shares with *Shelley* – witty put-downs. The difference is that Jane only aims them at people who visibly deserve them, in some way or other: to the appalling traditional agony aunt – who thinks the real problems in a woman's life are where to go on honeymoon and how to avoid runny home-made marmalade – she says 'Sex isn't something you bag coal in, you know.'

These examples give us the elements of a description of the series identity of *Agony*. It is based upon forms of gender role reversal and the incongruities these give rise to – or at any rate can be associated with; upon witty put-downs of those who deserve it, especially those who fail to see the world in the same terms as Jane; and upon self put-downs or rueful recognition of the battering that self takes in the course of trying to lead a decent life in trying circumstances.

A more complex example is Basil Fawlty. By common consent much of the series' success depends upon Basil's character: a snobbish, suspicious, repressed, aggressive paranoid who consistently creates the difficult situations which his paranoia sees as the direct result of other people's inefficiency, stupidity, selfishness or plain malevolence. The fire drill sequence, analysed earlier from the point of view of comic articulation, shows how his character is built up from the nature of the gags involved.

This sequence is triggered by the fact that Basil mistakenly sets off an alarm bell at approximately the time set for a fire drill – about which he has self-righteously reminded the guests a moment ago. As a result he feels obliged to explain the rather fine distinction between the two bells and between midday and midday minus two minutes to a series of guests arriving at short intervals to participate in the drill. Basil's mind often operates in a super-logical manner, exploring the ramifications of tiny pettifogging distinctions, and – as on this occasion – the results are that he gets caught up in a set of circumstances of his own making; here his explanation is so long that the two minutes are elided, as he is forced to recognise in a fit of pique. The humour of this situation derives from the series of implausibilities that structure it, as we have seen. From the point of view of character, it is Basil's obsessive pursuit of the most literal-minded interpretation of the situation (an alarm bell is not a fire bell – the famous 'semitone difference' – and 11.58 is not midday) that is both the source of the implausibilities and at the same time an important element in his character. His unpleasant self-righteousness needs this petty-minded insistence on tiny and unimportant detail to preserve itself; such behaviour is both the source of humour and psychological portrayal.

His obsessiveness and the self-righteousness that it reflects and defends continue to characterise his behaviour as he insists on carrying out the fire drill in as accurate a manner as possible, and gets increasingly frustrated at the guests' unwillingness to take it as seriously as himself. The phone bell that interrupts the blessed silence that follows is hilarious because of the implausibility of its timing at a moment when he is already feeling paranoid about the world getting at him. The humour of the situation, given in part by his exaggerated response (leaping in the air, bellowing down the phone and slamming it down) feeds directly into our knowledge of his character, for it is in so far as he behaves in this implausible and yet comprehensible manner that he is simultaneously hilarious and paranoid-obsessive. In general a lot of the humour of *Fawlty Towers* derives from the fact that what happens to Basil is precisely the last thing that he of all people needs to happen to him because he is the one person in all the world who is least capable of coping with it. In the gourmet dinner episode Basil is hurrying to bring the dinner from his friend's restaurant to the waiting guests, and of course his car chooses that moment to break down. Frustration under these circumstances is normal, but for someone like Basil the level of frustration reaches a dramatically higher pitch, and that extraordinary level is revealed in his response: he finds a large fallen branch and proceeds to bash the car with it, swearing at the car as if it was wilfully getting at him at the same time. Again, humour and character revelation are integrated into the same process, for it is the balance between plausibility and implausibility in his actions which is responsible for both.

As the fire drill sequence develops, Manuel accidentally sets fire to the kitchen (as a result of Basil's short-sighted order to go and do some cooking). Basil's response is disbelief, because he is so fixated on the notion that Manuel understands nothing and this hilarious response (he even locks Manuel in the burning kitchen) reveals exactly how obsessive he is, for it is his incapacity for seeing the obvious that underlines it. Here again, character is revealed in (humorous) response. Obsessiveness is not necessarily funny (think of Raskolnikov, or Othello) but it is peculiarly suitable for farce because it is so readily revealed in absurd actions.

The final example of the relationship between Basil's obsessiveness and the humour of *Fawlty Towers* is his apostrophe of God when he is unable to find the key to the alarm which will alert the fire brigade. Clearly he has mislaid it because of his obsessive attention to other unnecessary details; equally clearly, his inability to recognise this derives from the same source, and therefore his agonised 'Thank you, God! Thank you so bloody much!' is both the moment of hilarity and another rendering of his obsessiveness.

Another trait of Basil's character is his aggressiveness. Consider his telephone conversation with Sybil earlier in the German tourists episode. At the end of what is obviously a long string of nagging requests from the other end he asks 'Is there anything else you'd like me to do? Move the hotel ten yards to the left, perhaps?' The peripeteia and the implausibility of this crack obviously derive from the impossibility of the proposal; its plausibility is more complex, and derives from the implication that this possibility is no more demanding than all the other things he has been asked to do, an implication which reverses the significance of the preceding list. Instead of being a revelation of Basil's inadequacies (he was meant to have done all these things already) they become a revelation of Sybil's unreasonableness. Thus right in the heart of the mechanism of the logic of the absurd in this example is inscribed Basil's aggressiveness: it is the very absurdity of his challenge that marks it down as an aggressive act, for it is absurdity that enables it to reverse the burden of responsibility for the situation. Among other implications of this analysis is that the earlier objections to Freud's theory were well-founded: it is the semiotic mechanism of the absurd that enables the aggression to appear, in this example as in Freud's own (*Jokes*, pp.146 ff).

No doubt there is much more that could be said about the relationship between Basil's character and the humour of this series. However, this is only intended as a set of examples to illustrate a general theoretical point about the relationship between comedy and character. Basil's character is a result of the comedy of what he does and says, in other words a result of the selection of discourses about the world which are mobilised in the process of the absurd, discourses about what constitutes rational behaviour and normal behaviour towards others, which are mobilised in a particularly acute fashion. His ruptures of normality are extreme, but at the same time those elements in the situations which make them partially comprehensible (plausible) are correspondingly acute; on the one hand his actions are monstrously implausible, on the other they are none the less comprehensible, and this combination produces a comic tone which was completely fresh at the time, and thoroughly grounded in a consistent character who was none the less absurd for being consistent.

What we have seen in these examples is how the logic of the absurd is capable of providing the basis for an explanation of differences in comic identity, as well as the basis of an analysis of comic narrative;

apparently, therefore, this model is well-placed to serve as the grounding for a generalised survey of humour and comedy in all its forms. Indeed, the time has come to question in more general terms the scope of the logic of the absurd as an explanatory mechanism: what features of comedy is it capable of explaining? Assuming there are features of comedy which it cannot explain, what other forms of explanation are necessary? How are these forms related to the logic of the absurd? Since it is out of the question to write a general description of all the forms of comedy, what is needed is an analysis of those features of comedy which cannot be directly and entirely described using our model of comic enunciation. We are left essentially with two questions, which will turn out to be inter-related: in the first place, the question of the differences between the major forms of comedy – between farce and canonical literary comedy, for instance; and in the second, the question of how these forms have changed over time – the *history* of comic forms.

The differences between the major comic forms is not difficult to derive from the logic of the absurd, for we have seen that this logic is inherently related to narrative and to character, and the central differences between the various forms of comedy are those to do with these two aesthetic forms: what distinguishes farce from, on the one hand, stand-up comedy and on the other literary comedy such as Dickens is precisely differences of narrative and character, differences which could be summarised in the form of a diagram, thus:

Degree of complexity of articulation of narrative	Type of narrative and social situation	Type of comic character
None	Telling jokes in everyday life	None
Minimum: no narrative linking jokes	Stand-up comic in club, TV show, etc.	Relatively consistent comic persona

Intermediate: some narrative linking jokes	Comic sketches, silent screen farce	Stereotypical characters, positioned according to needs of punch line
Complex/maximum	Sitcom, literary or canonical comedy	Comic character in the fullest sense (although much sitcom is nearer the sketch where character is concerned.

Thus although there is no space here to pursue this question any further, we can see on the basis of the examples we have already analysed, and the theoretical materials already established, how it is possible to give an account of the differences between the different forms of comedy which are extant today, an account which derives in considerable part from the logic of the absurd. What is less directly related to this model of comedy is the history of these forms.

Two examples will demonstrate this.

The first is the form of the variety show as it is normally presented on British TV: a collection of short comic episodes linked – if at all – only by announcements by an MC, who may also take the opportunity to tell a few jokes on his own account, usually with a musical interlude. What determines this form? Certainly it is describable in terms of the logic of the absurd: it is a series of unrelated episodes in so far as there is no narrative linking them beyond the minimum levels of narrative normal in the structure of the single gag or in comic articulation. But of course it is immediately obvious that this description tells us very little indeed about why there is a form of entertainment of this nature available today, and to go any further we need properly historical materials. Vaudeville and variety derive from the form of the music hall as it developed during the second half of the nineteenth century in Britain (and seems to have been exported to America, where it connected with other forms of popular entertainment such as the medicine show and the circus), and already here the normal organisation of the evening's entertainment was a series of disconnected events – songs and comic sketches, conjuring, etc. – linked only by the announcements of the MC. Its origins lay in essentially amateur entertainments, but with success came the separation of performer from audience. The development of this form of entertainment in its turn cannot be explained in terms of the logic of the absurd, but needs to be referred to a series of other factors: the rise of working-class spending power to a level that would support an entertainments industry with a permanent professional personnel and specialised buildings, the public licensing system that encouraged the growth of a form that evaded the regulations governing plays and theatres and could take place in another venue, the public house and subsequent purpose-built venues.

Despite hesitations on both sides, this form of entertainment was adopted by the BBC in the inter-war years, and became a staple of popular broadcasting, at first featuring comedians and singers who had made their names in the music halls, but increasingly after World War II launching new names on the air. The basic format has remained relatively constant despite changes introduced on the basis of the technical nature of the new broadcast media – the possibility of reaction shots, for example, both changes the pace of comedy and broadens the possible sources of it in relation to the theatre, where the distance of the audience necessarily prevents this technique, which was of course used in the cinema long before television was invented.[1]

Nor is this the only change introduced by the broadcast format: in the theatrical versions of this form the 'headliner' acts, the stars, exercised relatively little control over the nature of the acts that figured on the same bill as themselves; the names on the rest of the bill could be extremely varied and as a result the emotional tone of an evening's entertainment might be far from homogeneous. Radio and television, on the other hand, have enforced a greater uniformity of tone on shows which are increasingly dominated by a single figure or team of comedians. The reasons for this are complex, and largely lie beyond the scope of this essay. In the early days of radio comedians were very wary of broadcasting because each of them had at their disposal only a relatively small amount of material, which in the music halls would suffice them for a whole season, perhaps longer, whereas the size of the broadcast audience meant constant renewal of material at a pace few could sustain. In the long run this problem was overcome by comedians and producers hiring comedy writers in ever-increasing quantities. At the same time, sound commercial practice makes predictability of audience response a prime consideration, and the domination of a well-known individual or team is good marketing. In part the reasons for these changes are technical: the possibility of assembling material on (video)tape over a period of days or weeks means that a single comedian or team can hire writers to put together sketches that they can record over an extended period, whereas the technical nature of the theatre prevented this.

The second example of the history of comic forms refers to the TV sitcom.

By common consent, the characteristics of the sitcom are these: the basic characters are the same in each episode; the relationships between them do not change from episode to episode, and therefore the situation is always essentially the same; the story always refers to some situation which, however farcically exaggerated, is a recognisable feature of the everyday social world of its audience. In this definition one element should be stressed above all others: the fact of repetition depends absolutely upon the fact of broadcasting systems, for although it is true that any other form of regular dissemination can produce repetition at this level – newspaper cartoons have many features in common with sitcoms – only radio and television have the type of space available in combination with a presumed regular audience which allows repetitive comedy at this length (although cinema cartoons and farce are obvious precursors here). Thus sitcom depends upon the broadcast format, clearly. But equally clearly the historical fact of broadcasting cannot be held responsible for the nature of sitcom: at the very least we would have to admit the debt that sitcom owes to earlier comedy forms: the sense of comic character and comic situation developed in the boulevard theatre, the comic rhythms of the revue or vaudeville sketch, for example. In fact, the history of the sitcom, in Britain at least, is relatively clear.[2]

Until the early 1950s British radio comedy was largely an imitation of music hall, albeit with elaborate sound effects that depended upon radio technology – the exception is the brand of 'nonsense humour' developed in *The Goon Show*, which shares the previously listed features of sitcom except the referencing of recognisable social situations. For reasons that relate partly to the increasingly central role of the scriptwriter, radio comedy started to explore the possibilities offered by miniature comic dramas featuring recurrent characters. A central feature of this process is the decision taken by the BBC leadership during the late 1930s, and reinforced by the wartime experience, to pursue two policies that had been avoided previously: firstly, increased regular scheduling of programmes to encourage audience building after the model of American radio – this had been largely rejected for ideological reasons until the late 1930s – and secondly to devote a considerable percentage of broadcast time to light entertainment.[3]

The radio shows that are usually credited with launching the sitcom in Britain are *Life With the Lyons* and 'The Glums' segment of *Take It From Here*; *Hancock's Half Hour*, which was later transferred to TV, was especially influential in extending the role that character played in sitcom, since it is Hancock's persona that is the central feature in the comedy of this series, and it is a persona with more psychological depth than was previously normal. Sitcom transferred to television relatively easily, despite obvious technical differences deriving from differences in the media. In large measure this is due to its adaptation to the broadcast format: regular scheduling of standard length and format items with easily recognisable recurrent features; a rhythm which is calculated to produce gags at a regular recurrent rate, and a peak – the comic hook – at a predictable point after (usually) just under half an hour; a range of subject matter and treatment guaranteed to amuse without producing more than the irreducible minimum of offence; a form of production which can deliver acceptable and predictable results at a budget that makes corporate sense.[4]

These two brief and schematic accounts of British broadcast comedy are not of course intended as a total explanation of comedy as we know it now – obvious omissions are such things as the performance

171

skills of the major players and the skills of the writing teams: to mention only one, sitcom would be a very different creature today but for the writing of Galton and Simpson, who were responsible for among other shows *Hancock's Half Hour* and *Steptoe and Son*. However, as elsewhere in this essay, the purpose of this material is not exhaustiveness, but the examination of the scope of a theory.

The logic of the absurd enables us to describe, with some precision, the mode of operation of a particular art form, not only in the sense of showing how the joke works – many psychological models have offered not dissimilar insights in the past, as we have seen – but also in the sense that it enables us to see how comedy builds up its effects and inserts them into other forms of narrative. On the basis of this model we are able to distinguish between different comic styles, as we have already seen, for central to the model is the way in which comic enunciation can only function by mobilising various discourses, according to its own norms. If we crudely group these styles into larger-scale categories, we may have available to us the basis for a history and sociology of humour; such categories would be based on considerations such as whether the humour in question was controversial or non-controversial at any point in time, on whether the audience for a given style was broadly based in the population or only appealed to a narrow section of it, on whether it was usually performed in contexts especially reserved for humour or whether it was part of some other wider context – and what this context might be.

Categories such as these are frequently used in writing about humour, but rarely do such analyses go beyond empirical impressions of this nature, perhaps backed up with quantitative audience research. What the logic of the absurd permits us to do is to show what it is in a particular style of humour that gives it its identity, and thus to postulate that it is this feature or features that is responsible for the elective affinity whereby it becomes the preferred style of the social group that is attracted to it. The empirical historical details sketched in earlier would then constitute the processes by which one particular set of comic styles – broadly speaking, ones that have been consensual since the late nineteenth century in Great Britain – came to be such. The important point here is this: no matter how much more empirical detail this historical skeleton was fleshed out with, such details would tell us nothing about *why* such-and-such a style was popular, it would only tell us how its popularity was organised institutionally, and while it is of course true that the power of broadcasting institutions is such as to play a considerable part in ensuring that their choice of style is the one that is accepted, and becomes the consensual style, it would be naive to imagine that this was the only factor at play in its acceptance – in the final analysis the product has to be *liked* by the audience.

The advantage of the logic of the absurd is that it is able to tell us something about how a given comic style builds up its effects, and thus about how it creates the pleasure it does. Of course, this is far from the whole story, for the history of the institutions involved plays a crucial role in determining comic identities, as we have seen. A viable explanation, therefore, will consist of an account of both processes, in combination.

Notes

1. For a fuller account of these processes, see the following: B. Took, *Laughter in the Air*, London, Robson Books, 1976; J. Palmer, 'Humour in Great Britain', in A. Ziv (ed), *National Styles in Humor*, Westport CT, Greenwood Press, 1987; M. Vicinus, *The Industrial Muse*, London, Croom Helm, 1974, Chapter 6; B. Waites, 'The Music Hall', Open University Course U203, Popular Culture, Unit 5, and P. Scannell and D. Cardiff, 'Radio in World War II', Open University Course U203, Popular Culture, Unit 8.
2. See B. Took, op.cit., for details.
3. See T. Bennett et al., *Popular Culture, Past & Present.*
4. Some of these points are discussed in B. Curtis, 'Aspects of Sitcom', in the BFI *Sitcom* Dossier.

9

Politics and Comedy
The Effectivity of the Absurd

The chapter on the theory of utterance closed with considerations on the effectivity of the comic, of which the bare essential is the production of subject positions for the speaker and the audience – which involve a kind of commitment – and the production of a position for the butt. In each case the positions are subordinate to the logic of the absurd. The production of subject positions is necessarily implied by the nature of the act of utterance, and thus comic utterance necessarily produces the subject positions of the absurd. These general principles tell us how the comic exercises its effectivity, but we still need to know what this effectivity is.

At one level it is a question of what a joke is about. In an interview in 1983 comedian Jasper Carrott describes seeing a performance by his fellow comedian Alexei Sayle:

> And it was like hitting me between the eyes with a red-hot poker. I mean, the things he was talking about! He cracked a joke about 'I've got my own personal charity – it's called "Save a London Child, Kill a Social Worker",' and there was this immense roar from the audience. I remember thinking, you can't do a joke like *that*. Not and get a laugh.

This story implies many things about the choice of comic material. Obviously it illustrates a principle put forward in general terms in the previous chapter: excessive contentiousness produces offence instead of humour, excessive politeness produces boredom; one of the arts demanded of the comedian is the ability to tread this dividing line. But it is possible to go further than this. The immense roar that made Jasper Carrott think derived from two sources, one would guess: firstly from novelty, secondly from the high level of aggression the joke contains; the two are not entirely separable since it is in part the level of aggression that is responsible for the novelty, but it is nonetheless possible to distinguish analytically between the aggression and the topic of the joke, the thesis that social work is the problem and not the solution. The impact this joke had on Jasper Carrott – it led him to re-evaluate his own act, and to change it – was a product of both aspects of it, of course, but it is significant (at least for our purposes, if not for Jasper Carrott's) that the non-comic thesis implied by the joke is in part responsible for its impact. This thesis is expressed in the mode of the absurd: the proposition 'Kill a Social Worker' is monstrously implausible as (if carried out) it would represent the maximum possible level of moral infraction, but it is plausible to the extent that if the thesis about the danger of social work is correct, it would indeed be a small part of a potential solution. The impact of the joke is probably a product of the fact that the audience had not clearly thought out for itself the thesis which is its presupposition, and thus found itself confronted simultaneously with the thesis and its absurd version. It is of course the absurdity of the proposition that makes it funny, but it is nonetheless the novelty of the topic, the serious thesis, that is partially responsible for the joke's impact – and Jasper Carrott's re-evaluation of his act as a result.

By the same token, circumstances may make it necessary for a comedian to drop certain topics from his repertoire. In the same interview Jasper Carrott explains his decision in the early 1970s to refrain from jokes about stupid Irishmen, and more recently from sexist jokes. In each case the decision was caused by the commitment not to offend a particular group, and by the evaluation that amusing others in this way was wrong. To select one group as a valid target and to refuse another is, in some sense of the word, a political act (even though Jasper Carrott refuses any particular political alignment), and it is the non-comic identity of the groups in question that is the basis of the decision. Clearly, the identity of the butt of humour, which is something non-comic, is central to the process of humour; but beyond this it is also a question of the attributes attached to the butt, of the discourses evoked in the process of making the butt into a humorous object, which are also – as we have already seen – something non-humorous: for instance, human dignity (pratfalls), monosemy (puns), the aleatory, etc. What is the effect upon such non-comic entities of being brought into the ambit of comedy? Is the result their subversion or their confirmation? Is the result uniform, is it the same in the case of the butt of a joke and in the case of a discourse evoked in order to attach attributes to the butt?

One of the most popular topics for humour is stupidity; such jokes are conventionally, but not inevitably, told about members of ethnic minorities, precisely the kind of joke that Jasper Carrott refuses to do. In these jokes, therefore, it is possible to distinguish between the overt butt of the joke – say, the Irish – and the belief system that is its presupposition: rationality; it is only in so far as we believe that intelligence, or rationality, is a normal attribute of mankind that such jokes are possible. What are the results, both for the belief system and for the butt, of being inscribed in comic utterance?

C. Davies has shown that such jokes are universal in the Western industrialised world, that the same jokes are told about various ethnic minorities, or other 'out groups', in different countries: about Belgians in France and Holland, about Boers in English-speaking South Africa, about Poles in the USA, etc. Davies argues convincingly that such jokes do not derive from racial prejudice, although there can be little doubt that told to or by someone who is racially prejudiced the pleasure of the joke would combine with the prejudice to produce an augmented pleasure. Were final proof needed that there is no *necessary* connection between racial prejudice and such jokes, the Danish convention of ascribing this stupidity to 'men from Århus' (an industrial and university town in the north of Denmark with no other distinguishing features, whose inhabitants are not the subject of any other form of prejudice in Denmark) would be sufficient. This does not of course reduce the degree of offence that such jokes may give to those on the receiving end, and Jasper Carrott's decision is no doubt right, especially given the variety of other forms of prejudice inflicted on the Irish in England. Davies goes beyond these descriptive considerations to ascribe an origin to such jokes, as we saw briefly in the introduction: it is the demands made upon the intelligence by the bureaucratic/rational society we live in – more exactly, the society Max Weber says we live in, since Davies' analysis is dependent upon this traditional sociological thesis. Ethnic stupidity jokes would therefore constitute a form of anxiety reduction by projecting fears about personal inadequacy on to an outsider group.

Clearly, for Davies, the overt butt of such jokes is only marginally implicated in this humour, as their selection is largely a matter of convention; indeed, some of the best stupid Irishman jokes I know have been told to me by an Irish friend who presumably feels in no way metonymically implicated. Moreover, stupidity jokes can easily be told *à propos* some other group: in Jasper Carrott's TV shows their target is *Sun* readers, and in at least one stage performance of *Accidental Death of an Anarchist* they were aimed at the British Royal Family. But it is not obvious what the variability of the target implies. On the one hand it suggests that the butt is irrelevant to the humour, whose main ingredient is the subversion of expectations of rationality; but on the other hand, if the choice of the Irish target can seem purely conventional this is certainly not so when the butt is the Royal Family – here we are in the presence of a deliberate and explicit attempt to implicate the butt in the process of the absurd. If non-conventional butts clearly are implicated, then it follows that the butt always is implicated unless something intervenes to prevent it. In other words, in the case of stupid Irishmen jokes the targeting of the butt has become neutralised, perhaps, through sheer repetition and the source of the pleasure lies entirely in the surprising mixture of plausible and implausible stupidity. But because such behaviour is ridiculous it is then perfectly possible to apply it to a non-conventional butt and under these circumstances the lack of a neutralising mechanism clearly highlights the target.

The discourses evoked in order to provide the butt of a joke with the attributes needed to make it ridiculous are logically distinct from the identity of the butt. This is clear from the empirical fact of jokes without a butt:

A van is driving up the motorway. Every half mile or so the driver stops, gets out, walks to the back of the van and bashes it hard two or three times with a pickaxe handle. Eventually the police spot him, follow him and pull him over to the side. 'Look', says the policeman, 'it's not exactly illegal, but . . . what on earth are you doing – why do you keep on bashing the back of your van?' – 'Well', says the driver, 'this van has a payload of 1½ cwt., and I've got a ton of canaries in there – I've got to keep them flying.'

The solution he has adopted to his problem is sufficiently ingenious to be far more implausible than plausible, but there is no question of there being a butt: this is – to use Freud's terminology – an 'innocent conceptual' joke, one which involves no aggression against a person, an institution, or a value.

This raises the question: what is the relationship between any discourse and its evocation in the form of the absurd? Could we say, for instance, that to evoke a discourse in the mode of the absurd is to commit an act of aggression towards it, to subvert the values it incarnates? There are two possible answers to this question. The first is that the contrary is true, that the evocation of particular discourses as the presupposition of an absurd event – that in terms of which it appears absurd – reinforces these discourses. If an old or ugly woman is made to appear ridiculous by being presented as making sexual advances, this presupposes that female sexuality is passive and associated only with youth and beauty: this is the implied precondition of finding her actions implausible; this conventional discourse is strengthened by its evocation as the presupposition of an absurd event, and to this extent humour would function as part of (sexist) ideology. This is by and large the conclusion reached in the analysis of various British sitcoms in the BFI *Sitcom* dossier.

The second answer is the opposite of the first. A pratfall is implausible in terms of human dignity; it is made plausible on each occasion by whatever causes it – a banana skin, for instance. The implausibility of the fall reinforces the discourse in question, as in the previous example, but the element of plausibility in the action pulls in the opposite direction: if it is plausible (in these circumstances, for this particular reason) that someone should do something undignified, then *to that extent* the portrayal of absurd actions constitutes an attack upon the discourse in terms of which the action is seen as absurd, here the discourse of dignity.[1] If the old woman is seen as absurd in terms of a certain

179

type of female sexuality, a certain discourse about female sexuality, nonetheless the countervailing element of plausibility undermines that discourse and that stereotype: for it consists in saying that there is no conceivable reason why this woman should not have the same sexual needs as any other. Indeed, this is no doubt exactly why such a joke would give offence to feminists: for them the plausibility syllogism would outweigh the implausibility, and the intention, manifest in the use of a stereotype they hate, of making this woman ridiculous would seem to them to implicate, by metonymy, all of womankind.

Both of these opposed answers are correct, but it must be stressed that the logic of the absurd indicates that one of the mechanisms is more significant than the other: implausibility outweighs plausibility in the form of the absurd, and therefore the discursive impact of implausibility is predominant, and the impact of plausibility is distinctly less. Not that this should lead us to disregard the latter, for it is the permanent, contradictory and simultaneous presence of the two syllogisms of plausibility and implausibility that is responsible for the particular impact of humour, and to laugh at something on the grounds of its absurdity is intrinsically to recognise the plausibility of the action as well as its implausibility; it is for this reason, as we have seen, that comedy is capable of being offensive.

We are now in a position to return to the role of the butt and ethnic stupidity jokes. To take an example:

A man from Århus goes to the cinema in Copenhagen to see a John Wayne film. During its course his neighbour taps him on the knee and says 'I bet you 100 kroner that John Wayne gets captured in the next five minutes' – 'Okay, you're on', says the man from Århus. Sure enough, three minutes later, John Wayne is ambushed and caught. 'Pay up', says the neighbour, and the man from Århus shakes his head ruefully and gives him 100 kroner. At the end of the film the neighbour taps him on the knee again and says 'Look, I can't take your money – I've seen the film already' – 'Oh, so have I', says the man from Århus, 'but I didn't think John Wayne would fall for the same silly trick twice.'

The implausibility derives from the nature of the film, which the man from Århus has failed to understand, thus indicating his stupidity. But it is the source of the plausibility that is more important in the present context. It has two potential sources: firstly, the fact that the man is from Århus, that is, stupid by nature – only such a man would make a blunder like this. The second source of plausibility is that *in a sense* John Wayne does do the same thing twice and to that extent the mistake is comprehensible – it is absurd, not nonsense or insanity. If the element of plausibility derives from the association of stupidity with men from Århus then the butt is heavily implicated as the object of comic aggression. But if the element of plausibility derives entirely from the novel interpretation of film, then the inhabitants of Århus are not implicated – and notice that neither of these interpretations increases the plausibility for in either case the event is equally more implausible.

What is perhaps most likely is that both sources of plausibility make a contribution, and in these circumstances the thesis advanced earlier makes sense: the conventional introduction of such jokes ('Did you hear the one about the man from Århus who . . . ?) would merely serve to call attention to the nature of the plausibility asserted in the punch line, and in this analysis would not implicate the apparent butt. Moreover, the sheer implausibility of the attributes attached to the butt may well militate against its serious implication in the alleged absurdity: to suggest that the man from Århus could actually misunderstand the nature of film, or to suggest that Reagan could really mistake nuclear war for Hollywood settlers and Indians, is to suggest something so implausible that any serious implication is unlikely. However, the opposite is equally possible: that this generalised, conventional stupidity is really felt to be attached to the butt even though the specific attribute in question may not be taken to apply.

That humour is intrinsically paradoxical is now clear. One side of its process – the implausibility syllogism – reinforces the discourse in terms of which the event is plausible; the other side tends in the opposite direction, its subversion. The butt is implicated in the absurd because he/she/it is an actant of the utterance, but the degree of such implication is far from certain, and this because of the play of plausibility and implausibility which is the basis of the process.

Thus semiotic theory is capable of explaining the impasses of commonsense and sociological theory referred to earlier. Regardless of the specifics of the joke in question, humour is both subversive and conservative, offensive and inoffensive, serious and ridiculous; it is its nature as semiotic process that ensures that this is so, and thus semiotics demonstrates why common sense is both paradoxical and correct in this instance. Common sense, however, would also assert that two opposed propositions cannot both be correct, but semiotics reveals that in the case of humour, because of its specific nature, this can in fact be so. And semiotics goes further: by revealing the inherently contradictory nature of humour, it points to the possibility of different subject positions that can be taken up by different audiences for humour. Although the appreciation of humour necessarily involves seeing the action in question as intrinsically more implausible than plausible, the ambiguity that derives from implausibility undermines the line between the implausible action and the butt of the joke. Perhaps the best example of this process is self-deprecating humour, where the joke consists in attaching an action that is implausible to oneself, or to some aspect of one's personality, such as one's belief system. Under these circumstances, the implausibility of the action makes it possible for the joker to assert that X is an aspect of his presence in the world, and yet not to believe it. When I was insulted by an aggressive football fan ('You look a right prat!') my answer ('That's because I am one') was just such an attribution: I attached an unflattering attribute to my persona, but clearly did not believe it; neither, I imagine, did any of the audience think that I believed it, even if they themselves did believe it.

Thus the logic of the absurd points to a variety of possible subject positions in a humorous statement. The intrinsic ambiguity that derives from implausibility makes it possible for any given audience either to consider that the action in question really does belong to the butt, or to regard the attribution as unreal, perhaps – as in the case of stupid Irishmen jokes – because the attribution is largely conventional. However, it may be that the type of jokes we have so far considered is not a random selection, and that these conclusions would not necessarily follow when derived from a different range of examples. In this respect it is interesting to compare a joke where racial insult is clearly intended, to a joke where it is questionable whether it is or not.

Firstly, a joke from *The Two Ronnies*: 'What do you get if you cross an aborigine with a plumber?' – 'A boomerang that says it will come back in the morning.' The butt, of course, is not aborigines, but plumbers, and the joke is part of that British tradition of jokes directed at people who do not do their jobs 'properly' – that is, to the satisfaction of those who employ them. But the humour derives from the absurdity of the attribute attached to the boomerang, not the attack on the plumber, and on the way the joke uses the well-known relationship between aborigines and boomerangs as a precondition of the joke's structure. One way of interpreting this joke would be to assert that the association of aborigines and boomerangs acts to reinforce a racial stereotype, the association of aborigines with the exotic and the primitive. Whether it in fact has this effect will no doubt depend upon the audience in question, and especially on the type of knowledge that they have of aborigine civilisation; nonetheless, it is clear that all other things being equal, it would indeed tend to do just this. Similarly with the hapless plumber (who metonymically implicates the working class as producers in general): the commonsense 'knowledge' that plumbers are not prepared to work late enough to finish the job is a precondition of the joke's structure, and it is in this form that plumbers are implicated as the butt. The essential point here is that in both cases what is asserted about aborigines and plumbers is entirely plausible – indeed, in the case of aborigines it is even true – and that the implausibility which is responsible for the joke's humour does not directly apply to either: it applies to the boomerang. In this instance the effectiveness of the joke in attacking its butt lies in the indirectness of the attack, in the use of the derogatory attribute as a precondition of the joke.

The second joke was told to me by someone I knew to be a racist, and in it the intention of racial insult is absolutely unequivocal:

A civil rights worker goes to Mississippi to investigate reports of racial assaults upon blacks in the area. One day he is taken by a sheriff to observe the investigation into the death of a black man found drowned. When they get to the river where he was found, it turns out the body is wound round with an enormous weight of steel chain. 'There you are!' says the civil rights worker. 'Try and deny that he was murdered and thrown in the river!'

'Damn fool!' says the sheriff. 'Trying to swim the river with all those chains he's stolen.'

The sheriff's interpretation is implausible for two reasons: firstly, nobody is sufficiently stupid to do what he says, for even if the man had in fact stolen the chains and did in fact try to swim the river with an excess weight, there is nothing in the situation to prevent him from escaping; secondly, everything in the preparation stage of the joke indicates that we are not meant to believe that his interpretation is correct, nor even that he himself believes it. Correspondingly, the sheriff's interpretation has an element of plausibility that derives from the stereotypical association of blacks and theft. Clearly this stereotype is plausible to racists: is it plausible to anyone else, or does finding it plausible necessarily implicate anyone who does so in racism? Probably so, and this implies that anyone who finds it funny is not totally immune, at the very least, to racial stereotypes. Thus the joke incarnates a racist insult by implying that any inane explanation of a black man's death is good enough, and in this process it is the absurdity of what the sheriff says that is central. But we should note another feature of this joke: it was told to me by someone I knew to be a racist, and therefore it was not difficult to interpret the joke as a racist insult. But it is possible, perhaps, that the same joke could be told by a black comedian, and used as an insult directed at white racism: here the inanity of the sheriff's 'explanation' would take on a different meaning, and in this process too it would be the process of the absurd that was responsible for the attribution of this meaning.

What we can learn from these examples is that the logic of the absurd is capable of producing a series of different subject positions for an audience *vis-à-vis* the butt of the joke. The most effective attacks are likely to be those in which the insulting attribute of the butt is assumed as a precondition of the joke, for here, typically, the insulting attribute seems entirely plausibly attached to the butt. Where the insulting attribute is attached to the butt in the mode of implausibility – as in the case in the joke against Reagan (' . . . wagons in the circle') – it is very easy to mentally separate the attribute and the butt, and therefore the attack is so much the less effective. But we should add to this that the identity of the speaker and the audience are essential: the audience must accept that what is asserted to be plausible and implausible in fact are such, and refusal to accept this will result in comic failure, often in the form of finding the joke insulting rather than funny. Which of these possibilities in fact occurs is beyond the scope of semiotic analysis, for it is a matter of the empirical circumstances in question – the identity of the actual speaker and actual audience – and only properly sociological analysis would be capable of dealing with these circumstances. However, although that is beyond the chosen scope of the present essay, it is at least possible to give some schematic indication of how such an answer might be sought.

C.E. Schutz cites an American political joke:

> A little old lady felt very strongly about NOT going to the polls and expressing a preference for candidates. She stated: 'I never vote, it only encourages them' (*Political Humor*, p.292).

The punch line of this joke also appeared in the form of graffiti on London walls during the 1983 election campaign, presumably put there either by an anarchist or by someone totally disillusioned by English politics. Schutz interprets this joke as being about ignorance: to him the old lady is stupid in her 'perverse irrationality', but the joke can also be interpreted, he suggests, to contain the message that 'when ignorant people vote, it does encourage ignorant politicians to respond to their ignorance with ignorant government'. My personal interpretation of the graffiti version of the punch line alone was that it was about justified cynicism and perhaps about a viable political tactic: how much validity would a government have if elected on a minuscule turnout? Far from revealing ignorance, the punch line would reveal a depth of political wisdom.

Let us discard the possibility that either (or both) Schutz or I are wrong about why we laugh: it is axiomatic that people's interpretation of their laughter (where it exists) is authoritative. The implication is therefore that Schutz and I laughed, genuinely, for different reasons: there are, in short, different ways of finding this joke absurd and therefore funny, and these different ways correspond *grosso modo* with different cultural values. Schutz is explicit about his commitment to Parliamentary democracy, and my political values are perfectly compatible with a high degree of cynicism about elections in England in the late twentieth century. If this principle is applied to jokes about Irish stupidity, it is clear that the evaluation of such jokes, the way in which or the reasons for which such jokes are found funny will vary with the culture of the audience. Freud's *Jokes* is full of Jewish jokes, which he evidently enjoyed, despite or perhaps because of his Jewishness. The same jokes told by a Nazi would clearly have a very different meaning, because the discourse mobilised in the joke form (ethnic characteristics) means something different in the two contexts.

Thus semiotics is not capable of telling us whether jokes about Irish stupidity contribute to racial prejudice against the Irish. What it is capable of telling us is how it can be that under certain circumstances – to be specified sociologically – such a process may occur, and why it is that no general conclusions on the subject can be reached. However, jokes about ethnic stupidity may not be a very far-reaching example to use in this context. If what we are seeking is some general formulation about the effectivity of the absurd, then it may be better to use examples where it is not possible to separate the message from the butt in the way in which it is usually possible in stupidity jokes, by regarding the apparent butt as merely a comic convention. In the cartoons illustrated such separation is not possible: the humour derived from the Tory faith healer, the Socialist faith healer and the Socialist Tradesperson is in each case inseparable from their actual political butts at the time of publication. Indeed, within the absurdity of the comic figures there is a tiny core of seriousness: Conservatism does not work, Socialism does. Or rather, more exactly, in each case the element of plausibility which balances the implausibility and makes the cartoons funny and not just nonsense derives from the presupposition that these political values operate. Of course, these 'demonstrations' that Socialism is superior to Conservatism are absurd: that is the whole point, that is why they are funny, and also why they are intensely ambiguous – a Socialist is as likely to find them offensive as a Conservative, for they could as easily be interpreted as a mockery of Socialism as its opposite. Nonetheless, the attitudes towards Socialism and Conservatism are distinguishable: the element of plausibility in the Norman Fowler cartoon is the Socialist belief that Tory health policies increase suffering and benefit only the rich, whereas the element of plausibility in the Socialist faith healer strip is the measure of faith in future possibility that all socialists must have.

Guardian, December 1983 © Steve Bell

187

A second example:

A man has a job as a lorry-driver's mate – loading up, occasional
relief driving, navigation, etc. And he is very depressed. His wife has
just left him, taking the kids with her, and they don't seem to like
him very much. He's dossing on people's floors because he can't
afford a room and can't get a council flat. And this morning he's got
a hangover as well. It's a beautiful morning and they're driving over
a viaduct over a wide estuary; the sun is gleaming on the water, sea-
gulls are wheeling and screaming overhead. The whole world seems
tasteless, and he looks at the height of the viaduct and he thinks
'Why not? Let's end it all now.' So he opens the cab door and jumps:
wheee . . . eee . . . eee . . . splat! And down he goes into the water,
barely conscious, waiting to die. Suddenly he realises that there's
somebody else in the water with him, pulling him back up to the surface, so he fights to stay down; but he's too weak, and they get him
to the surface. He splutters to the other man, 'Don't try to save me!'
'I'm not trying to save you!' says the other. 'Where do you work?'

In this joke the element of plausibility derives from the idea that unemployment breeds inhuman desperation, and as a result this otherwise monstrously implausible situation has a grain of truth about it. If
we examine it in the same terms as the previous jokes, we can see what
gives it its particular impact: the only conceivable butt is unemployment and what it does to people, since the 'rescuer' is totally anonymous, and therefore the implausibility of the situation cannot be laid at
the door of any other butt. As a result, it is impossible not to privilege
the origin of the plausibility in one's reaction. We should add to this
that the structure of the punch line is such as to urgently demand an
explanation (why does he ask where the man works?) and to allow only
one conceivable explanation. No doubt this is only a partial analysis, in
the sense that much of the joke's force derives from its blackness: the
implausibility derives from the proposition that the norms of sociability,
or solidarity, have indeed weakened to a quite remarkable extent, and
if this joke causes offence in some, it will no doubt be because they
can only see the logic of its implausibility, and cannot appreciate the
countervailing force of the element of plausibility. However, the cen-

tral point remains: in order to appreciate this joke it is essential to accept that unemployment can indeed produce such results – although whether this necessarily means that the person who laughs at the situation will also care very much about it is another matter, and one that exceeds the bounds of this essay – at this point one would have to start talking about particular audiences.

No doubt a joke and a few cartoon strips also constitute a slender base for a theory of the effectivity of the absurd, and the rest of this chapter is devoted to more substantial examples: Stanley Kubrick's film *Dr Strangelove or: How I Learned to Stop Worrying and Love the Bomb* (1963) and Dario Fo's stage show *Accidental Death of an Anarchist*. These two texts have been chosen as good examples of 'committed' comedy, that is to say, of comedy which clearly has an explicit non-comic value attached to it, and in each case a value which is also very clearly a political value.

The story of *Dr Strangelove* is relatively simple. An American Air Force General believes that the international Communist conspiracy has already succeeded in undermining the American way of life by fluoridisation of water, which 'rots our precious bodily fluids'; he therefore despatches the nuclear bombers of his command to attack the Soviet Union, using a plan devised to by-pass presidential authority in case a sneak Soviet attack should disrupt the chain of command; part of the plan involves the aircraft setting their radio receivers so that only messages preceded by a coded call sign can be received; only the general in question knows the code. The President orders a military attack on the General's base in order to get the code, and summons the Soviet ambassador to join. in a hot line conversation with the Kremlin, in which he tells the Soviet military how to shoot down their aircraft if they fail to recall them. The General commits suicide, but his executive officer works out the code; all the aircraft but one are successfully recalled. In the meantime, the USSR tell the President that they have installed a Doomsday Machine: a chain of extra-high yield atomic bombs are connected to a computer which is programmed to explode them, and thus surround the entire planet with radio-active dust for ninety years, if anyone invades the USSR; it is also programmed to explode them if anyone tries to tamper with the computer programme in any way. The aircraft which was not recalled cannot be, as a missile at-

189

tack has damaged its radio receiver, and it successfully completes its mission. The American leadership lay plans for a small section of the population to live underground until the radio-activity has cleared away, a section consisting largely of military and political leaders and a large number of beautiful young women, to increase the healthy population as quickly as possible. The film closes with the explosion of the Doomsday Machine, as Vera Lynn sings on the soundtrack 'We'll Meet Again'.

This story has clear links both with debates over the dangers of nuclear weapons and with a recurrent theme in director Stanley Kubrick's work. It is a standard theme in opposition to nuclear weapons that the danger of a war starting by accident is much more significant in the nuclear age than before, since nuclear weapons are machine controlled, response time is necessarily very abbreviated, and the results catastrophic and irreversible. And in other films, as in this one, Kubrick organises a story around machine breakdown. The obvious parallel is *2001*, but in *Clockwork Orange* too one of the themes is the mechanistic treatment of the hero, his reduction to a machine by a society that needs predictable and controllable behaviour. What is significant here is that a comedy film very clearly has a serious 'message' – the dangers of unintended chance catastrophe – which is presented in comic form; this is in part because *Dr Strangelove* is not an exclusively comic film, as we shall see. The focus of this discussion will be the effect that comic form has upon the presentation of a serious message.

In the first place, it is clear that there is a close relationship between the nature of the fundamental situation of the film (the 'machine breakdown' that threatens nuclear catastrophe) and the content of each of the gags that make up the comedy of the film; or – to use the terms of the logic of the absurd – there is a close relationship between the discourses that are mobilised in each gag and the discourses that compose the basic situation of the film. This is best demonstrated in examples.

When the Soviet ambassador is shown into the War Room in the Pentagon, he is assaulted by General Turgidson, who accuses him of trying to photograph secret charts; he replies that the General tried to plant the camera on him. The President is outraged: 'Gentlemen! You can't fight in here! This is the War Room!' Both the plausibility and

the implausibility of this remark derive from discourses that are fundamental to the structure of the plot. It is implausible because of the
identification of 'fight – war', plausible because war needs a high degree of organisation which must be conducted in a calm atmosphere:
in each case what is referred to is something that runs all through the
film – war and planning. In fact the paradoxical relationship between
war and calm, rational behaviour is frequently exploited in the film –
for instance in the hot line conversation between the President and the
Premier of the USSR, in which the President has to warn his Soviet
counterpart that nuclear bombs are on the way: 'Now don't get angry
Dimitri!'

A second example: General Jack Ripper – who dispatched the
bombers – eventually tells his Executive Officer why he is convinced
that the International Communist Conspiracy is undermining America
with fluoridisation: 'It was during the physical act of love', when he
suffered from impotence and was convinced that it was due to im-
purities in his 'precious bodily fluids' put there by Communist fluoride.
This is implausible for all the obvious reasons (lack of connection
between fluoride and impotence, the undesirability of Generals who
think like this), but plausible in so far as looking for excuses for impotence is understandable. This is linked with the general theme of the
film in various ways: in the first place, it is paranoia such as General
Ripper's – albeit that his is a severe case – which has caused the situation in which his action is possible. In the second place, it is the prime
example of machine breakdown – General Turgidson had instituted
Human Reliability Tests precisely in order to avoid this kind of situation. In the third place, the insanity of the general situation portrayed
in the film demands an equally insane explanation in order to keep it at
the level of comedy.

A final example: after General Ripper has committed suicide and
his Executive Officer has worked out the recall code he tries to phone
the President. General Ripper had all communications to and from the
base cut off, but he manages to find a public phone that is still working. However, he does not have the right change to make the call and
cannot remember what the different types of reverse charge calls are
called in America (he is English). The resulting frustration is hilarious:
it is highly implausible because no one ought to have to do this in such

191

a grave situation, but plausible because of Ripper's clampdown and because there is no reason to carry enough change to make a call to Washington when you are Executive Officer of an Air Force base. It is a further example of machine breakdown, the implausibility derives directly from the basic situation of the film, as does the plausibility: in every way this gag is tightly linked into the story as a whole.

This is not to deny that the film also contains many unfunny episodes (deliberately so, not by default): the assault on General Ripper's base has many scenes that are entirely serious, the missile attack on the aircraft is completely devoid of humour as is most of their successful attempt to deliver their bombs. Indeed, the bomber's 'successful' conclusion to their mission is characterised by a considerable degree of suspense. However, all of these 'serious' sequences are capped by gags: the best example is the bomber's final bomb run, in the course of which they find that the bomb doors are jammed; the Captain goes down to the bomb bay to release them manually, which he does incongruously perched on one of the bombs. As the automatic controls take over and the bomb falls he falls with it, riding it like a bronco, waving his stetson and cheering wildly: the suspense over the success of their mission is obliterated in the hilarity of its final moment.

We are now in a position to reconsider the question put at the beginning of this chapter: what is the result of using a specifically comic form to put across a political point? At a superficial level, the answer is obvious: the various actants of the story are made to do absurd things, things that are more implausible than plausible; this clearly implies a certain lack of reverence for them, and in so far as they stand in metonymically for real world personae who have authority – or at any rate power – this lack of reverence for the actants of the story may translate into lack of reverence for their real-life counterparts and for the power they wield; whether it actually does so is an empirical sociological question beyond the scope of this essay. However, it should also be stressed that nothing in this lack of reverence as formulated so far ties it specifically to the form of comedy: to make the actants of a story do evil things could induce a similar lack of reverence, perhaps. *The China Syndrome* sets out to achieve just this impact *à propos* a very similar topic. The lack of reverence deriving from the spectacle of evil differs, however, from the lack of reverence derived from comedy in that the former no doubt entails a component or fear lacking in the latter. This much is clear, and semiotics has little advantage over common sense, except in so far as it demonstrates *how* these results are possible.

However, it is possible to go somewhat further. *The China Syndrome* and *Dr Strangelove* are directly comparable not only in so far as they are about nuclear power, but also because both are about system malfunction and how human beings are able or unable to deal with the situations that result. *Dr Strangelove* is a comedy whereas *The China Syndrome* is a melodrama, and it is clear therefore that it is not the basic situation which is responsible for the impact of the films, but the different treatments which the subject is given; this too is obvious, but it has implications which are less so. We have already seen how tightly the various gags that compose the comic impact of *Dr Strangelove* are bound to the central situation, but it would have been better to say from the outset that this tight organisation of the gag themes, this constant mobilisation of an inter-connected set of discourses, is what in fact creates the central situation and, more importantly, creates it *as an absurd situation*. Although the narrative is in part non-comic, as we have seen, in so far as it is comic, and in so far as this comedy derives from certain interlocking themes, it is these intersections in the mode of the absurd, these intersections within the logic of the absurd, that are responsible for what a résumé would call the basic situation of the story. The logic of the comic aspects of the narrative is not that the theme of system breakdown creates the various gags that we have seen, but that the various gags, by mobilising an intersecting set of discourses, create the theme of system breakdown as *a comic theme* (as opposed to creating it in the form of a melodramatic theme, as in *The China Syndrome*). Thus, the film opens with a rolling caption which states that according to the United States Air Force, the situation portrayed in the film is impossible; in the film itself it appears to be part plausible and part implausible (the plausibility is augmented by the non-comic aspects, or episodes of the film) because each element of it is subjected to the logic of the absurd.

There are still further conclusions that are to be derived from considering the relations between politics and comedy in this light, but as they are to be conceived at a more general level, and will not apply only to *Dr Strangelove* but to the generality of such texts, they can be left until the analysis of another text has provided more examples.

Accidental Death of an Anarchist is a text which exists in various forms. It was originally a play written and performed by Dario Fo and Franca Rame in Italy, but has been transferred at least to the English stage, both the 'fringe' and 'West End' versions, and has also been produced on English television (Channel 4, Summer 1983). The two English versions with which I am familiar differ only slightly and such differences do not affect interpretation at the level to be pursued here; it also seems unlikely that differences between English and Italian versions will affect the interpretation, although differences between the performance situation in the two countries are sufficiently basic where this play is concerned to demand some comment.

The play is based on an actual event: a young anarchist was being questioned by the Milan police in the early 1970s and fell from the fifth floor window to his death in the street below. There was considerable suspicion that he was pushed or thrown by the police themselves, a suspicion which official enquiries failed to dispel. In Fo and Rame's version, a 'madman' is being questioned in the same police station some time after the anarchist's death, charged with impersonating a psychiatrist. While there he manages to impersonate another police officer and set his questioner at loggerheads with him; on hearing that a judge is arriving from Rome to conduct an official enquiry into the anarchist's death he decides to impersonate the judge and conduct the enquiry himself. He reveals very quickly that the official version of the event is riddled with contradictions; pretending to help the anarchist's interrogators construct a new sanitized version, he in fact leads them to invent more and more absurd scenarios.

At this point a Communist journalist enters, to interview the policemen; she reveals further contradictions in their stories. As the police were unwilling to admit that an enquiry was being conducted, the 'judge' poses as a ballistics expert for the benefit of the Communist journalist. Enter the policeman who was originally questioning the 'madman', and who realises that the ballistics expert is phoney; but since the other police do not want his 'real' identity (as judge) revealed in front of the journalist, they shut their colleague up every time he tries to denounce the 'ballistics expert', who by this time has acquired a bomb. In the confusion about identities, the most recently arrived policeman (who was not involved in the death of the anarchist) hand-cuffs the other two to pillars in the room. The madman/judge/ballis-tics expert manages to handcuff the last policeman as well, by which time he has been recognised by both the policeman who originally in-terrogated him, and the Communist journalist, who reveals that he is a 'Trotskyist extremist agitator'. He sets his bomb to go off in three min-utes and has a political argument with the Communist, in which she accuses him of inhumanity and he denounces the police as scum who deserve no better, alleging the coup against Allende as an example of how dangerous it is to leave thugs alive. He exits, giving the keys to the journalist, telling her to make up her mind whether she wants them to live or not. She hesitates, then leaves; the police are killed in the ex-plosion. The madman then reappears and explains that in the interests of a balanced presentation there is an alternative ending: the journalist releases the policemen, who then handcuff her, on the grounds that she now knows too much, and leave her to die.

The play is much more farcical than *Dr Strangelove* and contains el-ements of slapstick only marginally relevant to the central concern of the piece (the three policemen and the judge doing a mime of a train and breaking into 'Chattanooga Choo Choo', for instance). However, the plot is based upon three devices which enable the farce to have a minimum measure of plausibility: in the first place, the tradition of the 'divine fool', which enables us to accept that the 'madman' can attempt and succeed where no one else could; secondly, the device of the ju-dicial enquiry provides a framework in which essential information can be given and pressure put on the police; lastly, the device of journal-istic investigation plays the same role. None of these devices have any necessary connection with comedy, and just as the basic situation of *Dr Strangelove* was not in itself comic and had to be created through the comic construction of its constituent episodes, so too in *Anarchist*; indeed, its non-comic message is every bit as serious as that of *Dr Strangelove:* that the state, and especially the police, see their role as unconstrained by the law and are completely beyond control by the democratic process.

The general structure of the comedy in *Anarchist* is this: the police are invited to give an account of what happened that is sufficiently plausible to be the official published one; to do this it mut fit with the known facts. The versions they in fact construct are utterly implausible. Thus the middle section of the play, for example, turns around the question of whether the anarchist was depressed before he died, which is what the first official version of events stated; if he was depressed, why was he? Had the police been maltreating him? It turns out that they claimed he was responsible for a bomb at a railway station, and that they confronted him with manufactured evidence including a fake confession from one of his friends. This they feel unable to admit, and invent another scenario in which the anarchist is perfectly happy: because he is a railway worker they imagine remembering their childhood toy train sets, singing together, giving the anarchist a shoulder massage to relieve his stiffness, which by mistake turns into a karate chop to the neck, telling him funny stories which provoke gales of mirth, etc. Each of the components of this scenario is funny in itself – usually in the form of exaggeration – and their collective implausibility adds up to a massive indictment of the cover-up of which the police are clearly guilty.

The scenario is doubly implausible: in the first place it is comically implausible, in the sense that each contributory component is more implausible than plausible; and in the second place it is implausible that any policeman would actually give a moment's thought to trying to invent something so insane. For example: after discussing how it was possible for the anarchist to get half-way across a large room with three policemen in it, and over a four foot high windowsill, all without the four managing to stop him, it emerges that one of the four nearly managed to save him, catching him by the foot as he fell out of the window – his shoe came off in his hand. 'Wonderful!' says the 'judge': positive proof that they tried to save him; now there is no problem with an acceptable official account – provided the anarchist had three feet, for witnesses are quite positive that the body on the pavement below had two shoes on. The judge's irony explodes the police story, of course, but they try to invent a set of circumstances in which the presence of three shoes would in fact be explained: for instance, perhaps the anarchist had one foot much smaller than the other, which led him to wear an undershoe, and it was the overshoe that had come off as he fell – a truly monstrous implausibility, whose countervailing plausibility derives only from the fact that this extraordinary hypothesis would indeed explain the embarrassing third shoe, if it were possible.

The sheer implausibility of the explanation that is being offered has two functions: in the first place, its function is to cause laughter, by its place in the logic of the absurd; in the second place, it indicates the likely guilt of the policemen. But the explanation is not only implausible, it is also partially plausible, as we have just seen, and the plausibility is as much part of the political denunciation as the implausibility: if the implausibiity indicates the truth, the tiny element of plausibility underlines the fact that the police actually are looking for an explanation that could hold water in public. This is a tactic that Fo and Rame pursue through much of the play. The journalist asks the police to explain why they called an ambulance five minutes before the anarchist's death; the superintendent's response is 'So it's wrong to take precautions now, is it?' Again the comic implausibility is paralleled by a second layer in which the implausibility of the situation alleged (they were only being prudent) denounces the real situation (the anarchist was already in need of an ambulance). And in this instance too plausibility plays a part: the superintendent needs an explanation that makes sense, and he is trying very hard to find one.

The importance of the countervailing element of plausibility is shown with particular clarity in another gag: the ridicule of the third shoe provokes an acrimonious argument between the two senior policemen, each of whom thinks that the other is trying to pin all the blame on him alone: in the course of the argument the truth emerges (the anarchist was pushed). The argument is hilarious, for policemen are not meant to indulge in the kind of scurrilous accusation and counter-accusation that constitutes it, but there is no sense in which the implausibility of the situation denounces the reality: the implausibility makes it funny, but the political impact (these men really are unscrupulous thugs) derives from our certainty that their bad temper and lack of solidarity has led them to reveal the truth by mistake; in other words it is the tiny measure of plausibility in the situation – their bad temper – that gives the gag its political impact.

No doubt this political impact is somewhat diminished for an English audience: after all, it is a farce about stupid, evil *Italian* policemen, not about their English equivalents, and this is no doubt part of the explanation of *Anarchist*'s West End success – we may doubt whether it would have been as acceptable to a mainstream theatre audience if it had been about the police and army in Ulster. On the other hand, the play is carefully constructed so as to get the audience's sympathy at the beginning on the side of the clown who eventually turns out to be anything but a fool: his capers in the first ten minutes or so are non-controversial. In any event, the play had sufficient impact to prevent Dario Fo being allowed into the USA to perform; which he no doubt took as a compliment, if an inconvenient one; the ban has since been lifted.

We are now in a position to attempt a general answer to the questions about the effectivity of the absurd persistently posed, and as persistently deferred, in this essay. In the first place, a caveat: no attempt will be made to assess the actual effects of any piece of humour, for that is something that can only be examined in the context of particular situations. What we are discussing is not the actual effects, the efficacity, of humour, but its effectivity, that is to say, the form of pressure that humour exercises in any situation in which it is brought into play. This effectivity will then, in any given empirical situation, interact with all the other pressures that are in play in that situation, and the overall result will not be ascribable to the form of humour alone. From this caveat results a second restriction: the impact of any particular piece of humour would depend upon the discourses it mobilised, and in particular their degree of contentiousness for the audience in question, as much as upon the general form of humour, that is, upon the logic of the absurd. The decision not to examine any individual pieces of humour in this way involves restricting the analysis to the effectivity of the form of humour alone, of the logic of the absurd alone. The question to be asked therefore is this: what is the result of mobilising a discourse, or discourses – any discourses – in the form of the absurd?

We know that the essence of the form of the absurd is the combination of plausibility and implausibility, unequally balanced in favour of greater implausibility. Therefore, the key to our question must be: what is the result of mobilising discourses in such a way as to present any given person or event as more implausible than plausible? The results of such presentation are twofold.

In the first place, the attribution to a person or an institution of something more implausible than plausible necessarily involves defining an attitude towards that person which is less than reverent, an attitude which is essentially negative. Of course, the degree of this negativity is subject to great variation, from the hatred that underlies *Accidental Death of an Anarchist* to the gentle irony of certain sitcoms, such as *Butterflies*; nonetheless, the principle is general and clear. In this moment of negativity one of the essential components of the political process occurs: the statement of opposition. For political opposition does not consist essentially in the rational criticism of one's opponents – central though this may be to political success – it consists essentially in the will to oppose, the will to say 'No'. Thereafter it may well be necessary to define the grounds of such opposition, but the essential moment is the simple recognition that one does not want *that*, that what one wants is something different: the essential moment is no more than the will to opposition. To mark something with the indelible seal of ridicule is intrinsically to indicate the will to oppose it – even though it may be a very short-lived act of will.

This may sound like an over-valuation of the comic. However, it is only one moment in the definition of the effectivity of the absurd. The second moment is far more ambiguous. As we have already seen, to attribute something implausible to someone or some institution makes it difficult to believe in an intrinsic connection between the two, whence the possibility of laughing at something you believe in, and the possibility of self-deprecating laughter. On the other hand, the sheer implausibility of what is attributed disarms criticism. When one of the policemen in *Anarchist* suggests that the anarchist may have had one foot significantly smaller than the other, and that this would explain the unfortunate third shoe, he does something enormously implausible. If anyone responds, defending the police – the real police – by saying 'But policemen don't do that sort of thing', the obvious answer (between guffaws) is 'Of course not!'; rational criticism becomes impossible, hence the well-known principle that the only effective response to a joke at your expense is to cap it with another.

Why should this be so? In the first place, answering a joke seriously involves a change of register and invites the accusation 'Can't you take a joke?' But we already know that the chief element in the emotional tone of a joke derives precisely from the logic of the absurd, for that is what is responsible for the pleasure of humour, and therefore the fact that a serious answer involves a change of register is ascribable to the logic of the absurd; therefore it is no solution to the problem of why a joke is unanswerable. Therefore it is a question of the formal properties of the absurd, and the results of casting a representation of the world in this form. Two elements seem relevant. In the first place, a feature that jokes share with metaphor: closure. Any metaphor or any joke is a self-contained entity, in the sense that its meaning depends in the first instance on the internal relationship between its components. To take a simple example: Bob Hope's crack at Doris Day's expense about pre-virginity. The impact of this gag depends upon the relationship between 'before' and 'virgin', which is estabished within the syntagm. And the same is essentially true of any joke: at the punch line we feel that all the elements of the narrative that prepared this punch line have been brought into a satisfactory relationship with each other and with the punch line itself – at last we can understand where the story was heading.

The same is true of metaphor: Hamlet's 'slings and arrows of outrageous fortune' has an impact because of the way the two elements in the metaphor mutually support each other (this is in part a question of the rhythm of the line too) and only make sense in terms of their relationship to each other. A metaphor, or a joke, is a single unit of meaning in a way that is not true of an ordinary statement of predication – 'the table is brown', for instance – for here the terms are easily dissociable and replaceable. We can easily imagine an alternative predication such as 'the table is blue', or 'the earth is brown', whereas 'I knew Doris Day before she was twenty/a star/a philatelist' simply ceases to be a joke. It is no doubt for this reason that seventeenth and eighteenth-century criticism did not make a fundamental distinction between metaphor and humour, using the word 'wit' as a category which included areas of both, and that Pope's definition ('Nature to advantage dress'd', etc.) is focused primarily on the question of impact and how it is achieved.

The second feature of the form of the gag that is relevant here is the question of the balance between plausibility and implausibility. The absurd consists of a predication that is more implausible than it is plausible, as we know. Now the result of such a predication is that what is attached to the butt of the joke is an action, or attribute, that *cannot be*, and that precisely because it is fundamentally implausible: it cannot be that Doris Day *became* a virgin, yet this is precisely the attribute that she is saddled with in Bob Hope's crack, and it is plausible that it should be so because of her professional image – plausible despite the fact that it is also impossible. What can one do when accused of something that cannot be, that is, of something that has hit the maximum in irrationality? The answer is of course: nothing – or rather nothing rational, for a rational response to such a predication has no point of contact with what is predicated.

But it is necessary to go further: what is attributed in humour is not only implausible, it is also plausible; the policeman's explanation of the third shoe has an element of plausibility about it, therefore it is slightly likely that the policeman would say this, and thus the implausible action is all the more firmly embedded in the character. The plausibility of the action attaches it to the actant, the implausibility makes rational defence against this attribution impossible – or at any rate irrelevant and churlish, liable to attract the response 'What's the matter, can't you take a joke?': in this combination lies the source of the abrasive power of comedy. On the other hand, the massive implausibility of the attribution makes a link between the joke victim *qua* joke victim and the real referent in the outside world extremely problematic, as we have already seen. Hence the inherent ambiguity of the form of the comic: there is no way of going beyond this logical impasse, in which two contradictory alternatives seem equally true, for it is the contradictory nature of the process of the absurd that makes it inevitable that this contradiction should in fact be an immanent feature of the effectivity of the absurd.

More exactly, there is no way in which the semiotic study of the comic is capable of taking us beyond this impasse: at this point empirical studies of particular pieces of humour in the context of particular audiences is obliged to take over, for it is ultimately the nature of the audience which settles the question. If a particular audience is already ill-disposed towards the butt of a joke, then it will no doubt be inclined to accept the attribution of something absurd to the butt of the joke (an actant of the utterance); if the audience is not so disposed, then this logic is no longer compelling. This is not to suggest that this is the only relevant variable in the audience – clearly the question of the contentiousness of the discourses mobilised is also pertinent; this consideration should be taken only as an example. What semiotics is capable of telling us is how and why the process of humour is ambiguous in this way.

Notes

1. This is the logical underpinning of the defence of comedy (and various humorous institutions such as the Feast of Fools) traditional throughout the Middle Ages and the Renaissance: comedy and other forms of absurd behaviour served to remind mankind of its eminent fallibility ('the folly that is in us all'). The most famous example lis in Gerson's attack on the Feast of Fools in 1400, where he considers this thesis in order to refute it. See E. K. Chambers, *The Medieval Stage*, v.I, p.292.

10

Conclusions

In the previous chapter we have seen how the forms of political impact
– or effectivity – of which humour is capable are necessarily premissed
upon the mechanism which is fundamental to humour, the logic of the
absurd: essentially, we have seen that the ambivalence which necessarily results from the logic of the absurd implies no very strong commitment to the act of mockery – which is what makes self-mockery, for
example, possible. We are now in a position to extend this analysis
in the direction of the relationship between humour and culture in
general.

Our starting point is the notion of humour as a practice, in the Al-
thusserian sense: the transformation of a given raw material in order to
produce a given end product. Here the raw materials would be the
minimum semantic units of the various signifying systems, the end
product would be humour, and the practice would therefore be the
process incarnated in the logic of the absurd – the act of bringing-
together in a way more implausible than plausible. At first sight such a
formulation appears to acknowledge only the moment of production,
and implicitly exclude the moment of consumption, which we know to
be central to the process of humour. However, as Marx points out
(*Grundrisse*, p.92) the production of a commodity creates not only an
object for a subject (some thing for the benefit of someone), but also a
subject for an object – someone whose characteristics are such that
that object is useful for them: thus the consumer is implicated in the
moment of production as that sort of person who is able to benefit
from that category of object. What this implies about humour is that in
common with any other practice, the logic of the absurd must be exer-

cised in the context of a social situation of some sort, a situation composed of both producer and consumer, whether a formally designated comic situation such as a broadcast comedy show, or the informal ones of daily conversation and joke-telling.

Thus apparently we are in the presence of two practices: the logic of the absurd (the creation of humour abstracted from any social situation), and the application of this process to a social situation, whatever it might be. This separation, we might add, is written directly into academic studies of humour: sociology (and sometimes psychology) studying the application to the social situation, psychology, literary and film criticism studying the creation of humour in the abstract. However, in reality, we are in the presence of a single practice, for humour is inconceivable outside of some social situation or other, and this is written into its very structure. The distribution of roles in humour – event and spectator; or the speaker, the listener and the butt – is intrinsic to the structure of humour and is simultaneously the presence within humour of a social situation. That is to say, the enunciation of humour is simultaneously and inextricably a signifying process and a social process together.

This principle is rich in consequences. In the first place it enables us to ask what the logic of the absurd is capable of explaining. In the first chapter of this book we saw that current theorising on the subject of humour and comedy turned predominantly around two areas of debate:

- is humour something negotiated or something immanent to the moment of humorous arousal?

- should the analysis of humorous texts be based on minimum or maximum units of analysis?

The option pursued here was for analysis based on minimum units and the supposition that humour was immanent to humorous artefacts. Have the preceding pages justified this choice?

We have seen that it has been possible to isolate a mechanism – the logic of the absurd – that appears to be immanent to humour, and specific to it, and whose operations we have been able to observe in a wide range of examples. The first strength of this mechanism as an analytic tool is that it explicitly relates what goes on in the individual gag directly to other features of signifying systems: firstly, to the paradigms that give meaning to words and images; secondly, to the flow of the discourse and narrative within which the gag appears; thirdly, to the speaking subject, the person whose 'intention to amuse' is the focus of much psychological (in the broadest sense) theorising. As a result, this mechanism manages to by-pass many of the difficulties encountered by other models of the process of humour. In the first place, where the place of humour in narrative is concerned, we have seen that the individual gag can be articulated on to narrative flow in a series of different ways, all of them describable on the basis of the logic of the absurd because of this mechanism's inherent ambiguity. Thus all the problems about whether comedy interrupts narrative or not disappear – sometimes it does, sometimes it does not, depending upon the nature of the articulation between the logic of the absurd and the wider narrative framework. By the same token, the question of minimum or maximum unit analysis is solved: the use of a minimum unit is perfectly compatible with analyses based upon the notion of a comic rhythm, or any other conception of how narrative as a whole functions, since the logic of the absurd postulates only that this mechanism must be articulated in some manner or other on to a narrative, if there is in fact a narrative beyond the internal structure of the individual gag itself which is already a mini-narrative in its own right: a 'single event narrative', as the theory of narratology would have it.

The question of whether humour is immanent or negotiated is more complex. We have already seen, in Chapter 1, the logical objections to the idea that it is nothing but a process of negotiation: this would entail thinking of humour as totally random. But at the same time, the question of comic failure poses problems that must be faced by any theory operating in this area, for if humour is essentially immanent to the artefacts (jokes, gags, situations) in question, then one would expect responses to them to be universal; and yet we know from everyday experience that this is not so.

What are the possible causes for comic failure? Offensiveness, caused either by the topic of the joke or its occasion; incomprehension; banality – poor comic performance or invention; lack of receptiveness on the part of the audience – 'I'm sorry, I'm not in the mood for jokes', for example. Can these mechanisms be explained by the logic of the absurd? If they can, this would constitute the second strength of this notion as an analytic tool – the first was the relation it necessarily draws between gags and discursive contexts. Clearly offensiveness can be so explained: the logic of the absurd postulates that humour functions by bringing discourses into relation with each other, in an absurd way, and it is not difficult to understand that making topic X absurd, or making topic X absurd on such-and-such an occasion, or making anything absurd on such-and-such an occasion (say, a funeral) would cause offence to someone to whom that topic or that occasion deserved only serious treatment or behaviour. In each of these cases, the ground of the offence is that the process of the absurd (the creation of levity) is inappropriate.

Banality can be accounted for in the logic of the absurd by referring either to the fact that the joke in question is so hackneyed that it has lost its power of arousal for the audience in question, if not for other audiences – it no longer seems to them to contradict anything or to cause any surprise – or because the topic of the joke, the discourse or discourses, have no real meaning for the audience in question. The joke used earlier about Prague in 1968 ('not fraternally . . . 50/50!') rarely pleases anyone in Britain or the USA except those who have some experience of left-wing politics. In Europe, and especially Eastern Europe, it is far more widely appreciated; it is not that Britons and Americans don't understand it, but that the subject apparently does not matter enough to them. Lack of receptiveness is more difficult: the only reasonable hypothesis (reasonable from the point of view of the logic of the absurd, that is!) is that the meanings attached to different topics and to different activities vary with mood, and that under some circumstances the act of levity just does not make any sense.

What all of these explanations have in common is that in them the logic of the absurd plays a particular role. The form of each explanation is that under such-and-such a circumstance levity is inappropriate, and the logic of the absurd is able to show why this is so. Absurdity consists, according to this definition, of some person, situation, object or value being given attributes that are more implausible than they are plausible and to be accused of something implausible implies a reduction in status. Moreover, the fact that this implausibility should nonetheless be in some measure plausible attaches the stigma of implausibility even more firmly to its recipient. In more formal terms: it is the nature of comic enunciation, the relationship between speaker, listener and butt that demonstrates why humour fails, for the essence of the explanations just given is that in each case the butt fails to appear absurd to the listener(s) in question, and this affects their judgment of the speaker.

To the extent that these explanations go some way to accounting for comic failure, we may say that the logic of the absurd settles the question of whether humour is immanent or negotiated: there is a mechanism intrinsic to humour whose nature is such that negotiations are undertaken about whether any given statement in fact conforms to its protocols. That is, negotiation occurs, but on determinate grounds and on occasions selected for specifiable reasons. Now this raises a sociological problem: such an explanation fits well with what we know about the sociology of humour in societies such as our own (modern, industrial, Western) where – it is clear from evidence already cited in Chapter 1 – negotiation over the status of humour is a normal part of social processes; but do such analyses fit with what is known about the social structure of societies that are dramatically different from ours? Perhaps it is the case that the mechanism of comic enunciation is not to be found in these instances.

The key to such considerations is the relationship between semantic and pragmatic marking in the enunciation of humour. Linguistic analysis distinguishes between indicators of meaning that are entirely internal to a given statement (semantic markers) and indicators that derive from the context of utterance (pragmatic markers). Clearly the theory of enunciation posits that all statements and all acts of utterance (enunciation) include both sorts of marker; however, it is equally clear from sociological evidence that not all social situations are characterised by the same doses of these two forms of marker. To take an obvious example, if a TV broadcast is formally designated as a comedy (in newspaper listings, announced by the preceding voice-over or talking head announcement, etc) then this amounts to a pragmatic marking of such proportions that the semantic components of subsequent statements will inevitably be interpreted as comic (note that this does not preclude comic failure). Now we know from anthropological evidence that there are social situations, especially in tribal societies, where pragmatic marking of comic utterance is particularly insistent and widespread:

these are those situations that arise from 'joking relationships'.

Joking relationships are defined as relationships between categories of individuals where the essential 'content' of the relationship is levity, that is, a relationship where the normal, most appropriate form of behaviour is joking. It is normal under these circumstances that forms of behaviour that would be highly inappropriate with any other category of individual are considered (minimally) permissible here, and perhaps even obligatory.[1] For example in Luguru society, those in joking relationships are actively encouraged to marry each other, since the Luguru feel that the possibility of joking together serves as a release for the normal tensions of married life, and that in joking potential spouses can size each other up. If this does not sound significantly different from commonplace recommendations about a sense of humour in marriage in our society, reference to the forms of joking behaviour show that it is: joking behaviour commonly consists of obscene insults and trying to tear each others' clothes off (J.B. Christensen, passim). Similarly, among the Mayo and Yaqui Indians, among whom the expression of overt sexuality is stringently repressed, clowns perform acts of 'the grossest obscenity. The modest, shy and reticent Indians found the obscene joking uproariously funny' (C.P. Wilson, p.184). Indeed, their tribal clowns are 'comprehensively perverse': they stand naked in the snow and wear heavy robes in the heat of summer; they stagger under light objects but carry heavy ones with ease; they talk backwards and burble nonsense; they eat excrement and drink urine with apparent relish; they kick people who give them things up the backside to show their gratitude (ibid). In each of these cases what is happening is that acts which would be considered reprehensible, if not vile, under any other social circumstances are considered appropriate under the circumstances of joking relationships.

Such a social structure may be schematically contrasted with one where joking is possible between any individuals under any circumstances. Now it seems unlikely that any society would so strictly regulate joking that its every occasion and social framework was minutely prescribed ('only with mothers' second cousins, and only on feast days' – a fictitious example), and equally unlikely that any society would allow joking to occur under any conceivable circumstances, and regardless of the identity of participants – our own prohibitions on joking during (for instance) funerals would be a good example. However, we may perhaps be allowed to distinguish between types of social structure which tend to regulate the identities of jokers and the occasions for joking rather strictly, and those which merely exclude a relatively small number of such occasions and potential partners, such as our own.

If we consider the types of behaviour cited above, the difference in the position of humour in the two types of society becomes clear. In the tribal societies the mere fact of a joking relationship makes the grossest breaches of taboo acceptable; in industrial society this is not so, for it is difficult to imagine any social circumstances here under which courtship would consist of or even include obscene insults and tearing each others' clothes off, and it is difficult to imagine our clowns doing the kinds of things that Yaqui and Mayo clowns do. Moreover, whereas in those societies clowning is not spatially and chronologically separated from everyday life, in our society it is, on the whole – professional entertainers indeed have a licence to do things that most of us would not do, but only in the context of what is designated as 'entertainment'. Consider what happened to Lenny Bruce, who broke taboos in a way not dissimilar to the Yaqui and Mayo clowns:

> Bruce had attempted to purge sexual guilt by implying the uncomfortable syllogism:
> >   a) you think bodies are dirty;
> >   b) you think God made bodies;
> >   c) you must think God is dirty.
>
> (C.P. Wilson, p.183).

But Bruce's professional status did not save him from a conviction for obscenity and the refusal of an entry visa to Britain. The clowns of tribal societies, and those in joking relationships, are expected to breach taboo to the maximum: our professional humorists are only expected to do so within carefully defined limits.

An episode from Fellini's *I Vitelloni* (1953) illustrates one way in which this principle may be seen to apply in daily life in the industrial West. A young man makes an energetic pass at his employer's wife; the husband finds out and fires him; the young man tries to pretend that it was only a joke, but the explanation is lame and unacceptable. In a tribal society – we may guess – all would have depended upon the relationship and the circumstances: if the young man and the wife had been in a joking relationship, then the pass would *objectively* have been a joke; if the relationship and circumstances were other, it could not have been; no ambiguity would be possible, and the question of intentions would have been irrelevant, because entirely subordinate to the nature of the objective relationship between the parties to the incident.

Nothing further need be said here about societies which strictly regulate the occasions for humour, on the grounds that we may reasonably expect that here the fundamental mechanism of humour may well be very different and that it would therefore demand separate treatment; this is not to assert that it is in fact very different, merely to issue the caveat that if there are fundamentally different mechanisms of humour in the range of human societies, here is likely to be one of the boundaries between them. Specifically, we might guess – but no more – that where a society regulates the occasions for humour very little, humorous artefacts would have to be strongly semantically marked whereas in a society which regulates such occasions very strictly this strong pragmatic, contextual marking would make strong semantic marking unnecessary.

Here then we have the first application of the principle with which this chapter opened: the fact that humour is both a signifying process and a social process together enables us to estimate what the concept of the logic of the absurd is capable of achieving. Essentially the point is this: because the process of enunciation is a social process at the same time as it is a signifying process it is possible to use it to make statements about humour as a social process which would not be possible if enunciation was no more than a signifying process.

The second application of this principle relates to the concept of social function. Commonly, psychological, sociological and anthropological studies have attempted to suggest what the function or functions of humour are either within human society in general or within particular social contexts. Thus – for example – many studies suggest that common laughter at an object of fun or derision may increase group cohesion; that mockery may be used as a mild form of the censure of deviance; that the 'right to joke' under specified circumstances may mark out the place that individuals have in a hierarchy; that the relief that humour affords may remove or alleviate the stresses that are commonplace in certain social situations.[2] The conclusion of an essay on film and TV comedy is scarcely the place to comment at length on such propositions, but brief remarks can at least place the preceding pages in the context of such wider considerations.[3] Firstly, if the brief anthropological examples of the last few pages tell us nothing else, they should serve as a warning against hasty extrapolations from one set of social circumstances to the level of 'society in general'. Secondly, all ascriptions of a function potentially suffer from a common defect: if one defines X on the basis of its function (whether social, psychological or both), then by that very token one is prevented from distinguishing between X and anything else that serves the same function. We saw earlier how this has bedevilled discussions of jokes and metaphor, or jokes and dreams. Similarly, if one asserts that humour serves – for example – to take the stress out of stressful situations, how is one to distinguish between humour and anything else that serves the same purpose, such as getting drunk or going on holiday? Clearly the apparent answer to such an objection lies in the description of what is specific to each activity, but this does no more than indicate the root of the problem: what is needed in each case is an analysis of the specific nature of the activity in question which at the same time demonstrates *how* it is capable of fulfilling the function in question. Thus if one asserts that both getting drunk and humour are capable of taking the stress out of stressful situations, we need an analysis of intoxication which explains how it can do this, and an analysis of humour in the same terms. But at the same time we also know that humour serves other functions too, as does drunkenness, and the analysis of the specifics of both must be able to deal with these other functions at the same time as it deals with the one function where they overlap. In short, any analysis of humour which wishes to ascribe a function to humour must at some point offer a description of how it fulfills that function, a description which must also be compatible with analyses of how it performs other functions too.

What is perhaps more significant is that lurking behind this question of the relationship between structure and function lies another question which has been much debated in most philosophical discussions of humour, and which may be formulated in a brief and dogmatic way: is humour essentially subversive or conservative? This question lurks behind the others because each of the functions involves either the disruption of the social order or its conservation: in the cases mentioned above, it is always the conservation of the social order, or some aspect of it, but in other instances, as we shall see shortly, the function of humour is thought to be the disruption of the social order. In other words, the question we are now asking is this: is the nature of comic enunciation, the logic of the absurd, such that humour is essentially subversive or essentially conservative?

We have already seen that various answers have been given to this question. Among these would be:

– George Orwell's contention that essentially humour is a kind of miniature holiday, in which the 'Sancho Panza' side of our nature temporarily takes over, but thereby increases the long-term dominance of the 'Don Quixote' side; here humour is seen as essentially conservative.

– the Freudian view, in which humour undermines inhibitions and allows the forces of the id to roam free for a moment. Whether this conception sees humour as essentially subversive or as essentially conservative depends upon how one interprets the Freudian programme: if it is interpreted in terms of the slogan 'Where it was, there shall I be' – here the purpose of psychoanalysis is essentially to strengthen the ego against the depredations of the id – then humour would have to be evaluated as not essentially subversive, but as a minor mechanism of adjustment in the battle of everyday life. If, however, with the Lacanians, one regards this slogan as the locus of an illusion then humour may be more positively evaluated.

– the position by and large adopted by those who apply psychoanalysis to the study of the arts, according to which certain kinds of 'signifying practice' are inherently more subversive (and therefore more liberating) than others. Here the distinction is usually made between social realist comedy and 'crazy comedy': in social realist comedy, it is argued, the audience is placed in a position where anything that is a transgression of an established social code must be seen as a transgression, and therefore such comedy is essentially conservative – this is on the whole the position adopted by the BFI's *Sitcom* Dossier. On the other hand, crazy comedy (Jerry Lewis for example) is held to disrupt the process whereby meaning is assigned to features of the external world, penetrating the otherwise seamless web of ideology, and thus freeing the ego from the tyranny of 'the way things are' because the process of meaning assignation is central to the smooth functioning of ideology.

These conclusions depend upon far more than a theory of humour: the Freudian model depends upon a theory of mind, the 'signifying practice' model depends upon a theory of ideology, for example. However, a model of how humour functions may bear upon these conclusions nonetheless, since its mode of functioning has implications for what it can achieve, as we have seen. The model proposed here suggests that humour is neither essentially liberatory nor conservative, for its nature is such that it always refuses to make any commitment to any 'opinion' about anything (except of course the opinion that levity is appropriate under these circumstances); its very basis is ambivalence. In so far as it can be said to imply any attitude towards anything, it probably incarnates a will to opposition, as was argued *à propos* of *Accidental Death of an Anarchist*; but this will to opposition is a very feeble one, for it implies no action whatsoever, nor even any purely internal commitment to continued opposition to whatever is in question.

This said, however, there are two ways in which humour can, plausibly, incarnate real opposition. The first way refers to the distinction made by Mary Douglas between perception and permission of humour: to make a joke under circumstances where it is largely certain that it will not be permitted is to take a stand against the circumstances in question – getting drunk and clowning at a funeral, taking your trousers off during the Trooping of the Colour or a Veteran's Day Parade or walking up to the pulpit and telling a joke during Mass or Communion. All of these are activities which could possibly be said to be humorous in intention, but which would more or less certainly not be permitted as such in our society; similarly with jokes about subjects which are locally forbidden – jokes against the Army or racial purity under the Nazis, for example. To decide to make a joke under such circumstances implies a deliberate act of revolt which can be guaranteed to have some result or other, for reasons we have already seen when discussing offensive humour. In parenthesis we may note that such activities are exactly those not only permitted but encouraged on the part of court jesters in the Middle Ages – the one clear survival of joking relationships in our culture. Here the sociological circumstances are such that what is forbidden everybody else is explicitly permitted one person. The last court fool in Britain was at Charles II's court, and the last recorded domestic fool was kept until 1746.[4]

The second way in which humour can incarnate real opposition is when it is part of an organised sub- or counter-culture: if a joke with a particular butt is part of organised opposition to such-and-such an institution or person, it takes on a very different meaning to the meaning it has if it is 'mere entertainment'. As was said before, Dario Fo's play probably had a very different meaning in Italy to the one it had in the West End of London – though even under these anodyne circumstances one should not underestimate the degree of cynicism it revealed about the police, if nothing more. No doubt this is also the reason for Nazi persecution of the Weimar cabaretiers: they were part of an organised political opposition to the German Right in general. Equally the anti-Soviet jokes used as examples here would have a very different ring to them if told in the context of a Solidarity meeting in Poland, for example. Of course, these points about the way in which context affects the meaning of humour are equally applicable to any other cultural artefact that incarnates opposition; however, they are especially relevant to humour to the extent that the privileged position of the butt in humour makes joking an obvious way of expressing opposition.

At this point we are near the limit of what an examination of forms of humour and comedy is capable of telling us, and we need to place such a discussion in a wider framework; such a framework would have to consist of either – or both – a theory of mind or a theory of the social structure, and therefore the most plausible candidates are Freudian theory and the theory of ideology, for in both cases, in their modern versions, an attempt is made to link a theory of mind with a theory of the social structure.

Such an attempt in the realm of psychoanalytic theory would start from the mechanisms of jokes as Freud explores them in *Jokes and their Relation to the Unconscious*, and the way in which certain key concepts to be found there are developed in his later work. Our starting point is Freud's analysis of the different roles involved in joke-telling and humour. In 'Humour' Freud distinguishes between jokes and humour on the grounds of the different roles involved. In humour, as we have seen, there are only two: the spectator and the funny individual or situation. In the joke, on the other hand, there are three: the joker, the butt and the listener, and Freud insists on the centrality of the role of the listener – no one laughs at their own jokes except as an echo of the laughter of the audience. Recent re-interpretations of Freud's theory have questioned the centrality of the listener, underlining the distinction between a biographical individual who is the listener and the discursive role of the listener, which need not be incarnate in a separate individual. For instance, the listener can be conceived as no more than the instance of the Law, the instance where repressions take their form and have their effectivity. This is clear if one considers Freud's discussion of dirty jokes, which have their origin in sexual desire. Freud distinguishes three roles: the joker, who desires a particular woman, but the expression of whose desire is blocked by the unwillingness of the woman and the presence of another man (that is, the public); the woman; and the third party. The dirty joke is the expression of this desire made possible by the specific pleasure of jokes, which subverts the inhibition against the expression of desire; it is thus also an act of aggression against the woman, which gives pleasure to the listener by subverting his inhibitions too. The essential feature, in this analysis, of the listener is that he too gains pleasure through the subversion of inhibitions; but if this is indeed the essence of his role, then clearly there is no reason why it should be incarnated in a third person, since the same inhibitions are subverted in the joker himself.

Similarly, the butt of the joke – the woman – need not be incarnated in a particular biographical individual either: as Freud says, the canonical form of the dirty joke is man to man, with no women present; the butt of the joke is not a particular woman, but femininity, the object of male desire. Moreover, in other forms of joke at least, the butt of a joke can be the speaker himself (for example, jokes about one's own stupidity). And in many of the jokes Freud himself quotes, the butt is not a person but an institution or an idea: this is the case of what Freud calls cynical jokes. In each of these cases the roles in the jokes need not be played by distinct biographical individuals, for they may well overlap in the same individual.

It is tempting to assert that this distribution of roles is in itself capable of distinguishing jokes from non-comic statements: thus, if one took Freud literally and insisted that the listener was in fact a biographical other person, then this might distinguish the joke form from other statements on the grounds that other statements were not dependent upon the presence of this third person. However, this position is in fact difficult to maintain: in the first place, it seems unlikely that a bio-graphically distinct third person is in fact necessary to the role of listener. In the second place, we have seen already that many types of statement have the listener inscribed in them: 'Tom's coming to-morrow' can be either a threat or a promise. So the mere fact that jokes are marked with the presence of the listener is not sufficient to de-marcate them from other forms of utterance. On the other hand, the joke listener has a further characteristic that does distinguish him, potentially: the characteristic of the subversion of inhibitions. The dif-ficulty here is that inhibitions are subverted through the mechanism of the pleasure specific to jokes, which – as we have already seen – is the site of a strangely circular argument in Freud; and therefore the listener qua *joke* listener is indeed distinct from other listeners, but his distinc-tiveness derives from a particular semiotic mechanism that has to be specified separately.

In short the role of the listener does not suffice to delineate the joke. Is it possible to use the role of the butt to perform this task? The butt of the dirty joke is the object of aggression, as we have seen. Many other jokes that Freud quotes are directly aggressive, in the sense that the unconscious drive that is allowed free rein by the joke is aggression it-self, with no other drive hidden in it, such as sexual desire. Similarly, one could say that cynical jokes are a form of aggression, in the sense that they attack institutions and ideas. Thus the butt of the joke is always the object of aggression, and it is clearly not the case that all statements have a butt in this sense: does this amount to saying that the joke is to be demarcated on the grounds of the role of the butt? This position would be difficult to hold, for there certainly are other forms

of statement that are not jokes, but which are marked by the presence
of a butt: insults and polemic, for instance; the presence of a butt, in
itself, does not allow the demarcation of the joke therefore. What one
would need to do would be to separate the comic butt from other forms
of butt; this is indeed possible, but the necessary means is the logic of
the absurd, and thus it is not the butt but the butt inscribed in a particular semiotic mechanism that is distinctive.[5]

Thus far in these considerations Freud's conflation of all forms of
joke with what he calls 'tendentious jokes' has been accepted; the time
has come to ask whether this conflation is in fact justified, or under
what conditions it is justified. Freud's conflation is conducted in these
terms: that the essential features of all forms of jokes and jests are to be
found in the tendentious joke. The definition of a tendentious joke is
that the pleasure it gives serves the purpose ('Tendenz' in German) of
releasing some drive otherwise subject to repression. The opposite of a
tendentious joke for Freud is an innocent joke, a joke in which the
pleasure derives from the joke technique alone and which serves no
further purpose. However, this distinction is considerably undermined
when Freud considers the role of innocent conceptual jokes (that is,
jokes where no Tendenz is served, but where the joke is not purely
verbal):

> Jokes, even if the thought contained in them is non-tendentious and
> thus only serves theoretical intellectual interests, are in fact never
> non-tendentious. They pursue the second aim: to promote the
> thought by augmenting it and protecting it against criticism (p.183).

In this passage therefore, Freud is asserting that even if a joke appears
not to serve any purpose associated with the unconscious, it nonetheless is, for all jokes protect the thought they contain from rational adult
criticism; thus only jests are really innocent – that is, non-tendentious
(ibid). But even this distinction (jest/joke) is undermined: jests as well
as jokes 'prolong the yield of pleasure from play', by finding a way of
neutralising the voice of criticism; this is achieved through the combination of sense and nonsense, as we saw in Chapter 1. Therefore, 'in
jests what stands in the foreground is the satisfaction of having made
possible what was forbidden by criticism' (p.179). Clearly jokes and

jests, innocent and tendentious jokes all have something central in common: they subvert the norms of rational adult criticism. Indeed, as we have already seen, this is how they can serve the interests of the drives of the unconscious.

No doubt such criticism of Freud – minor terminological inconsistencies – will seem carping. But the purpose of these remarks, appearances notwithstanding, is not in fact critical: it is to explore a series of implications of Freud's thought which are only latent in the text of *Jokes*. The key point is this: that adult rational criticism is itself an inhibition. The function of both jokes and jests, Freud says (p.180), is to lift 'internal inhibitions', to give access to 'sources of pleasure which have been rendered inaccessible by those inhibitions'. If this statement is to apply to both jokes and jests it is logically essential that adult rational criticism should also be considered as an inhibition, for that is all that jests subvert. Moreover, throughout the long section on the psychogenesis of jokes, Freud consistently gives the subversion of criticism the same characteristic as the subversion of other inhibitions, the characteristic of reduction of psychic expenditure. That is to say: all forms of comic statement that Freud refers to in *Jokes* have one fundamental feature in common: they all subvert the inhibition of rational adult criticism, thus giving a form of pleasure peculiar to them and which enables them to 'come to the aid of' the other instincts or drives of the unconscious. We have also seen, in the semiotic elaboration of this process, that the essential means that comic utterances use is the play of the signifier. Thus one could say, in a sense, that all jokes and jests have a butt: normal usage, since it is normal usage that is subverted in all of them and since it is this subversion that provides their peculiar pleasure.

The purpose of these pages has been to show that only one feature of jokes and jests, of all forms of comic utterance, is universal in them and distinguishes them from non-comic utterances: the subversion of the inhibition of criticism. Neither the distribution of actantial roles nor the subversion of other inhibitions can play this role: such is the implication of Freud's analysis, even though it goes somewhat against its letter. With this principle once established, it is then possible to accept what is conventionally held to be the core of Freud's theory of jokes, that is, the subversion of inhibitory norms regulating sexual, aggressive, cynical, etc., behaviour. To repeat: the purpose of these pages was not criticism (in the usual negative sense) of Freud; indeed, the most that Freud can be accused of is inadequate development of certain of his own insights. The purpose is rather to pursue latent implications of Freud's theory; to do this we need to consider one final criticism of Freud's text.

The most telling criticism of Freud made by Todorov is this: the reduction of psychic economy that is typical of jokes derives from the subversion of rational criticism through the 'return to primitive non-sense'.[6] This nonsense, Todorov argues, is posited as the opposite of critical rationalism, and these two concepts are a binary pair, mutually defining and excluding all other possibilities. As a result any statement must either be in accordance with the norms of critical rationalism or will be nonsense. This binary opposition excludes the space of the symbolic, whose existence Todorov asserts (rightly). No doubt this is something of an over-simplification of Freud's thought, since – as we have seen – Freud in fact locates the pleasure-giving capacities of jokes and jests in the mixture of sense and nonsense, not in nonsense alone. Nonetheless, it is true that Freud does not theorise this combination of sense and nonsense, which remains a problematic concept as a result; yet Freud asserts it, as the basis of his theory, and we are expected to accept it as a self-evident truth. Todorov is right, no doubt, to stress that Freud conceives of the space words occupy on the basis of two fundamental characteristics: meaning, which is given in the terms of adult rational criticism; and nonsense, which is ectopic and therefore the limit of rationality, which cannot therefore have any immanent features of its own: its features are simply the negative counterpart of rationality. No doubt this binary division of words (and non-verbal discourse too, by implication) is inadequate; nonetheless, it is this division which will serve as a starting point for the final stage of our investigation, the placing of the semiotic mechanism of humour in history.

What is the nature of this adult rational criticism that is subverted by jokes and jests? Freud gives us certain indications. In the first place, it is adult: it belongs to the psychogenetic phase in the course of which the pleasure of play (in the childish sense) is no longer possible as the reality principle now counter-balances the pleasure principle. This is not to imply that the pleasure principle is eliminated from the psyche:

on the contrary it still has free rein in the unconscious. Thus critical rationality is a feature of the conscious mind, of the adult mind adapted to the real outside world, opposed to the childish mind which is still prey to the drives of the subconscious, which is still of course to be found in the adult too. In the second place, rational adult criticism is inseparable from language. Freud distinguishes – in a way that becomes clearer in his later works – between word-representations and thing-representations. Neither of these two terms is identical to the concept of the signified, for thing-representations are as much signifiers as are word-representations: thing-representations are representations of the outside world buried in the unconscious and are therefore pre-verbal signifiers, whereas word-representations are verbal signifiers located in the conscious. In dreams and jokes, Freud says, word-representations are treated as if they were thing-representations, that is to say treated according to the laws of the subconscious, subjected to displacement and condensation.

The case of the fetishist who needed something shining on his nose in order to achieve sexual satisfaction is an instance. Freud demonstrates that the origin of this need lies in a pun: as a child the patient displaced his curiosity about the mother's phallus into a 'glance at the nose'; the patient was German, but as a child had been bilingual in German and English; the German phrase for something shining on the nose is 'ein Glanz auf der Nase'; his childhood English completely forgotten, the 'glance at the nose' had punningly become 'Glanz auf der Nase', and the origin of the fetish was thus explained.[7] Here word-representations (Glanz – shine; glance – look) have been treated as thing-representations, treated not according to their meanings in the linguistic sense but according to their physical properties, that is, their sound, in the same way, that is, as meaning is displaced in the subconscious from one signifier to another. The implication is that representations are not *normally* treated in this way at all, but are treated according to a norm which prescribes a relation of direct equivalence between signifier and signified, in other words a relation of denotation: for the essential feature of this equivalence is that it leaves no space between signifier and signified in which the play, the slippage, of condensation and displacement can occur.

It is only in the various circumstances where psychic activities succeed in avoiding the censorship of inhibitions that such a treatment of words becomes possible: the primary processes of the unconscious operate on the principle of obscure echoes, whose polyphonic relationships are utterly different from those typical of words as used by the conscious. Word representations, moreover, are intrinsically linked to the process of the conscious mind, to thought: it is in the passage from thing-representation to word-representation that images acquire the 'index of quality' or seal of the conscious, as Laplanche and Pontalis put it: 'Word representations are introduced in a conception that links verbalisation and coming to consciousness'.[8]

Thus critical rationality possesses a series of characteristics: it is based on the reality principle; and denotation is its condition and its instrument. Now we are in a position to give a precise definition of the status of jokes and humour in Freudian thought: they work by subverting the reality principle and the mechanism of denotation, defined as what fixes the signifier to the signified in order to give it total coherence, and which therefore works in a direction opposed to any polyphonic relationships. However, where jokes and jests are concerned the reality principle only plays a limited role: for the childish impulse that has to be repressed by the reality principle and has to be subverted by the joke is precisely the sense of play applied to the process of signification. What the childish mind demands, what the pleasure principle demands, is the play of the signifier, and this play of the signifier is repressed by the reality principle just as are the other primary processes. Thus the focal point in this process, the point at which subversion occurs in all forms of comic utterance, is the relation of denotation.

The exploration of this path through Freud's ideas brings us to a point where it is possible to say something about the relations between comic enunciation and the social structure. Comedy and humour function essentially by subverting the norms of denotation, the norms by which meaning is unequivocally assigned. The significance of this discovery in turn depends upon the role that the process of unequivocal meaning assignation is held to play according to any given theory. Conventionally, in recent theorising, such 'play of the signifier' is held to disrupt ideology, and this for a reason that can be clearly, if dogmatically, stated. According to Althusser's theory, ideology functions

221

by constituting subjectivity, in the phenomenological sense of this phrase: something which is characterised as being the source of all meaning in the world, and therefore both authoritatively and unproblematically the source of experience. It is in and through ideology, in other words, that individuals are made into individuals, Althusser argues. Now the Freudian model of humour offers a way in which this seamless web can be fractured: for ideology functions precisely by referring meaning to the point where the experience of subjectivity (still in the phenomenological sense) is the site of another process, the process which Lacanians call 'suture', the stitching together of the faces of 'personality', which in fact can never be brought into a state of total cohesion. Here, then, is one way of exploring the potential meaning of humour and comedy. However, there are various empirical considerations which cast doubt upon its value.

In the first place the question of the negotiation of humorous meaning. Freud himself is quite explicit that jokes depend upon audiences in the sense that they sometimes fail to be appreciated. However, this empirical observation is not entirely consistent with his main assertion, that jokes undermine inhibitions and give free rein to the drives of the id: for the failure of jokes clearly shows that on many occasions the mechanism is blocked by something else. If we ignore failure caused by incomprehension as irrelevant in this context, we are nonetheless left with the significant instances of failure through offensiveness and through banality. Banality can perhaps be explained in a way that is easily consistent with the Freudian model: the audience's experience of humour and comedy itself, in other words of its semiotic mechanism, is such as to reduce the effectiveness of its surprise as an act of subversion of inhibition. Offensiveness is more difficult, for *ex hypothesi* it suggests that some psychic mechanism has prevented the play of the signifier from subverting inhibitions, in other words, the inhibitions in question have been proof against their attempted subversion; but this is precisely what is excluded as a possibility by the original thesis that the role of jokes is to subvert inhibitions.

In the second place, considerations about the nature of comic performance. It is well-known that professional comedians are extremely careful about the pacing and the ordering of the jokes they tell: that – crudely speaking – they attach great importance to 'getting the audience on their side'; commonsensically, we may guess that this is because nearly any joke is going to risk offending someone, and that the better the joke, the more likely it is to do so. In so far as this is true, we could say that the structure of comic performance is intended to minimise the risk of causing offence (and maximise the possibility of arousing mirth, of course). Indeed, it is probably unnecessary to refer to professional comic performance in order to make this point: anyone who tells jokes in everyday life, or who merely wants to make funny remarks in the course of ordinary conversation, knows as a matter of common sense that a certain amount of care is needed over the choice of topic and moment before trying to inject levity into the occasion. From these considerations we may derive two points: firstly, that jokes rarely if ever have much meaning in isolation from the social context in which they are told, and this social context essentially consists of the audience being 'warmed up'; secondly, that humour and comedy are very fragile, and constantly risk failure just because they fail to subvert inhibitions.

What these arguments suggest is that it is unwise to unequivocally insist that the play of the signifier is capable of any specified effect regardless of the context of utterance. No doubt this is paradoxical, for the theory with which we are concerned here is based upon the assertion of the centrality of this context. But what is significant is that the context of utterance is not just psychoanalytically structured, but also sociologically; and this in two ways: firstly, the institutional framework in which humour or comedy is produced; secondly, the sociological characteristics of the participants in the comic process – speaker, butt and audience. Such a consideration points us even more firmly in the direction of the theory of ideology, and perhaps more specifically in the inflection of it constituted by recent applications of Gramsci's theory of hegemony.

In this theory ideology is conceived of not as a seamless web, as in Althusser, but as the site of struggle, where the meaning of any individual 'lexical item' or artefact or practice would be determined not by reference to some established paradigm of meaning such as 'representing' the point of view of such-and-such a class, in its turn defined by its place in the mode of production, but by reference to the role that it played in the class struggle at any given point in time and place. Thus the meaning of a given artefact might change according to the place and time it was created, to the purpose for which it was used, and to the identity of the participants involved in its consumption. The theory of humour proposed in these pages fits well with such a conception, for it is absolutely basic to its thesis that humour is ambivalent, that in and of itself it involves no commitment to anything except the act of levity and that its meaning changes dramatically according to the circumstances of its utterance.

Notes

1. The *locus classicus* for an analysis of this phenomenon is A.R. Radcliffe-Brown's 'On Joking Relationships' and his 'Further Note on Joking Relationships', both in *Structure and Function in Primitive Society*, 1952. See also D. Handelman and B. Kapferer, 'Forms of Joking Activity: A Comparative Approach', 1972.
2. See C.P. Wilson, *Jokes: Form, Content, Use and Function*, 1979.
3. See my forthcoming *Taking Humour Seriously*.
4. See J. Palmer, 'Humor in Great Britain', in A. Ziv (ed), *National Styles in Humor*, 1987.
5. The classical Greek author Lucian, in an essay on slander, points out that there are necessarily three roles involved: the slanderer, the person who is slandered, and the listener; without the butt of the slander, and without a listener, there is no slander. Lucian compares slander to comedy in this respect. (*Works*, Loeb edn., v.1, p.367) The idea comes from Herodotus, Book 7, section 10.
6. T. Todorov, 'La Rhetorique de Freud', in *Theories du symbole*, 1976, p.313.
7. See J. Lacan, *Ecrits*, 1966, p.522.
8. Laplanche and Pontalis, *Vocabulaire de la Psychanalyse*, 1967, p.418.

Bibliography

AGEE, James, 'Comedy's Greatest Era', in *Agee on Film*, v.1, London, Peter Owen, 1963.

ALTHUSSER, Louis, *Lire le Capital*, Paris, Maspéro, 1968.

ALTHUSSER, Louis, 'Ideology and Ideological State Apparatuses', in *Lenin and Philosophy*, London, New Left Books, 1971.

APPIGNANESI, Lisa, *Cabaret*, London, Methuen, 1984.

APTER, M.J., *The Experience of Motivation*, London, Academic Press, 1982.

APTER, M.J., and SMITH, K.C.P., 'Humour and the Theory of Psychological Reversals', in *It's a Funny Thing, Humour*, ed Chapman and Foot, Oxford, Pergamon Press, 1977.

ARISTOTLE, *Poetics*, ed. Lucas, Oxford University Press, 1968.

BARTHES, Roland, *Elements of Semiology*, London, Cape, 1967.

BARTHES, Roland, 'L'Ancienne Rhétorique', *Communications* 16, 1970.

BENVENISTE, Emile, *Problèmes de Linguistique Générale*, 2vv, Paris, Gallimard, 1966 and 1974.

BERGSON, Henri, *Le Rire*, Paris, Presses Universitaires de France, 1940.

BFI Dossier No. 17, *Television Sitcom*, British Film Institute, 1982.

BLACK, Max, 'How Metaphors Work', in Sacks (ed), *On Metaphor*.

BRIGGS, Asa, *History of Broadcasting in the United Kingdom*, 4vv, Oxford University Press, 1961-79.

BURCH, Noel, *Theory of Film Practice*, London, Secker and Warburg, 1973.

CARROTT, Jasper, 'Carrott's Lip', *Time Out*, no.695, 15 December 1983.

CHAMBERS, E.K., *The Mediaeval Stage*, 2 volumes, Oxford, at the Clarendon Press, 1903.

CHRISTENSEN, James Boyd, 'Utani: joking, sexual license and social obligation among the Luguru', *American Anthropologist*, v.65, 1963, pp.1314-27.

COHEN, Jean, 'Théorie de la Figure', *Communications*, 16, 1970.

COHEN, Ted, 'Metaphor and the Cultivation of Intimacy' in Sacks (ed), *On Metaphor*.

COOK, Jim, 'Narrative, Comedy, Character and Performance', in BFI, *Television Sitcom*.

CORNEILLE, Pierre, *Horace*, in *Théâtre Compet*, ed. Maurice Rat, Paris, Editions Garnier, n.d.

COURSODON, J.-P., *Keaton et Cie*, Paris, Seghers, 1964.

CULLER, Jonathan, *Structuralist Poetics*, London, Routledge and Kegan Paul, 1975.

CURRAN, James, *Mass Communications and Society*, London, Edward Arnold, 1977.

CURTIS, Barry, 'Aspects of Sitcom', in BFI, *Television Sitcom*.

DAVIDSON, Donald, 'What Metaphors Mean', in Sacks (ed), *On Metaphor*.

DOUGLAS, Mary, 'The Social Control of Cognition', *Man* (new series), v.3, 1968, pp.361-76.

DURGNAT, Raymond, *The Crazy Mirror*, London, Faber, 1969.

EATON, Mick and NEALE, Steve, 'Psychoanalysis and comedy', *Screen*, v.22, no. 2, 1981, pp.21-43.

EDGAR, David, 'Interview', *Theatre Quarterly*, No. 33, Spring, 1979.

ELIOT, T.S., *'The Love Song of J. Alfred Prufrock'*, in *Collected Poems*, London, Faber, 1963.

EMERSON, Joan, 'Negotiating the Serious Import of Humor', *Sociometry*, v.32, 1969, pp.169-81.

EVANS-PRITCHARD, E.E., 'Witchcraft', *Africa*, v.8, no. 4, 1955.

EVERSON, William K., *The Films of Laurel and Hardy*, Secaucus NJ, Citadel Press, 1967.

FREUD, Sigmund, *Jokes and Their Relation to the Unconscious*, Pelican Freud Library, Harmondsworth, Penguin Books, 1976.

GRIFFITHS, Trevor, *Comedians*, London, Faber, 1976.

GUREWITCH, M., *Comedy – The Irrational Vision*, Ithaca NY, Cornell University Press, 1975.

HALL, Stuart, 'Culture, the Media and the Ideological Effect', in *Mass Communications and Society*, ed J. Curran et al., Edward Arnold, 1977.

HANDELMAN, Don and KAPFERER, Bruce, 'Forms of Joking Activity: A Comparative Approach', *American Anthropologist*, v.74, 1972, pp.484-517.

JEFFERSON, Gail, 'A Technique for Inviting Laughter and its Subsequent Acceptance Declination', in G. Psathas (ed), *Everyday Language*, Irvington Publishers Inc., 1979.

KERBRAT-ORECCHIONI, Catherine, *L'Enonciation de la Subjectivité dans le Langage*, Paris, Presses Universitaires de France and Armand Colin, 1980.

KERBRAT-ORECCHIONI, Catherine, 'L'Ironie comme Trope', *Poétique*, v.11, Feb., 1980, pp.108-27.

KRAL, Piotr, *Le Burlesque, ou Morale de la Tarte à la Crème*, Paris, Stock, 1984.

LACAN, Jacques, *Ecrits*, Paris, Editions du Seuil, 1966.

LACLOS, Choderlos de, *Les Liaisons Dangereuses*, in *Oeuvres*, Paris, Editions de la Pléiade, Gallimard, n.d.

LAHUE, K. and GILL, S., *Clown Princes and Court Jesters*, Cranbury NJ, A.S. Barnes, 1970.

LANGER, Suzanne, *Feeling and Form*, Routledge and Kegan Paul, 1953.

LAPLANCHE, Jean and PONTALIS, J.-B., *Vocabulaire de la Psychanalyse*, Paris, Presses Universitaires de France, 1967.

LOVELL, Terry, 'A Genre of Social Disruption?', in BFI *Television Sitcom*.

LUCIAN, *Works*, Loeb Classical Library, 1913.

MARS, François, *Le Gag*, Paris, Editions du Cerf, 1964.

MARX, Karl, *Grundrisse*, Harmondsworth, Pelican Books, 1973.

MAST, Gerald, 'The Comic Mind: Comedy and the Movies', in *Film Theory and Criticism*, ed. Mast and Cohen, pp.458-68.

MAST, Gerald and COHEN, Marshall (eds), *Film Theory and Criticism*, Oxford University Press, 1974.

METZ, Christian, *Film Language*, excerpts in Mast and Cohen (eds).

MILNER, Jean-Claude, *L'Amour de la Langue*, Paris, Editions du Seuil, 1978.

MORRISSON, Bill, 'Conversation Piece', interview with Sue McGregor, BBC Radio 4, 5 January 1984.

ORWELL, George, 'The Art of Donald McGill', in *Collected Essays*, London, Heinemann, Mercury Books, 1961.

PALMER, Jerry, 'The Damp Stones of Positivism', *Philosophy of the Social Sciences*, v.9, no.2, June 1979, pp.129-48.

PALMER, Jerry, 'The Function of le Vraisemblable in French Classical Aesthetics', *French Studies*, v.29, no.1, Jan. 1975, pp.15-26.

PALMER, Jerry, 'Humor in Great Britain', in *National Styles in Humor*, ed. A Ziv, Westport CT, Greenwood Press, 1987.

PALMER, Jerry, *Taking Humour Seriously* (forthcoming).

PRICE, Christopher, *Listener*, v.94, no.2427, p.541.

RABATÉ, Jean-Michel, 'Enunciation in the Field of the Psycho-analytic theory of Language', unpublished mimeo, University of Dijon, Faculty of Foreign Languages.

RACINE, Jean, *Britannicus*, in *Théâtre Complet*, ed. M. Rat, Paris, Editions Garnier, n.d.

RADCLIFFE-BROWN, A.R., 'On Joking Relations' and 'A Further Note on Joking Relations', both in *Structure and Function in Primitive Society*, London, Cohen and West, 1952.

RICOEUR, Paul, 'The Metaphorical Process as Cognition, Imagination and Feeling', in S. Sacks (ed), *On Metaphor*.

RIMMON-KENAN, Shlomith, *Narrative Fiction: Contemporary Poetics*, London, Methuen, New Accents, 1983.

ROBINSON, David, *Chaplin*, London, Collins, 1985.

ROBINSON, David, 'The Italian Comedy', *Sight & Sound*, v.55, no.2, Spring 1986, pp.105-12.

SACKS, Sheldon, *On Metaphor*, Chicago IL, University of Chicago Press, 1979.

SAUSSURE, Ferdinand de, *Course in General Linguistics*, London, Fontana, 1974.

SCANNELL, Paddy and CARDIFF, David, 'Radio in World War II', Open University Course U203, Popular Culture, Unit 8.

SCHAEFFER, Neil, *The Art of Laughter*, New York, Columbia University Press, 1981.

SCHUTZ, C.E., *Political Humor*, Cranbury NJ, Fairley-Dickinson University Press, 1976.

SMITH, Neil and WILSON, Deirdre, *Modern Linguistics*, Harmondsworth, Pelican Books, 1979.

TODOROV, Tzvetan, 'La Rhétorique de Freud' and 'Freud sur l'Enonciation', both in his *Théories du Symbole*, Paris, Editions de Seuil, 1976.

TOOK, Barry, *Laughter in the Air*, London, Robson Books, 1976.

TORRANCE, Richard, *The Comic Hero*, Cambridge MA, Harvard University Press, 1978.

VICINUS, Martha, *The Industrial Muse*, London, Croom Helm, 1974.

WAITES, B., 'The Music Hall', Open University Course U203, Popular Culture, Unit 5.

WATERMAN, J., *Listener*, v.101, n.2602, 15 March 1979, pp.373ff.

WHITEHOUSE, Mrs Mary, "*Who Does She Think She Is?*", London, New English Library, 1971.

WILSON, C.P., *Jokes*: *Form, Content, Use and Function*, London, Academic Press, 1979.

ZIV, A., *National Styles in Humor*, Westport CT, Greenwood Press, 1987.

Index